THE MISSING MILLIONAIRE

KATIE DAUBS

THE MISSING MILLIONAIRE

THE TRUE STORY OF AMBROSE SMALL AND THE CITY OBSESSED WITH FINDING HIM

McCLELLAND & STEWART

Library and Archives Canada Cataloguing in Publication data is
available upon request

ISBN: 978-0-7710-2517-4
ebook ISBN: 978-0-7710-2518-1

Jacket design by Terri Nimmo with Andrew Roberts
Jacket photo: City of Toronto Archives, Fonds 1244, Item 7069
Text design by Andrew Roberts
Typeset in Goudy by M&S, Toronto
Printed and bound in Canada

McClelland & Stewart,
a division of Penguin Random House Canada Limited,
a Penguin Random House Company
www.penguinrandomhouse.ca

1 2 3 4 5   23 22 21 20 19

 Penguin
Random House
McCLELLAND & STEWART

There is no city that does not dream
from its foundations. The lost lake
crumbling in the hands of brickmakers,
the floor of the ravine where light lies broken
with the memory of rivers. All the winters
stored in that geologic
garden. Dinosaurs sleep in the subway
at Bloor and Shaw, a bed of bones
under the rumbling track. The storm
that lit the city with the voltage
of spring, when we were eighteen
on the clean earth. The ferry ride in the rain,
wind wet with wedding music and everything that
sings in the carbon of stone and bone
like a page of love, wind-lost from a hand, unread.

"THERE IS NO CITY THAT DOES NOT DREAM,"

ANNE MICHAELS

To the reporters who told this story the first time around,
and the archivists and librarians who kept it safe.

CONTENTS

◇

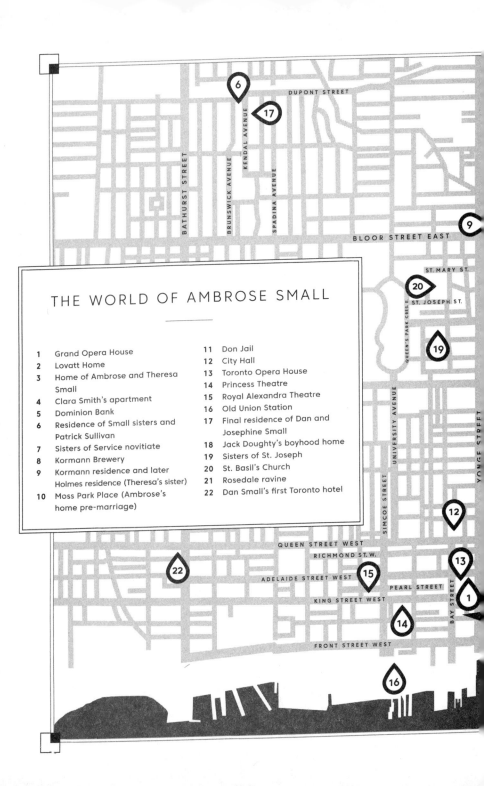

THE WORLD OF AMBROSE SMALL

1 Grand Opera House
2 Lovatt Home
3 Home of Ambrose and Theresa Small
4 Clara Smith's apartment
5 Dominion Bank
6 Residence of Small sisters and Patrick Sullivan
7 Sisters of Service novitiate
8 Kormann Brewery
9 Kormann residence and later Holmes residence (Theresa's sister)
10 Moss Park Place (Ambrose's home pre-marriage)
11 Don Jail
12 City Hall
13 Toronto Opera House
14 Princess Theatre
15 Royal Alexandra Theatre
16 Old Union Station
17 Final residence of Dan and Josephine Small
18 Jack Doughty's boyhood home
19 Sisters of St. Joseph
20 St. Basil's Church
21 Rosedale ravine
22 Dan Small's first Toronto hotel

GLEN ROAD

AVONDALE ROAD

PARK ROAD

ELM AVENUE

MAPLE AVENUE

ROSEDALE VALLEY ROAD

CHURCH STREET

JARVIS STREET

SHERBOURNE STREET

WELLESLEY STREET EAST

CARLTON STREET

GERRARD STREET EAST

BROADVIEW AVENUE

RIVER STREET

SHUTER STREET

QUEEN STREET EAST

KING ST. W.

BAY ST.

MELINDA ST.

JORDAN ST.

YONGE ST.

WELLINGTON ST. W.

SMALL AND KORMANN CONNECTIONS

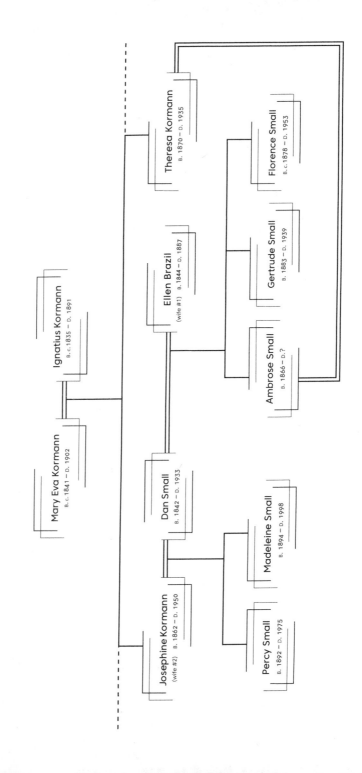

Ignatius Kormann
B. c. 1835 – D. 1891

Mary Eva Kormann
B. 1841 – D. 1902

Theresa Kormann
B. 1870 – D. 1935

Ellen Brazil
(wife #1) B. 1844 – D. 1887

Florence Small
B. c. 1878 – D. 1953

Gertrude Small
B. 1883 – D. 1939

Ambrose Small
B. 1866 – D. ?

Dan Small
B. 1842 – D. 1933

Madeleine Small
B. 1894 – D. 1998

Josephine Kormann
(wife #2) B. 1862 – D. 1950

Percy Small
B. 1892 – D. 1975

THE MISSING MILLIONAIRE

———————◇———————

TORONTO, 2019

Ambrose Small's city is still here in pieces. You can find his mansion on a leafy Rosedale street or walk by the trio of skyscrapers he knew so well at King and Yonge. In his day, they were a source of civic pride, among the tallest buildings in the British Empire, and they housed banks and railway offices. A century later, one is a hotel, while the other two are office towers filled with financiers and lawyers, with a mattress shop and pharmacy at street level. His theatre on Adelaide Street was torn down before the Depression, and now there is a glass banking tower in its place, a building so tall that no matter where you are, there it is, pointing to the spot where the story begins. The Grand Opera House.

Ambrose Small knew everyone had secrets. People might say they liked highbrow theatre, but he knew they'd be happy enough to sit in a dark room with a thousand strangers watching a pair of likeable goofs singing ditties of the old country. As the ringmaster of one of Canada's most powerful theatre networks—headquartered at the Grand Opera House—Small made his millions by catering to humanity's desire for cheap escape. In 1919, when he was fifty-three years old, he sold it all for $1.75 million. The next day, he vanished from the theatre, never to be seen again.

The people who knew what that Toronto felt like, what it sounded and smelled like, are nearly all gone. The horse manure, coal dust, and factories have disappeared too, but the lilacs and chestnut trees bloom every spring, and the sewer pipes still snake below the ground, so ancient that they sometimes rupture, the past bubbling to the surface. But never Ambrose. Never the solution to the mystery.

If he had been nicer, a theatre critic once said, maybe they would have looked harder for him. A hundred years have hardened the image of Ambrose Small into a vengeful, petty businessman—and he was that, certainly—but there are details buried in newspaper stories that make him seem more of a human being and less of a caricature. He had trouble sleeping. He had a hangnail problem.

Ambrose didn't crave the spotlight like the actors on his stage. He built hidden rooms at his theatres, paid for indiscretions with secret accounts, refused to open his books when he was sued, and grew richer on backroom bets that left no trace.

Like any good theatre man, he knew that audiences love a mystery. When I imagine Ambrose Small, he is laughing at me for thinking I could know him, for thinking I can know how this ends, for thinking this ever ends.

ONE

AMBROSE SMALL IS MISSING

TORONTO, CHRISTMAS 1919

Ambrose Small was so good at slipping away—from business terms he didn't like, from women he'd grown bored with, from sticky situations of all kinds—that no one gave much thought to his absence in December 1919.

The city had been dusted by a layer of snow, there were pine garlands on the street lamps, and the department store ads were crowded with Grafonolas, radios, and dainty things for the woman in your life: "Surely There is Someone to Whom You Will Give a Camisole This Christmas."

The theatres were in the middle of their busiest season. The Royal Alex—the city's most prestigious house—had a musical comedy, and Ambrose Small had booked a two-week stint of *Little Red Riding Hood* for his Grand Opera House. The Grand had once been Toronto's premier theatre, but now it was the discount option, a place to see a respectable second-rate show for a reasonable price, and *Red Riding Hood* was packing them in every night as the woodsman killed the wolf and the cast sang sweet melodies of yesterday to celebrate the triumph of good over evil.[1]

It was the perfect box office bait for the holidays, but Ambrose Small wasn't counting the receipts. Nobody had seen him in weeks, and the rumour was that Ambrose had just closed a $1.75 million deal for his theatres. "If true, this is the biggest theatrical deal ever consummated in the Dominion of Canada," one New York trade magazine mused. "For, to begin with, the story runs that the entire holdings of A.J. Small . . . and the A.J. Small booking agency, have been taken over."[2] It was true, but Ambrose wasn't around to confirm the details. The company that had bought him out was called Trans-Canada Theatres Limited. Anchored in Montreal, Trans-Canada was in the midst of a country-wide shopping spree for theatres, with plans to build where it couldn't buy. Instead of relying on the Broadway barons, it would bring high-class productions from England.

The plans had a touch of grandeur because they were dreamed up by railwaymen. The son-in-law and son of Baron Thomas Shaughnessy, the newly retired president of the Canadian Pacific Railway, were both involved in the project. Nobody had ever mastered the cross-Canada network, owing to the sheer size of the country and the obstacles along the way: the mountains, the sparsely populated prairies, the unpredictable weather. It had always made sense for Canadian theatres to link up with the American states to the south in regional circuits.

Any theatre man would have told you it was overly ambitious, but Baron Shaughnessy's involvement, even indirectly, gave it the stamp of legitimacy. He was something of a miracle worker with lost causes and long shots. He had helped save the Canadian Pacific Railway from financial ruin in the 1880s. He was a master of liquidity, postponing payments until the last possible moment and looking for any discrepancy between work promised and delivered to lobby for a discount.[3] While his methods had nearly ruined his suppliers, they had saved the railway.[4] "His predecessors had been great railroaders, but Shaughnessy had been a hard man, and intolerant, a great mogul in the world of transportation," one journalist said.[5]

A mogul was good, but most of the men involved in the deal were financiers who didn't know stage left from stage right. "I have had many obstacles in the way," Trans-Canada's president and Shaughnessy's son-in-law, H.W. Beauclerk, wrote to Small. ". . . this is a peculiar business transaction which it is very hard to explain favourably to a number of our financial people, as they have had no experience whatever in this line."[6]

Ambrose probably knew their plan was doomed, but this was his chance to escape a business that was becoming more difficult to control. The Great War had been hard on the box office, the Spanish flu had frightened people away from public places, and the actors were demanding better wages and working conditions.[7] (Charlie Chaplin and the rest of the silent film stars, trapped inside a canister of film, were easier to deal with.) Railway travel was becoming more expensive, and the travelling show was looking a little tired. So were his theatres.

Some of the older reporters came up with Ambrose. As cub reporters, they'd had a front-row seat as he finessed his way out of the working class. Some of the guys said he'd backstabbed his way to the top, but he had plenty of admirers who saw the way he'd worked, quietly and diligently like a spider, gathering theatres and booking contracts, weaving his web across the province. He was a good friend if he liked you, a "very vindictive man" if he didn't, and downright "nasty," if you went behind his back.[8]

Ambrose didn't have the best theatre in Toronto, but he controlled dozens across the province. He was the middleman who arranged schedules for out-of-town productions, which in turn offered a steady flow of shows to smaller theatres who couldn't attract them on their own. His network was unavoidable if you wanted to make money on the road in Ontario. Trans-Canada wanted to buy that power—and after a summer of haggling in 1919, they agreed to pay Ambrose $1.75 million: $1 million in cash and $37,500 a year for the twenty years after that.

Ambrose had the upper hand and he knew it. He was slow to share the paperwork and deeds, and by the time the deal closed, there were all kinds of things the Trans-Canada men still didn't know when it came to the theatre's daily operations. Ambrose's personal secretary, Jack Doughty, was moving to Montreal to work for Trans-Canada, so it wasn't a huge worry.

There was a giddiness to Ambrose once he had the $1 million cheque in early December 1919. It was a nonsensical sum in a city where most men made $25 or $30 a week.[9] Housing was scarce in Toronto, and the cost of rent, food, and fuel ate up wages as quickly as the factories churned out stoves and tractors. Homes were crammed with children and boarders. You lived with your parents until you married, even if that meant staying until your thirties. Ambrose had been thirty-six when he finally left home after marrying Theresa Kormann in 1902. He could have moved out sooner, but there wasn't much point since his father lived downtown near the theatre.

The couple lived in the wealthy enclave of Rosedale, north of downtown. They had a roomy mansion with a cook and maid. There were no children, but they found pleasure in their first-class trips to Hawaii, Italy, and Egypt. As years went on, Ambrose also found pleasure in the arms of the chorus girls—and at least one long-term mistress during the war. There were usually a few women he could give a camisole to at Christmas.

Because of his tendency to go off the radar, his disappearance wasn't treated with much seriousness at first. People in the know figured he might be down at the racetrack. Maybe with his girlfriend, Clara. The deal closed on December 1, and the last time anyone saw him was the early evening of December 2. A few of his business contacts bounded up the Opera House stairs to chat with him in early December, only to find his office locked.[10] Word trickled out, and reporters began to ask questions. His theatre managers were probably dealing with more mundane problems already—another star drunk as a skunk, some scenery held up at the border. He'll be back, they said, like he was the family cat on the prowl. But privately, some worried. He usually sent telegrams.

An undated photo of Ambrose Small at his desk at the Grand Opera House.

Edward Flock, the sixty-something lawyer who helped Ambrose close the deal with Trans-Canada was imagining all kinds of terrible ends for his client as Christmas came and went. Maybe Ambrose was beaten and mugged on his way home from the theatre. Maybe the miscreants dragged him to the bottom of the ravine that isolated Rosedale from the rest of downtown.[11]

"What news of our friend. Answer quick," Flock telegrammed the Grand's manager, James Cowan.

"NO WORD YET AT OFFICE OR HOME AM WORRIED," Cowan replied on December 26.[12]

Small's wife, Theresa, knew of her husband's tendency to romance other women, and said she wanted to keep his absence quiet because when he eventually came back, he would be furious to discover she had made a fuss. The police had been poking around since the middle of December, but nobody was ready to print the "missing" posters. It was still easy to imagine Ambrose Small waking up in a sunny locale, the curtains rustling in the breeze, a couple of empty champagne bottles on the floor. His favourite place had always been the edge of good taste.

———

Toronto started the new year as it always did, with a municipal election. The leading contenders for mayor in 1920 were Alderman Sam McBride and incumbent Tommy Church. Both men wanted to wrest control of the privately run streetcar company—and place it into public hands. They spent the day being driven around, shaking hands with returned soldiers, calling out Happy

New Year.[13] (Mayor Tommy Church—a popular Conservative voice—was more convincing, evidently, and was given another year.)

In England, where a few hundred Canadian soldiers were waiting to be discharged from war service, Prime Minister David Lloyd George welcomed in the New Year by reminding his countrymen of the historic signing of the Treaty of Versailles. "Whether the New Year shall be rich with promise or laden with despair depends upon ourselves. We have reached the time when a concentrated effort is essential to the rebuilding of the world."[14]

Sir Arthur Conan Doyle was one of the millions who had lost a son to the Great War. In his New Year's message, the

Toronto's downtown as it looked during the final years of the First World War.

creator of Sherlock Holmes proclaimed that the "age-long mystery of death" would be solved within a generation, and the spiritual world would be universally acknowledged.[15] The Great War had swallowed an entire generation, and Toronto was another city of the missing. On January 3, 1920, its citizens woke up to read about another vanished man.

"Startling Disappearance of Toronto Millionaire Causes Grave Apprehension," read the headline of the *Toronto World*, next to a photo of Ambrose. It was an older photo, but a good likeness. His cheekbones looked sculpted in stone. His hair was thick, receding a little at the temples, but his skin was taut and smooth, his features hawkish and intense. His walrus moustache hid his mouth, but he had trimmed it shorter since the war. "The World has for some time known of Mr. Small's disappearance," the story read, "and of the search that was quietly being made for him, but believed, with his friends, that the missing gentleman would turn up, or that some definite word of his whereabouts would come to hand at any moment." Just above the report, the paper attached an editor's note to explain that they were only writing about Ambrose "in the hope that it may lead to some clue as to the whereabouts of a prominent and wealthy citizen."[16]

Every paper jumped on the story. The *Evening Telegram* had the most beautiful photo of the lot, taken before the war. Ambrose was standing in a Venice piazza with one hand in his pocket and a pigeon in his outstretched palm. The Smalls had gone to Venice in 1912 for the grand reopening of St. Mark's Campanile, the famous bell tower of the basilica that had collapsed ten years earlier. "To live there is to live a poem," Theresa wrote of Venice. "There is no whir and rush of cars and carriages, no click of horses' feet, no twentieth-century hurry of life."[17] Theresa loved visiting the historic churches and gliding along the canals in a gondola.[18] She had snapped the photo of her husband just as his overcoat blew open in a gust of wind. Ambrose was perfectly still, trying not to scare the bird, with shoes so shiny they gleamed in the grubby newsprint. "In Venice then; where is he now?" the headline asked.[19]

People were keen to speculate with the kind of plot lines Small would have booked for an Ontario-wide tour. Perhaps he was having a dalliance with a chorus girl like the 1912 farce *Don't Lie to Your Wife*. Had he been murdered in a harem swimming pool like the wicked and rich Wazir in *Kismet*? The general sense was that the mystery would be solved any day now, so why not have a guess in the meantime? The war had been a nightmare and the transition to peace was not going well. At first, veterans returned to parades and celebrations, but then they had to fight for jobs, compensation for their injuries, and a place to live amid a housing shortage. Many had to battle memories, and if they wanted a drink, they had to be careful about it since the province had banned public alcohol consumption while they were fighting. Many were wounded, recuperating without antibiotics, waiting for prosthetic limbs to be built and face masks to hide hollows carved by shrapnel. There was so much time, and nothing to do but talk. Jawing about a missing millionaire—and where he might be—was a better way to pass the time than worrying about the fate of the world.

If you were in the know—one of the theatre staff who drank whisky in the coal hole of the Grand Opera House—you might have heard what the caretaker found when he went to clean the boss's office the day after Ambrose was last seen. It was filthy. The leg of his rolling chair was broken and the big boxy telephone had been ripped from the wall. There were cigarette butts scattered on the ground, but Ambrose didn't smoke.[20] A few days later, the caretaker was finishing the last of his chores, when the phone rang, late at night.

"Is that the Grand Opera?" a man asked.

"Would you like to know where Mr. Small is?"

"Why certainly," the caretaker said.

"Well keep your mouth shut," the man advised, "or you will be in the same place as him."[21]

TWO

THE HALL OF STRANGE DELIGHTS

TORONTO, 1874

The first object of Ambrose Small's desire was not the girl next door but the theatre next door. The Grand Opera House was a slice of Paris on Adelaide Street, topped by a pleasing mansard roof the same colour as the sky at dusk. On nearby King Street, you could shop for jewellery and silk dresses and catch up on gossip about the city's best families. On Adelaide Street, concerns had always been more practical. There were blacksmiths, stables, and factories where workers churned out Oxford shirts and billiard tables. Horses carted goods and people, and the stench of manure ran sickly sweet on a hot day.

When the theatre was built near Yonge Street in 1874, it was an aspirational bit of architecture. People knew the coal dust would come for it eventually, but a city could dream, and the Grand Opera House was the proof. By that time, fewer than a hundred years had passed since British settlers had imposed their grid and values on the forested swamp that had been home to Indigenous people for thousands of years. The word *Toronto* was the settler take on the Kanienkehaka word for the ancient fishing weirs one day's portage upstream: *Tkaronto.*

The land had been the bottom of a glacial lake during the last ice age, and when Ambrose and his family arrived in Toronto in the 1870s, it didn't feel like the underwater world was very distant. Navigating Toronto with a horse and cart was terrible in the mud of spring and fall, and dirty and dusty in the dry days of summer. Winter brought the only relief, when sleighs sliced through the snow and the rivers froze over. The early reviews from visitors were not great: ill built, tactless, vulgar, no match for "second-rate towns in England."[1] The city had an inferiority complex from the beginning.

After the railways came in the 1850s, industrialization* spread through Toronto's factories, drawing more people from the countryside to build stoves, pianos, furnaces, candy, carriages, glue, shoes, cabinets, corsets, barbed wire, brassware, artificial limbs, and hoop skirts. As men hammered and sawed and drank away the nights, the city grew. There was little help for the unemployed, aside from a couple of charities that provided a

---

* In his comprehensive book about the city in its early years, *Toronto to 1918* (1984), historian J.M.S. Careless notes that industrialization began in the 1870s. In 1871, there were 530 manufacturing enterprises in Toronto; ten years later, there were 2,401. He credits the fact that Toronto was already a centre of capital and labour that was also known as an entrepreneurial place, with businessmen taking advantage of the growing "transport hinterland" to ship their products across the province.

goose at Christmas or a cemetery plot if your child was run down by a runaway horse or killed by a dread disease.[2] The working classes had sawdust-covered taverns, and the rich threw lavish dinner parties to showcase the beautiful things their money could buy: live music, fine cuts of meat, and endless bottles of bubbly champagne.[3] The dinner party circuit was where a group of artistically inclined citizens started talking up the idea for a first-class theatre.

Toronto's first major theatre was the Royal Lyceum—a "queer little theatre" built on the south side of King Street, home to the city's first resident stock company.[4] Many people found the theatre too American, and in that respect, too morally loose.[5] The upper crust shook their heads at the "dirty, filthy rabble" who saved up their pennies for a magician at the Royal Lyceum theatre or a show at the St. Lawrence Hall.[6]

Toronto had its share of travelling circuses, magicians, choral singing, and lectures, but halls were crowded "almost to suffocation."[7] A proper theatre—or an "opera house," as they were called, was not only a necessity, it was a ticket to the international recognition Toronto craved. The most passionate advocate was Robert Harrison, a prominent criminal lawyer who defended his clients from the full spectrum of charges, whether it be sheep stealing or murder. At dinner parties, Harrison and his friends talked up the transformative power of Shakespeare as the gas lamps burned low under the strain of an entire city celebrating the end of the week.

The Grand Opera House was designed by a New York architect in Second Empire style. It opened in 1874, the same

year eight-year-old Ambrose Small moved into town. The theatre's marquee was wedged between storefronts leased to a
rotating cast of barbers, hatters, restaurateurs, and barkeeps. It
was called Mrs. Morrison's Opera House in the beginning,
after the theatre's first manager, Charlotte Morrison, the one-
time star of the Royal Lyceum.

When British theatrical sensation Adelaide Neilson starred
in the romantic melodrama *The Lady of Lyons* that first year, it
felt like Toronto had arrived. "The house was crammed. The
excitement very great," Harrison wrote in his journal. "Baskets
of flowers were presented to her together with two canaries in
two separate cages."[8] But audiences were fickle, and some days
hardly anybody showed up.[9] There were weeks when the gas
engineer would light a scene only to find that the supply was
shut off, and Mrs. Morrison had to hustle someone down to

The Grand Opera House circa 1885.

the gas company to pay the bill.[10] A wealthy politician named Alexander Manning took over in 1876, bringing in a management team from New York. The theatre was rechristened the Grand Opera House, and there was always a steady supply of high-class shows. It all went splendidly until it suffered a very Victorian fate in 1879: it burned to the ground.

Naturally, *Macbeth* was involved.

The Bandmann Company had staged the Scottish play one evening in late November, but the potash, nitrate, and shellac were still brewing in the witches' cauldron long after curtain call.[11] The chemicals sizzled and popped late into the night, when the Grand's on-site employees had finished their nightly tasks and were slumbering in the apartments on the top floors. Nobody knew exactly how it happened, but it's likely that a spark hit a drape, the drape brushed against the wood, and the flammable interior, masked by the theatre's overcoat of brick, became a roaring swirl of flames.

Fires were a horrifying but regular part of life. Toronto had lost much of its business core in 1849 to a blaze, and it would happen again in 1904. Theatres were usually built on the cheap and lit by gas or calcium lamps that had a tendency to explode.[12] The inside of the theatre was a pyromaniac's paradise: wood everywhere; rich, flammable draperies; and scenery made with oil-based paint.[13] A few years before the *Macbeth* fire, a New York theatre inferno had killed three hundred people.[14] (Luckily for the Grand, the crowds had gone home, but there was still a body count.) The *Globe* reporter began his story by noting the devastation "to the gayety of English Canada," before he took readers to the morgue, where the Grand's "humble" carpenter, his wife, and his child, who had been sleeping in their apartment at the top of the building, were "burned to a crisp."[15]

Manning didn't waste time rebuilding. Several of the theatre's walls were still standing, and the Grand came back to life in fifty-one working days, with iron bones, wide staircases, and staff apartments equipped with fire escapes on the main level. "I have spared neither trouble nor expense to make the new Grand Opera House the safest as well as the finest theatre in the Dominion," Manning wrote to the *Globe*.[16] The inside of the new theatre was adorned with painted gold walls and deep crimson fabrics. The stage curtain was painted with a scene of the Temple of Jupiter at Athens.[17] A chandelier fuelled by gas and electricity illuminated the gallery.

The opening show for the "fire-proof" Grand was Shakespeare's *As You Like It*, and Toronto's ladies received a commemorative program of blue silk. Before the play began, British actress Adelaide Neilson—the Toronto favourite who had been showered in flowers and canaries in 1874—returned to read an ode to the Grand.[18] It was particularly stirring when she spoke about the fire and the indomitable spirit of the city that had rallied to rebuild.

> So the wild flames rose through the quiet night
> From faintest flicker into fiercest light. . . .
> Twas a brave fight; alas' in vain; the dawn
> Told that the Hall of Strange Delights was gone.
> What if our Romes be burned—we build once more.

And marble stands where stone was seen before.
The world in this, as in each bygone age,
Sees its great friend and teacher in the stage.[19]

After the fire came the Smalls. Dan Small, a rural hotelier who had moved to Toronto a few years prior, took over two storefronts to the west of the marquee.[20] At number 13, he opened the Grand Hotel, with excellent accommodation for fifteen guests and a "beautiful saloon."[21] At number 15, he opened Small and Company Wine Merchants.[22] His teenage son, Ambrose, helped at the bar, emptying the warm beer from glasses and sweeping sawdust from the floor at the end of the night. Next door, the Grand had a new manager named Oliver Barton (O.B.) Sheppard, a "spirited" fellow who gave Toronto the "intellectual stimulation" of the world's greatest actors.[23] Did anybody expect that Ambrose would one day be more famous than the thespians who came for a nightcap? The theatre staff knew the likeable teen, but nobody really gave him much thought. Nobody imagined he would one day own the theatre. And nobody thought that he would vanish from its strange corridors.

THREE

THE SMALLS OF ADJALA

Adjala Township was rich in wheat, cattle, and Irish accents. It was part of Simcoe County, a large swath of rolling, farmable land north of Toronto where people tended to settle with their religious brethren. Everyone knew that Adjala was a "first-rate township" for Catholics: "They predominate in the proportion of Two to One!" read one 1856 advertisement.[1] When Ambrose Small's paternal grandparents, Daniel and Sarah, left King's County, Ireland, in the 1830s, Adjala seemed like a good place to start fresh. The name was beautiful and foreign to Irish ears, honouring an "Indian Princess" as the county directory said. They were some of the earliest settlers, and the forest around them was suffocating in its density.[2] The Smalls built a log cabin in the southern part of the township, within walking distance of the Catholic church in the hamlet of Colgan.

Many strange things happened in Adjala, if you asked the Protestants in the surrounding towns. There was that time the Catholic priest allegedly told his congregation who to vote for in the election and roared that he "would curse all or any of his flock" who disobeyed him.[3] Then there was that tense week in 1866, when Protestants were convinced that the Fenians planning to invade Canada were in cahoots with the "murtherin' villains" of Adjala, and the lot of them were conspiring to kill the local Protestants and divide up the land among their own.[4] The rumour was so widely believed that four hundred Protestants on horseback gathered in the dark with pitchforks, muskets, and tree branches one night, believing the attack to be imminent.[5] When a few scouts cantered into Adjala to see if trouble was brewing, the entire township was asleep, except for a few barking dogs. "It's a bit funny when you think of it," recounted a farmer who was waiting to attack Adjala that night. "All these people in Ajala [sic] sound asleep, never dreamin' how close they were to war."[6]

The county directory didn't mention any of these antics, and instead painted Simcoe County as a cohesive place, low on crime and high on morality—but people there quarrelled just like anywhere else. The occasional murder and arson made the paper, usually the result of a drunken brawl over broken promises or unpaid debts. When the train came through the province in the 1850s, it didn't roll through Adjala. The horse was the best way to get around, favoured by local priests and angry Protestant mobs. The local equine population was helped along by the Small family stallion, who made the rounds every year.[7]

The Smalls did well as the forest tumbled to the ground and fields of wheat, barley, and beans defined the landscape.[8] Brick homes replaced the log cabins, land values increased, and not every son could inherit the family farm. That was okay for the Smalls, who had six children—five boys and one daughter—as the family was known for politics and business in addition to farming. Dan Small, one of the younger boys in the family, followed his older brother Peter into the world of innkeeping.

In 1865, when Dan was twenty-three, he married Ellen Brazil.[9] Ellen was a Catholic girl from the nearby community of Bond Head. She was the oldest child in a family of five, and her family had moved around after her father died—she had even spent some of her teenage years in Toronto.[10] Dan and Ellen ran Small's Hotel in Bradford, a town twenty-five miles east of Adjala that was a prominent stop on the railway that connected Toronto to Lake Huron.[11] Their first child, Ambrose, was born in the winter of 1866 and baptized Catholic. A few years later, the Smalls moved to Bolton, where Dan ran another hotel.[12] In 1874, they were one of the thousands of families who showed up in Toronto, hoping to make a living in the city growing with manufacturing wealth.[13]

Dan Small was "hopelessly ambitious," and the Smalls settled on the western stretches of Queen Street.[14] It was the outskirts of town, a few blocks away from the Asylum for the Insane. Dan Small leased the National Hotel and tavern at the corner of Queen and Bathurst Streets. It was a modest building, sturdier than the shacks down the road, but not as nice as the brick building that housed the barber and feed store next door.[15] The family lived in the hotel with a rotating cast of sleeping strangers and a family dog.[16] There were lots of Catholics in the city, but they were in the minority. Most of the Smalls' neighbours were Protestant. It wasn't novel for Dan, who had spent the last few years running hotels in Protestant towns—but the power dynamic was more pronounced in Toronto. Historically, Ireland had been more Catholic than Protestant—but the migration to Canada was reversed—Protestants dominated the demographics, especially in Ontario.[17]

It's hard to pinpoint when the trouble began between the Catholic and Protestant populations of Ireland, but King Henry VIII didn't help matters when he created the Anglican Church in the sixteenth century and imposed his religion on his kingdom, including Ireland. The forced conversion didn't go over well, so the king dispatched loyal Protestants to plant themselves in the north, on the confiscated land of rebel Catholics.[18] The monarchs who followed continued the Protestant demographic expansion project.

There had been a glimmer of hope for Catholics when King James II took over the British throne in 1685. The new king was a recent Catholic convert, but Protestants consoled themselves because the king's daughter Princess Mary was still a good loyal Protestant. When the king's new wife gave birth to a son, the tiny Catholic baby worried Protestants. They invited Princess Mary's husband, William of Orange, to oust his father-in-law and restore Protestantism to the realm.[19] The bid succeeded* and life in Ireland continued to be harsh for Catholics. Under the

---

*   It would be celebrated in Protestant garrisons like Toronto for centuries to come.

penal laws, they couldn't own land or access education, and they had a "self-appointed counter revolutionary force of loyalists" ready to keep them in their place, should they attempt any uprisings.[20] The Loyal Orange Lodge was founded in Ulster in 1795, and named for the Protestant community's favourite usurper, William of Orange.

When mass migration to North America started to pick up in the early nineteenth century, many of the Irish Protestants left a polarized country behind, bringing their love of William of Orange, and their suspicions about Catholics to Upper Canada.[21] As William J. Smyth details in *Toronto: The Belfast of Canada*, they built Orange Lodges across the land. These were "ideological garrisons" where you could air your suspicions about the Pope, but they served a practical purpose too.[22] There was no social safety net in those days, so lodge dues went to men struggling with illness, the death of a spouse, or job loss.[23] There was whisky in the winter and picnics and parades in the summer.[24] English and Scottish Protestants were gladly received—so long as you were Protestant, you were welcome.[25]

The migration from Ireland marked the beginning of what one historian calls Ontario's "long orange walk"—an era of Protestant dominance that lasted for nearly a century, entrenched by powerful Orange mayors, premiers, police, lawyers, and judges.[26] In Toronto, the Protestants ran the show, and many didn't trust the Pope, believing that he was "bent on regaining the prestige and authority" he had lost in an increasingly secular world.[27]

When boatloads of Irish famine migrants showed up in Toronto mid-century, the Orange Order renewed their vigilance amid the surge in the Catholic population.[28] Toronto was a British place. A Protestant place. "The Belfast of Canada," some of them said, namedropping the Protestant stronghold in the north of Ireland.[29] Charles Dickens, who visited Toronto back in 1842, said it was a pity that old grudges ran hot, with "the most discreditable and disgraceful results." There was murder, rowdiness, violence, and tension. In 1866, at the height of the Fenian scare, an Orange newspaper warned of a Catholic plot to murder Toronto's Protestants. Military volunteers caught up in the drama yelled "To Hell with the Pope" as they walked by the Catholic bishop's home.[30] Violence was sporadic, and most people were not extremists. Most people wanted to get along.

The Smalls arrived sometime in 1874, and their formative early years in the city were marred by an event that was later called "the last gasp of physical confrontation" between the city's Catholics and Protestants.[31] It began in Rome, when Pope Pius IX declared 1875 a "Jubilee Year." It was a rare but special chance for Catholics to be pardoned of all sins, and parishioners had to make pilgrimages to different churches in the city and make certain prayers to cleanse their souls.[32] The marching started that summer, but the tension erupted in the fall, when an Orange crowd threw stones and fired pistols into the air.[33] The "Jubilee riots" were widely condemned as a shameful outbreak of "intolerant bigotry"[34] by the Protestant rabble.[35]

In this Toronto, where municipal employees were given a day off every July for the Orange parade, the Smalls were quietly Catholic. Dan Small still sent his taxes to the Catholic school board, and the census taker recorded the family religion as "R.C."

when he stopped by every ten years.[36] In 1880, the family—which now included Ambrose's younger sister Florence—moved downtown, taking over the hotel and bar next to the Grand Opera House complex.[37] Depending on business, Dan would sometimes take over the adjoining storefront to sell liquor. As a teenager, Ambrose attended De La Salle College, a Catholic all-boys academy a few blocks east. He was second in his class in English grammar and natural philosophy, and third in geography.[38]

Ambrose was smart, but his attention was diverted. For whimsy, you couldn't beat the Grand Opera House next door. The touring show was still unreliable in those days. Companies crossed North America on the railway. Contracts could be easily broken, attendance could be soul crushing, and transporting a troupe of actors ate up cash.[39] The staff at the Grand doubled as casting directors, recruiting down and out men to be actors in the "eatifying" scenes, and herding college boys to fill out the ballroom dances.[40] It wasn't strange to see the janitor filling in for a bit part, or to have the star of the show suspended from a painful hoist for two excruciating minutes, a look of pained serenity on his face, because his ascent to heaven was tripped up by faulty rigging.

Ambrose sold newspapers out of the family storefront,[41] helped at the saloon, and worked as an usher, seating people for whatever the delight of the week was—like the trick horse show, where a blind horse named Uncle Ruth untied knots and understood over one hundred words. By eighteen, he had a job behind the curtain as assistant treasurer.[42] A journalist who knew him back then said that Ambrose had created a matchmaking pamphlet that so impressed the Grand's manager, O.B. Sheppard, that he offered Ambrose a job.[43] Another story credits Sir Henry Irving, the looming British actor who was said to be the inspiration for the character Count Dracula. Irving came to town in the 1880s for *Macbeth*, and he apparently saw a young Ambrose selling tickets on the wood-plank sidewalk. He talked to Ambrose, who said he might become a lawyer. "The show business needs smart boys like you," Irving said. "Stay in this business."[44]

Ambrose came of age as the kerosene and gas lamps were replaced by electric light. Patrons at the Grand could hire "one horse hacks" for fifty cents to any part of the city. It was an age of progress, but science had only begun to unravel the mysteries of the body, and his mother, Ellen, was unwell. The Small family lore was that Ellen never recovered from her pregnancies very well. Her final daughter, Gertrude, had been born in 1883, and sometime afterward, Ellen was diagnosed with chronic Bright's disease.* A scientist named Richard Bright had identified the complex kidney problem back in the 1820s—but by the time you saw blood in the urine, it was too late. Death always won.[45]

Some of the medical advice—like avoiding the chill and damp—was not suited to life in a drafty Toronto hotel. Other treatment options were more accessible but not curative. Stay in bed. Apply a few leeches on your back to suck out the toxins. Drink cream of tartar water to cleanse the organ.[46] Build up your blood with cod liver oil and malt. Take arsenic and mercury for the nerves,[47] and morphine when the convulsions came.[48] Antibiotics were a faraway dream, and so was a kidney

---

*   Modern diagnosis: kidney disease, or in some cases, diabetes.

transplant. Doctors were told to "throw more hopefulness and cheer into the treatment of this disease than is generally done," as if a smile might distract from looming death.[49] Ellen died a few days after Christmas 1887, forty-three years old. Ambrose was twenty-one, Florence was ten, and Gertrude was four. Their mother's body was placed in the Catholic cemetery's dead house to await the spring thaw. Somebody in the family— Dan, probably—slipped the wedding ring from her finger before the casket closed forever. It was meant for Ambrose. One day he'd marry, and his mother would be there through this ring.[50]

Ambrose threw himself into his work at the Grand, where he was promoted to treasurer, counting up the receipts from shows like *The Pearl of Peking* (with costumes from China) and *The Fugitive* (a great New York success). His boss, O.B. Sheppard, was twenty years older, with a wife, children, and boundless charm. Like the Small family, O.B. had traded rural life for a job in Toronto. He was an outdoorsman who liked horses, and when the theatre season wound down every summer, he worked for the government as a game official in the north country. He had been an alderman on city council for a few years, and he and his wife were both interested in pioneer history. People respected him so much that a baby was once abandoned on his doorstep in a wicker basket, instead of at a church or a convent.[51] O.B. leaned into his reputation and made sure to arrive early before every show so he could charm his guests like a priest welcoming his flock.[52]

For five years, Ambrose managed the accounts behind the scenes, an "affable and efficient" young man.[53] His stint at the Grand came to an end in 1889 when Ambrose and O.B.

had a "violent quarrel" and O.B. fired him.[54] Small was twenty-three years old, and he had probably been too pushy with ideas that didn't suit his boss's old-fashioned sensibilities. Ambrose packed up his office and vowed that he would one day seek his vengeance when he returned as the theatre's owner.[55] A few more theatres had opened since the Grand made its debut, and Ambrose walked two doors west looking for a job at the Toronto Opera House, a theatre born from the husk of a roller rink.

The rollerskating craze hit North America in the 1880s, and a handful of rinks popped up downtown. To the pious, they were cavernous halls of sin where young girls were corrupted by clasping the "ungloved hands" of strange men. There was also talk of boys dying "from brain exhaustion" associated with the sport.[56] When the trend petered out, a pair of Detroit business-men, Mr. Jacobs and Mr. Sparrow, transformed the Adelaide rink into a theatre. They went after a more lowbrow market than the Grand—offering a "menu of sobs and villainy" along with cheap musicals.[57] Ambrose was hired as treasurer in 1889 and went to war with his old boss for the city's entertainment dollars.[58] He added more seats and tried to pick value shows that would delight and frighten. Some say he raised the standards of cheap theatre; but the offerings were so lurid that one old theatre worker thought audience members with high blood pressure ought to stay home for the sake of their health.[59]

Ambrose was an up-and-comer, eager to impress friends and strangers alike. He drank with the reporters and tried to help the stagehands get a better pay deal. The men behind the curtain appreciated his help, calling him a "true friend" as they presented the "exceedingly popular" Ambrose with a token of thanks after big-name shows.[60] When a young Irish actor finished his two-week stint at the Toronto Opera House, he was so grateful for the sellout crowds that he presented Ambrose with an inscribed diamond pin.[61] His career had taken off, but it wasn't enough. There were whispers about his unseemly ambition. After a few years at the Toronto Opera House, Ambrose became manager.[62] It wasn't a simple promotion: the rumour was that Ambrose had slandered the former manager until he was fired.[63]

Hector Charlesworth had been charmed by Ambrose, but now the theatre critic began to pay closer attention, wondering if his "amiability was something of a mask."[64] "Like all the younger newspapermen I was on friendly and even intimate terms with the new manager," he said.[65] But he began to notice that Ambrose "did not enjoy the trust" of travelling managers who came through town. The word among the travelling shows that stayed in Toronto for a week was that you didn't want to leave your nightly share of the box office receipts under the control of Ambrose J. Small. Money had a habit of disappearing from his safe. And it wasn't just that. Now that he had a bit of control, Ambrose was obsessed with keeping it.

One of Charlesworth's good friends at the *Globe* worked for Small on the side as a public relations man. The reporter was good at both jobs, and Ambrose wanted him full-time at the theatre. After he turned Ambrose down, hateful, defamatory letters began to arrive at the office of the *Globe*'s editor-in-chief. Charlesworth saw the letters and recognized the work of Ambrose right away: "Paper and typewriting were the same, and the handwriting was hardly disguised,"[66] Small didn't deny it. "From that night, though for newspaper reasons I was obliged to maintain civilities, there was no further cordiality between Small and myself," he said.[67]

Not long after, another of Charlesworth's friends had a troubling run-in with the theatre manager. The friend was "one of those Bohemians" who drifted between the newspaper and theatre worlds.[68] When he went looking for work in New York as an advance press agent one season, he realized he had been blacklisted. Ambrose, upset by some perceived slight, had written to all of the theatrical companies to say the man was a lazy, no-good fool. He left New York in a rage. His anger did not subside on the long train ride home; nor did it abate as he walked up the grooved stairs of the Toronto Opera House. He burst into Small's office and pointed a revolver at the blue-eyed devil in the tailored suit and said he was going to "finish" him "for good and all." Small's cronies leapt on him.[69]

Ambrose was rattled. He could have apologized or changed his ways. Instead, he paid someone to build a cage around his desk.[70] In his memoir, Charlesworth included a handful of anecdotes about Ambrose Small's acts of "wanton treachery" and ungentlemanly business practices.[71] He was a terrible correspondent and an unyielding negotiator, which earned him his fair share of lawsuits. Having ordered dozens of chairs from Chicago, he refused to pay when the job went over budget. Same with the brickwork for a theatre in Hamilton. Then there was a woman who was angry when her photo magically (and falsely) appeared in a program as the leading actress in *The Fatal Flower* and Ambrose did nothing about it. "Miss Annie Webb of Toronto issued a writ against

Ambrose J. Small," the *Globe* reported, ". . . claiming $2000 for libel in publishing a copy of a photograph of the plaintiff in a programme he issued. . . . Miss Webb denies any connection with the opera company."[72]

With each accusation, the nice young man faded away, but Ambrose didn't forget him. Inside his daybook, where he scribbled down important details of the day's business, he had a few of the old stories folded into a protective sleeve at the back.[73] The stories celebrated the kind, mediocre man he had been at the beginning of his career, the "third most popular" treasurer in North America.[74] The daybook surfaced in 1929, a decade after he vanished. Two boys found it as they rummaged through a garbage heap for treasures. By then, the idea of Ambrose Small as a decent person had been buried underneath actual garbage and the crushing weight of his mythology. The *Star* newspaper sent a photographer to snap a photo of the boys and their discovery. Then the world went back to the comfortable narrative: Ambrose Small, mean-spirited man of mystery.

It was always easier that way.

FOUR

MRS. AMBROSE SMALL

At first glance, Theresa Kormann and Ambrose Small seemed comically mismatched. She was the charitable, pious do-gooder. He was the rule-breaking bon vivant. But they were both ambitious children of Toronto entrepreneurs.

Theresa's father, Ignatius, was born in Alsace in 1835, which had been French or German, depending on the most recent war. He came to Canada as a young man in the middle of the nineteenth century and met his wife, Mary Eva, in Waterloo, a community where you could find schnitzel just as good as in Germany.[1] The couple married and moved to a hamlet sixty miles north called Carlsruhe. It was named for the German city of the same name (although their version started with a K), wedged between the French border and the Black Forest. The southern Ontario farmland was mostly flat with soft rolling hills, and Ignatius was the village's first postmaster,[2] divvying up the mail each week for the hamlet's scattered residents. He spoke French, English, and German and soon came to the attention of the movers and shakers of Grey County.

When local member of Parliament Alexander Sproat heard that Ignatius was heading back to Europe in the summer of 1870, he floated the idea of employing the "very well-educated man" to recruit German and French settlers on Canada's behalf. Sproat raised the matter with George-Étienne Cartier, a Quebec politician who had helped wrangle the Confederation of Canada three years earlier. Sproat would have written to the prime minister "but for his severe illness." (It's suspected that the well-lubricated John A. Macdonald had acute pancreatitis in the summer of 1870.³) "[Ignatius] now resides in the Township of Carrick," Sproat explained, "where there are a very large number of Catholics. If we could make him an emigrant agent, he would do a lot of good."⁴

Ignatius Kormann became a salesman for the Canadian dream. At taverns and restaurants in France and Germany, he talked up Canada's rich farmland and boundless opportunity. He was well regarded by the government, but there were occasional complaints—like that time one of "Mr. Kormann's German settlers" allegedly murdered a local in a Quebec village and caused "much excitement and fear" among the old settlers, who complained that they had been forced to huddle together at night for safety.⁵ In addition to the Europeans Ignatius cajoled across the Atlantic, he and Mary Eva added new citizens to the country roughly every two years, consulting their Bible for good Catholic names. By 1871, there was Francis Xavier, Josephine Maria, Henry, Joseph, Maria Magdalena, Francis Ignatius, and

Maria Theresa, seven months old.[6] (Elizabeth, Emma, Mary, and John were still to come.)

A few years later, the family had moved to the outskirts of Toronto, where Ignatius worked as a butcher, a sausage maker, an importer of French wines, and a "commercial traveller."[7] In the early 1880s he and Bavarian Lothar Reinhardt took over the Walz brewery, naming it Reinhardt & Co. Brewery. Reinhardt was a formally trained brewer,[8] and they modernized the plant with steam engines and cranked out thousands of barrels of lager beer a year, "unsurpassed for purity, quality, flavour and uniform excellence."[9] Few things riled people in Toronto more than booze, but German-adjacent brewers had a small advantage with the moral reformers—their lagers were seen as a lighter "temperance" beverage.[10] When Reinhardt moved on, Kormann bought him out and renamed the brewery for his family: Kormann Brewery.[11]

Ignatius and Mary Eva bought a sturdy brick home at the intersection of Bloor and Yonge Streets in 1885. Their dining room had an onyx table with beautiful linen and silverware. Fine oil paintings decorated the walls, and the ledges were lined with Mary Eva's fancy bric-a-brac.[12] Robert Simpson, the wealthy retailer who had made a fortune on his mail-order department store, lived down the street. The family was on the rise—the older sons were working as clerks, piano tuners, and bookkeepers, and the Kormanns had enough money to send two of their younger daughters[13] to St. Joseph's Academy, a Catholic boarding and day school near the provincial parliament buildings, a ten-minute walk from their home. The school was run by the Sisters of St. Joseph.

The religious congregation was founded in France in the seventeenth century, but a few sisters came to Toronto from the United States in 1851 to care for the sick and vulnerable. They filled the city's infrastructure gaps,* opening an orphanage, schools, and later, four hospitals. They also taught in parish schools as well as in their own academy, where Theresa and her classmates were the future of Catholic Toronto, foot soldiers in lace and pearls. In addition to their academic lessons, the sisters taught the women "the exact width of a ladylike smile, the exact rhythm of a curtsey, the exact position of the head, feet and arms and hands, while sitting, standing and walking, the exact intonation of polite speech."[14] St. Joseph's Academy was not far from the Kormann home, but Theresa boarded there for her final year of study.[15] Grades were read aloud at a monthly assembly, discipline was dispensed by hairbrush, and both visitors and mail were heavily regulated.[16] The closest thing to a prom was the annual library ball, where the women dressed as their favourite literary figure.[17]

Theresa loved to write. Years later, she penned a story seemingly inspired by her academy years for the alumni journal. The story was about an intelligent teenage student named Ethel heading home for the Christmas holiday, and Theresa

---

*   The Sisters of St. Joseph were instrumental in supporting the city
     through many of its early struggles. They helped sick and dying famine
     migrants who arrived in Toronto, as well as the orphans created by
     those deaths, and also helped during the diphtheria epidemic of the
     1890s. They founded St. Michael's Hospital, St. Joseph's Hospital,
     Our Lady of Mercy Hospital, and Providence Hospital.

described the ringing bells on the horse-drawn carriage, creating a merry scene. The protagonist, Ethel, had beautiful black eyes and was "her father's pet."[18] When Ethel arrived home, there was a bouquet of roses and a big present under the tree with a pearl ring inside and a card inscribed "From your first lover." Ethel tried to hide the gift from her father, embarrassed by the inscription.

"Who is he, my Little One?" her father asked.

Ethel cried. She didn't know who sent them.

"Her father took her in his arms, kissed her, and said, 'My little sweetheart, who ever loved you before your father? Am I not your first lover? It was I who sent the roses."

Before her 1887 graduation, Theresa posed for a photograph with four other students who could afford the luxury.[19] She was the moon-faced graduate with the soft, delicate features standing on the pelt of a jungle cat. Her hair was pinned in a loose updo, a garland of flowers pinned to her chest.

1887 was a big year. Sir John A. Macdonald held on to power in the federal election, Toronto's first pro baseball team won their league with the help of slugger Ned "Cannonball" Crane,[20] Theresa graduated in the early summer, and Ellen Small died at Christmas. The Kormann and Small families were likely connected through their downtown businesses: Ignatius Kormann brewed beer and Dan Small sold it by the pint at his hotel and tavern.[21]

They were close enough that a few years after Ellen died, the Kormanns' eldest daughter, Josephine, married the widower Dan Small, a man twenty years her senior.[22] (Shortly after the wedding,

Ignatius died unexpectedly, leaving the brewery to the care of his wife and children.) At twenty-eight, Josephine became a stepmother to children who were closer to her own age. Ambrose was twenty-five, and Florence and Gertrude were fourteen and eight. Josephine was soon pregnant: Percy was born in 1892, Madeleine followed in 1894, and the family made some lifestyle changes. Dan finally gave up the hotel and saloon at the theatre and opened a liquor store a few blocks north.[23] The Smalls moved into their first proper house, on a short stub of a street called Moss Park Place in the Garden District downtown, near Queen and Sherbourne Streets and the Kormann Brewery.[24]

As the new century dawned, Josephine was busy with her family, and Theresa, a single woman of thirty, travelled the great cities of Europe, honing her singing voice with the French and Italian masters. The Toronto papers said Theresa's voice sounded like the very essence of youth: clear, healthy, and hopeful.[25] "While abroad she won many complimentary paragraphs from European Journals," the Sisters at her old school proudly noted. Theresa had even been given the chance to sing at the Basilica in Lourdes. "Dear Teresa is a true child of St. Joseph's—very grateful and very faithful."[26]

By the standards of her time, Theresa was inching past marrying age, but there was a promising candidate close to home. Ambrose Small, the stepson of her sister, was a few years older, handsome and ambitious, and technically a Catholic. By now, he had risen through the ranks of the Toronto Opera House from treasurer to manager to lessee— the first local to do so in "some years," the *Star* said, marvelling at his achievements.[27] He had reformed "the Home of blood and thunder" with high-class entertainment at low prices and looped the theatre into an existing American theatre circuit, which guaranteed a steady supply of shows. Small liked the idea of the circuit and started making deals with other Ontario theatres, building a network of his own.[28] He partnered up with Detroit theatrical promoter Clark J. Whitney to learn the ropes. They had profit-sharing agreements for theatres they were both involved with.[29]

Ambrose had done a good job making the Toronto Opera House relevant, but there was more competition every year. A new theatre called the Princess had opened on King Street, a few blocks northwest of the Grand.[30] It was the city's first modern theatre, one of the "prettiest opera houses on the continent," with a large stage, electricity throughout the building, and seats that were designed so that every person had a good view. It was "one of the best equipped and most thoroughly tasteful houses of amusement in America," the *Globe* said on its opening weekend in 1895.[31] The Grand had well-earned prestige, but the Princess was gaining momentum.[32] On the eve of the 1901 season, the *Star* made note of a management shakeup in Toronto's theatre world. O.B. Sheppard, the elder statesman of the Grand Opera House, had jumped to the Princess and taken his booking connections with him. That meant there was an opening for a manager at the Grand Opera House, so Ambrose swooped in to make the best of it: "This old-established theater may expect a new impulse from his activity," the *Star* noted.[33]

Theresa Small

The season kicked off during the Toronto Industrial Exhibition (renamed the Canadian National Exhibition in 1912). Every year, the exhibition drew tens of thousands of people to Toronto to marvel at cutting-edge technologies, horse races, and pheasants that were better than any birds you might find in the old country.[34] It always coincided with the opening week of Toronto's theatre season, which shut down during the unbearable heat of summer. O.B. had a matinee performance of *Way Down East* at the Princess—a "simply homely" story of a woman's life. The show was a sensation with the ladies and proved "that the Princess will be as popular with the high-class matinee goers as the Grand was in its palmiest days."[35] Ambrose had the comedy duo of Ward and Vokes yukking it up at the Grand with a "farcical extravaganza" that featured twenty-three musical numbers.[36] Ambrose knew it would be a difficult go in the crowded entertainment landscape. A burlesque theatre, the Star, had opened around the corner, and the Shea brothers, from Buffalo, had a popular vaudeville theatre on Yonge Street. Small knew the Princess would have an impressive season, so he played the quantity game instead. He quietly built his empire, securing leases and contracts in small towns like Ingersoll, Chatham, and Stratford.

His most important acquisition was tucked into the social pages of the newspaper in 1902. Ambrose was engaged to marry Theresa Kormann: the devout Catholic daughter of a small Toronto brewing empire. Theresa's father, Ignatius, had died in 1891, and now her mother faced a terminal cancer diagnosis. Mary Eva, who had been running the brewery with her sons since her husband's death, died two weeks before Theresa's wedding, leaving behind an estate of $72,000, including real estate, stocks, horses, and about $30,000 cash.[37] "Deceased was a woman of great force of character which was shown conspicuously in the successful administration of the large business in which she became the head on the death of her husband," the *Globe* noted. "In the social circle in which she moved Mrs. Kormann was much loved for her tenderness of heart and warm friendship."[38]

Ambrose and Theresa had a subdued wedding at St. Basil's Church* a couple of weeks after Mary Eva was buried. Theresa wore a silk crêpe de chine gown studded with lace medallions and pearls, and held a clutch of white roses and ferns as she walked down the aisle with her brother, passing paintings of biblical violence on the walls. Candles flickered for her dead parents and the dead of the parish, and the soft light caught the diamond sunburst in her dark hair—a gift from Ambrose. Ambrose held Theresa's hand and delicately jimmied the wedding ring in place—he'd had it made specially, using his mother's old wedding ring.[39]

Mr. and Mrs. Ambrose Small returned from their honeymoon to their new home in Rosedale. It was a three-storey brick mansion with a separate staircase for staff—hot in the summer and drafty in the winter, with stained glass windows, wainscoting,

---

* The church, run by the Basilian Fathers, was an important symbol for Toronto's Catholics. Captain John Elmsley—a late in life convert to Catholicism—donated the land and requested that his heart be entombed in the west wall when he died in 1863. It is still there to this day.

and engraved brass door knobs. Their new neighbourhood radiated wealth. The streets were romantically landscaped, curving this way and that, the imposing homes decorated with embellished stone work, heavy pillars, and stained glass.[40] Ambrose had a growing business, and Theresa had several thousand dollars she had inherited from her mother's estate, along with a few stocks and bonds that she'd purchased before their marriage.[41]

At her first official reception as Mrs. Ambrose Small, there was a "spring-like softness in the air." Theresa wore her wedding gown and accepted the compliments of her new neighbours. There were crimson roses and lilies of the valley and dainty snacks.[42] Years of teas unfurled ahead of her, with tables resplendent with flowers, and society ladies murmuring their approval. Some of the neighbours were descendants of the landed gentry, but many were the new class of leaders—politicians, lawyers, doctors, industrialists. Toronto money was best respected when it had a few generations to "mellow," but you could speed it along with the right kind of socializing and charitable work.[43]

Ambrose didn't care much about rules. His main concern was money, and not long after their wedding, two things happened that would entrench his plans to make more of it. Clark Whitney, his business partner in the Ontario circuit, died in March 1903, and several days later, the Toronto Opera House—managed by Ambrose—was destroyed by fire. The blaze was blamed on faulty insulation of an electric wire. A janitor smelled smoke before he went to bed, but he couldn't find the source of it, and neither could police. He woke up gasping at 4 a.m. when the room he shared with his wife and children filled with smoke.

As fire and smoke snarled through the theatre, and the janitor piled his furniture into a tower for his family to climb to escape through a skylight. It was "as thrilling as any of the most sensational scenes that had been depicted on the theatre's stage," the *Globe* said.[44] A Detroit company owned the charred remains, and Ambrose Small, who leased the building, told the papers it would be rebuilt.

It reopened that November as the Majestic with the romantic religious musical *Mary of Magdala*, an appropriate blend for Ambrose and Theresa's first anniversary. "It is not perhaps a work of genius," the *Globe* reported on opening night. "The theme is the regeneration of a woman's soul through the saving grace of the influence of Jesus of Nazareth." One of the leading actresses of the American stage, Mrs. Fiske, played Mary Magdalene. (The reviewer thought Mrs. Fiske did an admirable job, even if she had a quick, nervous way of speaking. Judas was played with a sinister edge, top notch indeed.[45]) Although they didn't own the theatre when it burned to the ground, one historian noted that the blaze encouraged Ambrose and Theresa to embrace geographical diversity in their future theatrical assets.[46]

Theresa used some of her family money to help Ambrose purchase theatres he had been leasing, including the Hamilton Grand Opera House (1903) and the London Grand Opera House (1905).[47] They soon owned the Majestic too, and Ambrose continued to acquire leases in smaller cities. With his old business partner dead, Ontario was his for the taking—no profit sharing involved.[48] (Whitney's heirs did sue for a portion of the profits. Small didn't want to divulge any of his business details, so he didn't file a statement of defence. An appeal court eventually sided with Ambrose, ruling that the death dissolved the partnership.[49]) Small went full tilt. He entertained Broadway producers on yachts; he had a telegraph company wire election results to his theatres so the audience could keep up with Prime Minister Wilfrid Laurier's victory in 1904; and, in 1905, he was rumoured to have a $200,000 offer to purchase his first love—Toronto's Grand Opera House.[50]

It was soon his, and the money poured in like a capitalist's fairytale. He showed authentic pictures of the San Francisco earthquake with piano accompaniment, and signed an endorsement deal for Bell pianos. There were summer trips to New York and Quebec. The Smalls had one of the first motor cars in the province and built one of the city's first garages in their backyard. The treasured family car had the macabre distinction of being one of the city's first to run over a pedestrian. Ambrose

High Park, 1912

loved to drive, but it was the chauffeur at the wheel that day in 1906, driving Theresa, Josephine, and Dan Small home from an afternoon in High Park. The driver ran over a nurse who was waiting for a streetcar before her shift at the asylum. As with most pedestrian deaths in the early days of automobile excitement, Jane Porter was blamed for her own demise.[51] The death didn't sour Ambrose's enthusiasm for the open road. He liked to buy two new cars every year. He also purchased extravagant gifts for his wife: pearl necklaces, diamond pins, a sealskin coat trimmed with chinchilla, and a silver fox fur coat when the chinchilla coat wasn't good enough.[52]

Ambrose Small sent his New York contacts postcards from his yearly summer travels around the world before the First World War.

When the theatre shut down in the heat of the summer, Ambrose and Theresa lounged on steamship cruises to Europe and Asia, which featured diving shows at the pool. His friends said that Ambrose only relaxed on the water, rocked asleep by the waves in his first-class suite. At the time, most people traversed the ocean to serve in a war or bury their mother in the old country, but the Smalls travelled for pleasure. Ambrose sent postcards of Hong Kong gamblers, Japanese theatres, and Hawaiian surfers to the booking agents in New York, and Theresa brought her camera, dreaming up the presentations she would give when she returned. She had a reputation as one of Toronto's best "woman speakers," and she always returned to St. Joseph's Academy to talk about her travels. The sisters who listened to her tales of faraway lands swore they could feel the scorching Egyptian sand underfoot, see the long shadow of the camel at sunset.[53] Theresa brought a little piece of the world home to Toronto, and the religious sisters always presented her with a bouquet of roses, which she dutifully left at the chapel so they could breathe out their fragrance for the Lord.

FIVE

NAPOLEON AND HIS EMPIRE

The powerbrokers behind the scenes of the theatre business were more dramatic than any character on stage. Consider Abe Erlanger, the most frightening member of the Theatrical Syndicate. He collected statues of Napoleon in his New York office and perfected the French dictator's battlefield stance, "hands behind his back, feet spread apart, and a brooding scowl on his face."[1] "He was eccentric, perhaps a touch mad, and certainly a terrifying character," one historian noted.[2] The Syndicate, as they came to be known, was a group of six men who pooled their clout to take control of the theatre industry at the close of the nineteenth century. They had hatched their plan in a New York City restaurant in 1896. They didn't like the way that managers, actors, and booking agents played them against each other, so they created a centralized booking agency, forcing everyone to sign contracts.[3] Theatres that wanted a steady supply of shows, and travelling companies that wanted a guaranteed month on the road—they would all have to come through the Syndicate. By 1905, the group controlled hundreds of theatres in North America and played an all-or-nothing game.[4]

Many thought they had saved the industry from chaos—but others thought their greed would destroy the theatre.[5] The Syndicate did everything they could to stamp out those voices. When the *New York Dramatic Mirror* questioned the monopoly, Erlanger—who liked to speak in the thundering cadence of a Shakespearian king—banned the trade newspaper from his theatres, and said he would fire any actor caught browsing its pages.[6] (Generally speaking, criticizing the Syndicate ended with banishment or unemployment.)

The Syndicate seemed unstoppable until the Shubert brothers began gathering their own theatres in upstate New York at the turn of the century. Sam, Lee, and J.J. Shubert were Syndicate clients, but they dreamed of building their own network and, one day, producing their own shows. Erlanger and company weren't worried at first, but as the Shubert power grew, Erlanger accused them of breaking a contract and pronounced them "finished in the theatre world."[7]

Sam Shubert—who had many allies among blacklisted theatre companies and actors—called for an "open door" booking policy without repercussions. The not very subtle implication was that of course you'd want to deal with the Shuberts over the Syndicate.[8] Sam was in his twenties, a slight man with black hair and elegant features. He had sold newspapers outside a theatre as a kid, and then became treasurer and rose through the ranks. Like Ambrose, he had a quick mind that seemed to reverberate through his entire body. "He is very slight and twitchy,

I should think he might weigh eighty pounds. His muscles are never still," one theatrical magazine observed. "When his face is not twitching, his fingers are, or his feet."[9]

Sam was the de facto leader and problem-solver. That's what the twenty-six-year-old was doing in May 1905—heading to Pittsburgh to convince a theatre to grant the Shuberts their lease for the upcoming season. His overnight train was rumbling through the sleeping countryside of Pennsylvania when it grazed a train parked on the siding and hurtled off the tracks. The battered passengers escaped through the windows, but the worst was still to come as the flames from the wreck licked a rail car on the siding, loaded with "blasting powder."[10]

The people who lived nearby said the explosion felt like an earthquake, but at the scene it felt more like a missile. The railway cars were splintered and smouldering amid the twisted iron of the tracks.[11] Survivors escaped into nearby farmers' fields through smoke and flames, passing unfortunates who were already "burnt to a crisp" or "cremated on site."[12] Sam Shubert was dragged from the train by his booking manager. His family and doctor all rushed to the hospital in Harrisburg, and J.J. was at Sam's bedside to hear his brother's dying words. The sentence is a matter of some debate, but one version served the Shuberts' sense of drama: "Sam died with an indictment of Erlanger on his lips, telling J.J. to let Lee know that his rival had murdered him as surely as if he had shot him to death."[13]

"Officially he was a neutral in the conflict," one trade magazine said of Sam. "Report has it, however, that he was elaborating, at the time of his death, a plan to overthrow the Syndicate by organizing a chain of theatres that would practically make him independent and it is said that this plan may still be followed by his brother."[14] After Sam's death, J.J. and Lee continued to gather theatres and sign contracts with stars who had been shut out of the Syndicate houses. They didn't have their brother's charm, but they had a knack for promotions. In 1906, they rented circus tents for the "farewell tour" of famous French actress Sarah Bernhardt to drive the point home that she was a slam-dunk and that the Syndicate men were not only evil, they were fools to blacklist her from their theatres.[15]

The rivals battled for years like this, trying to top each other's productions and limit their reach. When the Syndicate scored a hit with the elaborate *Ziegfeld Follies* in 1907, the Shuberts came up with the *Passing Show*, a musical revue with beautiful dancing girls and bright stars.[16] The Shuberts liked to think they occupied the moral high ground, but they eventually wielded the same kind of power and habits as the Syndicate. They were micro managers obsessed with keeping costs low on the road, and were known for replacing their big-name stars with members of the chorus when the shows reached the smaller towns.[17] They banned critics who gave unfavourable reviews, and just like the Syndicate, they created their own newspaper to criticize their detractors.[18] The escalation of the theatrical war between the Shuberts and the Syndicate created an arms race across North America, as new theatres popped up in cities and towns.[19] Each group tried to get an edge or run the other out of town, and Toronto was another battleground in their continental game of Risk.

DOWNTOWN THEATRES CIRCA 1914

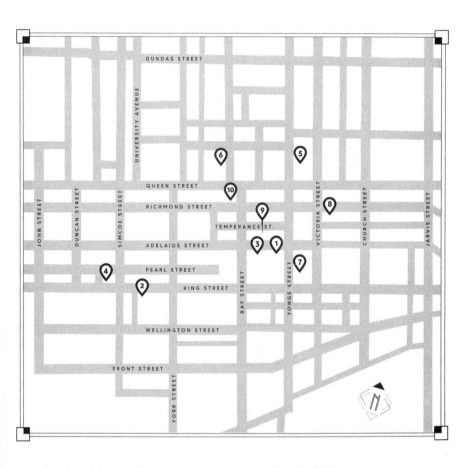

1 Grand Opera House
2 Princess Theatre
3 Majestic *(Formerly Toronto Opera House)*
4 Royal Alexandra Theatre
5 Loew's and Winter Garden

6 Shea's Hippodrome
7 Shea's Yonge/The Strand
8 Shea's Victoria
9 Star Theatre
10 Gayety Theatre

The annual Toronto directory—the thick-as-a-brick precursor to the phone book—had a list of amusements easy to find in the "A" section, below the city's "ammonia manufacturers." There was the Princess for first-class theatre, the Grand for second-rate stuff, and the Majestic for cheap matinee melodrama. All three were fuelled by Syndicate shows, but Ambrose accepted the occasional Shubert production in his "open time." (He was one of the few who could do that, owing to the reach of his provincial network.) The Shea brothers, out of Buffalo, had a couple of vaudeville theatres, and there were the Gayety and the Star for the more risqué burlesque shows. The theatre that would outlast them all came in 1907.

The Royal Alexandra was built by Cawthra Mulock and his business partners. The Toronto papers called Mulock the "boy millionaire." He was in his early twenties, handsome as a film star, rich as a railway baron. He studied at the best private schools and became impossibly wealthy when a great-aunt died with a $2.7 million estate and left most of it to him.[20] Mulock donated his riches to hospitals and the like, but his most famous investment was his exquisite temple to the arts on King Street West: the Royal Alex. Unlike the Grand Opera House, its face on King Street was devoted to theatre alone. There was no saloon or barber shop to "mar the unity" on the street.[21] With its delicate embellishments, it looked like a jewellery box.

As Robert Brockhouse relays in his history of the theatre, Mulock approached Ambrose to see if he wanted in. Ambrose declined, but it was said that he suggested Lawrence "Lol" Solman in his place.[22] Lol was a few years older than Ambrose, but both men had spent their formative years downtown. In 1871, when Lol was almost ten years old, there were 157 Jewish people living in Toronto, and Lol's family (plus one boarder) represented nine of them.[23] They lived in the east part of downtown, where Lol's father was a cigar and clothing dealer as well as chairman of the building committee for the Holy Blossom synagogue on Richmond Street East.[24] When the house of worship opened in 1876, it was a "red letter day in the history of the Jewish congregation of Toronto," the *Globe* said.[25] Solman had been an errand boy and a baker's apprentice, had lived in Detroit for a spell to run a mail-order business, but he was best known as Toronto's amusement king, the man who helped build a theme park on Toronto Island with a diving horse show, a roller coaster, and a Ferris wheel.[26] He also owned a stake in the ferry service that brought people to the Island, which was where the real money was.[27]

Solman knew very little about the theatre, but he had good business instincts. He became manager of the Royal Alex, as well as a partner. When he made the trip to New York to ask Abe Erlanger if he would consider sending his best stuff to the Royal Alex instead of the Princess for that first crucial season, Erlanger practically laughed in his face. The Syndicate already had Toronto covered, but they were attempting to make a go in the city's vaudeville market and Erlanger suggested that Solman sign up for the Syndicate's newly created stream of magicians, tap dancers, and hypnotists.[28] The thought of those characters at the glamorous Royal Alex was an insult, and Solman said he'd talk to the Shuberts instead. Erlanger figured it wouldn't be long before bankruptcy came for the Royal Alex crew, and he could swoop in to buy their theatre. "I like Toronto," he supposedly said. "I may even purchase a summer home there someday and I think I'll buy the Royal Alexandra and use it as a stable for my horses."[29]

Cawthra and his partners had deep pockets, and the Royal Alex opened in late August with the Shubert blockbuster *Top O' Th' World*, which was meant to out-dazzle the Syndicate's *Wizard of Oz*. A few more splashy musicals and comedies followed, but the Shuberts didn't have enough shows to fill that first season. The Royal Alex had to lower its prices and make do with local stock companies—not exactly what the backers had in mind, but it staved off financial ruin.[30] Within a few years, the Royal Alex had become Toronto's top theatre. "Finest theatre in Canada," the stationery read by 1910, under the direction of the Shubert brothers and with Lol Solman as manager. (Lol Solman and the Shuberts formed a company called Entertainments Ltd. to control the theatre's operations. Solman had 51 per cent of the stock; the Shuberts held the rest.[31])

Ambrose and Lol had little in common when it came to management style. Solman had one theatre to manage, so he could spend more time curating for Toronto's conservative tastes.[32] He advised the Shuberts which actors had the best followings. ("Don't send Madam Kalich," he wrote.[33] Toronto had thousands of Jewish people by now, but Solman knew that the popular Yiddish star was not going to be a sellout in the Protestant-dominated city.[34]) Solman also advised the Shuberts which social issues (suicide, drugs) would turn off the waspy audience or run afoul of the censors. The city censors were newspapermen who had been empowered by the police to shut down indecent shows. They watched shows on Mondays (often with preachers and priests beside them) and suggested changes to axe any suggestive behaviour.[35] "What is the use of sending shows to Canada if a show is stopped every time a girl has bare legs?" the New York producers complained. "It is getting so now that they will want fur coats on everybody."[36] Managers like Solman learned to work with these morally righteous critics, and to anticipate their whims. Burlesque shows like *Chuckles*, he wrote to the Shuberts, were "distinctly unpleasant" and not suitable for a Toronto audience.[37]

Ambrose Small also catered to the censors. Volunteer censor Reverend John Coburn had two seats available to him any time he wanted, and Coburn went to the Grand often, advising Ambrose and his staff on script vulgarities that would embarrass God-fearing members of the audience.[38] "It was highly amusing to many of my friends that a Methodist preacher was given such power in a theatre," Coburn later wrote. But the system worked well, he acknowledged: "There had never been any complaints as to the character of the plays staged at the Grand."[39]

With such a large network to manage, it made sense that Ambrose would minimize risk where he could. While Solman would criticize the meat of the shows, Ambrose stuck to practical concerns unless a show was bad enough to hurt his bottom line: "Someone should take Lee Shubert to one side and ask him to get some real actors for 'The Road to Yesterday,'" he wrote to a New York contact in 1909.[40] The play was a mystical romantic comedy about an unhappy couple who have flashbacks to their lives three hundred years ago—but the real stars of the show had likely peeled off by the time the tour reached the border.

The theatre season followed a reliable rhythm. It began in August when the Exhibition brought thousands of people to Toronto. Offerings grew more serious in the fall, and the Christmas season was the busiest time, with family fare like *Peter Pan*, minstrel shows, and melodramas.[41] The season ended in June with "amusettes"—photo projections accompanied by music or lighter fare that didn't require much exertion as the summer heat began to intensify.[42] Life on the road was risky: bad weather, train delays, scenery snafus, and drunk actors could all wreak havoc on the finely calibrated schedule.[43] Ambrose tried to anticipate trouble. He knew that snowstorms were likely for a good chunk of the season, so he built a buffer into the schedule—Orillia was nice padding for the jump between North Bay and Guelph.

Small could book shows with anyone because of his reach. With the Royal Alex on the scene, he couldn't run a Shubert show in Toronto, but across Ontario, his theatres were the biggest, the best—the only game in town. By 1909, there were dozens of theatres on his letterhead: "The most carefully booked territory in the world," he crowed in his promotional material, showcasing a map of the province criss-crossed with railway tracks, dotted with theatres.[44] (He owned only a handful of the theatres. Some he leased, and others he locked into booking contracts.)

With the A.J. Small company, a travelling show could play a new town every night, which they needed to do to make money. The split was usually 30 per cent of the box office for him, 70 per

MOST CAREFULLY BOOKED TERRITORY IN THE WORLD

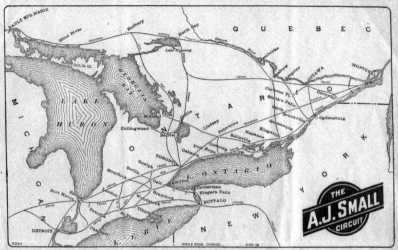

Note the new outlet into the Copper Country by way of North Bay, Sudbury, Blind River and the "Soo."

Magnificent new theatres at North Bay and Sudbury, both of which points are situated in a very rich mining country and good for capacity with everything that plays them. Also the smaller town of Blind River.

The "Money Route" to the West is now via OTTAWA, RENFREW (new $75,000 theatre just opened), PEMBROKE (new theatre building), NORTH BAY and SUDBURY, thence into the Copper Country by way of the "Soo" or on the Canadian Pacific Railway to Winnipeg.

ALL COMMUNICATIONS TO

A. J. SMALL,
Grand Opera House,
Toronto, Canada

Promotional material for the A.J. Small theatre empire.

cent for the touring show. He brought dozens of delights (and hundreds of stinkers) to mining towns and factory cities,[45] and with the New York bigwigs, he talked up small Ontario municipalities like they were his underrated daughters. He was aggrieved when American companies had the nerve to cancel on a city like Ottawa when something better came along, like

GENERAL OFFICES

THE A.J. SMALL CIRCUIT

A. J. SMALL, SOLE PROP.

ALL COMMUNICATIONS TO THE

GRAND OPERA HOUSE

TORONTO, CANADA.

TORONTO - Population 400,000 GRAND OPERA HOUSE MAJESTIC THEATRE	
OTTAWA - Population 100,000 RUSSELL THEATRE GRAND OPERA HOUSE	
HAMILTON - Population 90,000 GRAND OPERA HOUSE	
LONDON - Population 60,000 GRAND OPERA HOUSE	
KINGSTON - Population 25,000 (GOING MORE TO OWN FROM) GRAND OPERA HOUSE	
ST. THOMAS - Population 18,000 GRAND OPERA HOUSE	
PETERBORO - Population 20,000 GRAND OPERA HOUSE	
ST. CATHARINES Population 20,000 GRAND OPERA HOUSE	
BRANTFORD - Population 25,000 GRAND OPERA HOUSE	

Grand Opera House, Galt.
Opera House, Woodstock.
Opera House, Belleville.
The New Theatre, Brockville.
Opera House, Guelph. Opera House, Stratford.
Opera House, Chatham. Opera House, Berlin.
Academy of Music, Lindsay.
Grand Opera House, Barrie.
Opera House, Orillia.
Grand Opera House, Collingwood.
Opera House, Midland.
Opera House Napanee. Music Hall, Cornwall.
Opera House, Renfrew. Opera House, Coburg.
Opera House, Smith's Falls.
Opera House, Carleton Place.
Opera House Pembroke.
Opera House, Perth. Biou Theatre, Picton.
Opera House, Petrolia.
Opera House, 'Port Hope.
Opera House, Sarnia.
Grand Opera House, Sudbury
Royal Theater, North Bay.
Lyric Theatre, Cobalt.
Plaza Theatre, Haileybury.
Opera House, New Liskeard.
Savoy Theatre, Open Sound.
Opera House, Meaford.

TORONTO, Apr. 30th, 1912. 19

CANADA

Mr. Edw. Thurnaer,
  New York.
Dear Eddie:-/
    Yours here and would suggest the following for "The Red Rose":-

Ottawa	Aug.	29-30-31
Brockville	Sept.	9
Smiths Falls		10
Kingston		11
Belleville		12
Lindsay		13
Peterboro		14
St.Catharines		23
Galt		24
Hamilton		25-26
Woodstock		27
London		28
St. Thomas		30
Stratford	Oct.	1
Owen Sound		2
Guelph		3
Brantford		4
Barrie		5
Orillia		7
North Bay		8
Sudbury		9
		10
Pt. Arthur		11
Fort William		12

The company will have to lose a night in making the jump from Sudbury to
Port Arthur - and there is not a town big enough to break the jump.
        Yours very truly,

Boston. "It's really the worst piece of show business I've ever been up against," he wrote to the Shuberts on one occasion. "As you can quite understand I naturally feel rather badly over the treatment I have received."[46] Under his care, Ontario had been elevated "to a position second to none on the theatrical map."[47] All of the leading producers wanted "time" in Canada, and it was all thanks to Ambrose Small. "He is an indefatigable worker and the smallest detail in every booking is given his personal supervision," one theatrical man wrote in 1912. "He is still a young man and has the greatest confidence in the circuit which he controls."[48]

Ambrose was the king, but he had sat through enough Shakespeare to know that the king was never safe. One attempted coup came in 1909, when a group of mysterious backers were willing to finance a theatrical network, but only if they could avoid dealing with Ambrose Small and his fees.[49] The backers told H. Stuart Raleigh that if he could succeed in one small Canadian city, they'd give him more money. Raleigh was a confident New Yorker who knew show business. The former actor–playwright–manager–private eye accepted the challenge with relish.[50] How hard would it be to outsmart Ambrose Small?

Raleigh moved to St. Catharines in the summer of 1909. The factory city was surrounded by orchards and canning operations, and just down the road was the roar of Niagara Falls. "When I took over this house I found that Mr. Small a Theatrical Manager of Toronto had been booking same for several years and fooling the people so often with rotten shows that the very name of Small to the people in this town is like a red flag to a

wild bull," he explained in a letter to a friend.[51] In the summer of
1909, Raleigh renovated the theatre and tried to convince the
Syndicate and the Shuberts to send him something sensational.[52] But nobody wanted to come all the way to St. Catharines
for a one-night stand.

The Shuberts had expressed interest, but no contracts were
signed. And the Syndicate—out of loyalty, or maybe just for the
fun of it—sent Raleigh's letter, requesting a few bookings, to
Ambrose. In response, as Raleigh told a friend, Ambrose "wrote
[him] a nasty letter and stated that he could not see his way to
book any attractions at this house as he was partly committed
to build a Theatre in St Catharines and besides, he understood
that I had made the remark that I did not care for any of [his]
attractions." Raleigh confessed, "Well I did make such a statement. Small will send you about one Syndicate attraction a
week and 5 rotten shows which he books himself. Small is
determined that I shall come to him and beg him to book the
house and accept whatever he will give me."[53]

As the nights turned colder, Raleigh was on the verge of
ruin. He asked his friend in New York to appeal to the Shuberts,
as he couldn't afford the train fare to beg in person. Upon hearing this tale of woe, J.J. Shubert wrote to Raleigh, "Mr. Small,
it seems, is in position to control the routes of attractions play-
ing Canada, therefore, you are handicapped to a great extent,
and it is my earnest advice that you make some sort of a deal
with him. While I do not approve of Mr. Small's methods, in
order for you to have a profitable season, you must get more
attractions than we can send you ourselves."[54]

Lots of people shook their head over Ambrose Small's antics. His name was in the newspapers for all the wrong reasons—like the time he accused an employee of stealing, or the time he was forced to pay eight hundred dollars to a grieving mother whose son was electrocuted behind the scenes.

He gambled on horses and lingered at the blackjack tables at the underground casinos the police were always wringing their hands over.[55] He liked to use the alias "Mr. Kelso" when he made bets at the track.[56] (The real Mr. Kelso was a social crusader who founded the Toronto Humane Society and the Children's Aid Society.) When one of his relations from Adjala gave him money to make a bet at the Woodbine race track, the old timer was excited when his horse won. The next time he saw Ambrose, his rich cousin had bad news—he hadn't had a chance to make the bet. "The story was of course false, the bet had been placed, but having collected the winnings Ambrose Small was physically incapable of parting with the money in his pocket," Hector Charlesworth wrote.[57] "He was one of the largest betting operators on the race tracks of America, and it was popularly understood that he was one of a small international ring which usually had a race 'fixed' before they ventured their money on it."[58] He was the smartest kind of gambler: one who didn't trust his money to chance.

Ambrose's office at the Grand was halfway up the stairs from the lobby, off a small stub of a hallway. His personal secretary, Jack Doughty, sat in the front half, and Ambrose in the back corner, and the furniture was arranged so it would be "impossible for even a good marksman to get a bead on him."[59] He also had a private staircase leading to the lane, so he could make a speedy exit. The Grand was a "curious rookery of a place," cloaked in gilt and crimson, and according to lore, there was a secret love nest hidden behind "thick burgundy curtains" off the main office.[60]

Ambrose was said to have a private boudoir in his London theatre, too. He purchased the London Grand Opera House around 1905, proudly putting his face on the program, along with instructions for the evening: Women were kindly asked to remove their large hats, unless they were old and sick and worried about catching a cold.[61] London was said to be one of Ambrose's favourite cities, a two-hour train ride to the west of Toronto. Ambrose gave the theatre his special attention, along with the ladies, in the secret room tucked behind his private balcony off stage right.[62]

Ambrose Small did not manage his sprawling empire alone. Jack Doughty helped run the show and stepped in when the boss was away. Ambrose stayed in touch, sending cheques and instructions: if anyone asked where he was, "simply tell them you 'don't know,'" he once wrote to Jack from a hotel in the heart of lower Manhattan, near the theatres and department stores.[63] Jack was about ten years younger than Ambrose, and came of age as the city became a financial hub and needed administrative types to keep the money moving. When Jack was in his early twenties, he started at the Grand Opera House as a stenographer. By 1907, he was Ambrose Small's personal secretary.

Jack grew up on River Street, in the eastern part of downtown, beside the Don River. His parents, George and Agnes, had been born in Scotland and had come to Toronto after several years in the United States.[64] George was in the metal business and made his living collecting and reselling scrap and wool extract downtown, and Jack grew up surrounded by his doting sisters Eliza, Jeanie, and Barbara.[65] He had a much older brother Will, and also a sister Agnes, who had married and moved west. The Doughtys were a close-knit bunch. When Jack grew up and married, he lived two doors down from his mother. Jack's wife, Berthe, died of pneumonia a month after childbirth in 1911, leaving Jack—then in his mid-thirties—with three infant children. His family rallied to help, with his mother and sister collecting breast milk at the hospital every day to feed the newborn twins. The twins were named George and Berthe—but the little girl did not make it to her first birthday.

Through all the turmoil, Jack worked for Ambrose. "Japan is great. Best yet," Ambrose wrote from a luxurious vacation a year and a half after Jack's wife died. "Hope yourself and the children are O.K."[66] Typically, they proposed an Ontario-wide schedule for a theatre company, drew up contracts, and finalized rates. Small liked to get his 30 per cent cut—although for the spectacular shows he was willing to take a smidge less, but he felt like "a chump" anytime he did.[67] His margins were tight, he'd say as he dictated the dispatch to Jack. Didn't these New York producers know that he was being incredibly generous already? Sometimes, Ambrose drew up contracts with the figure he originally wanted, and if his deception was spotted in person by a road manager, Ambrose gave his own performance, summoning Jack into his office to scream at him for his "mistake."[68]

A network of spies reported their intelligence to Ambrose like they would to any powerful mafia don. In 1908, a railway contact tipped Ambrose off when the Grand Trunk Railway reimbursed an American opera company for a delay that made them miss a show in London. Small wrote to the opera company to ask about his share of the refund, which he calculated at $225.07.[69] The opera boss sent apologies, and later, the cheque. Their accountant, he explained, had been in a sanitorium.

Ambrose did a lot of good for the industry. He lobbied the Canadian government to make border-crossing easier for touring American productions, but he always made sure he got the credit. He liked to constantly remind the New Yorkers how important he was to their success. "You know yourself that I was the only circuit manager in the entire country to keep my houses open to the Shubert shows a couple of years ago when all of the other men were on the fence," he told the Shubert brothers in 1911.[70]

No matter how bad the plays were, Ambrose expected the press to rave. When Toronto reporters travelled to New York, Lol Solman and Ambrose Small sent telegrams to the New York theatrical men to make sure the wide-eyed Canadians were "fixed up" for a few shows and a good time.[71] But not everybody knew the deal. A rookie Toronto reporter once reviewed a slapstick comedy at the Grand Opera House "with an unfortunate fidelity to facts."[72]

"I was told politely but firmly, that accuracy in reporting of theatrical entertainment was something prejudicial to the interest of the advertising department," the reporter recalled. There was another thing. "Mr. Ambrose J. Small was both surprised and hurt."[73]

WAR

Toronto had long been a manufacturing boomtown, and when gold, silver, and nickel were discovered in the rocky landscape of northern Ontario, it became a hub for mining finance.[1] By 1910, most of the world's nickel came from Sudbury, and the money flowed back to the stockbrokers, banks, and law firms on Bay Street. Ambrose capitalized on the mineral rush by adding theatres in northern Ontario to his network. His "money route to the west" ran through Ottawa, Renfrew, and Pembroke on the Canadian Pacific rail line, and then it was straight into mining country and the "magnificent new theatres at North Bay and Sudbury."[2]

Toronto was becoming the unavoidable centre of everything.[3] Toronto annexed its border communities, growing large in land and population. There were more office jobs and more women working. Each time a female citizen was spotted in an unlikely career, she was treated like a sideshow in the newspaper: Look at the policewoman: see her gentle constitution with the lowborn criminals! Observe the female truck driver:

she is the prettiest of her sisters and uses her feminine wiles to escape speeding tickets! Have a gander at the latest crop of lady lawyers—who will find a man?

There were Catholic priests who watched the dawn of the "age of women" with unease. They heard stories of women who missed church on Sundays, ate meat on Fridays, stole jobs from men, visited Anglican churches for fun, apologized to their liberal friends about the Catholic Church, and—worst of all—had sex outside of marriage.[4] When a group of American women asked for the Church's blessing to create an alumni association for graduates of Catholic schools, some religious powerbrokers saw an opportunity. "With their Catholic faith and principles, our Alumnae should be able to restrict the too liberal interpretation of what is called the emancipation of women," the archbishop of New York wrote in a congratulatory letter to the group.[5]

As a proud graduate of St. Joseph's Academy, Theresa Small signed up for the International Federation of Catholic Alumnae in 1914. It was an exciting time to be a woman. In the papers, there were always stories about equality and the vote, but Theresa was usually found a few paragraphs over, giving one of her "delightful talks" about the "Charms of the East" to a woman's group, or, with the ladies of the Imperial Order Daughters of the Empire, teaching immigrant children English and the merits of "British fair play and British sympathy."[6] She never made any public statements about the vote but clearly believed in empowerment through education. This Catholic women's group, with its more modest aims, suited her perfectly.

The IFCA wanted a set of Catholic encyclopedias and Catholic newspapers in every school library, and more Braille books for the blind. More crucially, in these days of social unrest, they wanted to extend the influence of Catholic women around the world.[7] Theresa signed up for the press committee and was elected governor of Ontario. It was mostly just Toronto ladies, but the title was nice.

The group's annual conventions were lavish affairs at the fanciest hotels of the Midwestern U.S. and the eastern seaboard.[8] The guest speakers were usually men who congratulated the women on their achievements but reminded them about the evil seduction of "progress." As Theresa sat in those twinkling ballrooms, she was told that her most important role was keeping the home safe and her family happy. The speakers were important types—politicians and judges—and they railed against the latest salvos in the culture war, the titillating legs in the "beach bathing" pictures, the indecent photos in newspapers, the crimes committed by the "motherless." At the St. Louis convention, one feisty politician told the ladies that the movies were now the fifth-largest industry in the United States, after steel, and the world's morality clock was set to "sex-o'clock."[9]

"You women should know that it is only the women who have been made the subject of lure in these pictures, frilled up and made more attractive than naturally they would be, with all due respect," he said, calling for censorship.[10]

It was a vile, vicious, dirty world, and the women debated how they could help steer children away from the devil and his minions in Hollywood.

Did they know that Theresa's husband was responsible for his fair share of chorus girls? (All above board of course, with minor modifications, as requested by the censor. According to volunteer censor Reverend Coburn, "Toronto for many years had the reputation of having the cleanest stage of any city of its size on the North American continent."[11]) Theresa was every-thing a good Catholic woman should be—charitable, smart, devout—but she "never permitted her religious feelings to inter-fere with box-office receipts," a *Toronto Star* journalist wrote in his 1974 book on the case.[12]

If anyone doubted her morals, she silenced them at the 1916 banquet. The Baltimore ballroom glittered with electric lights, the air was sweet with roses, and the female orchestra played "charming melodies" of the South.[13] After the dinner plates were cleared away by hotel staff, Theresa was called onto the stage. The master of ceremonies told the crowd that although an age of progress was dawning, Mrs. Ambrose Small would take them all back to what truly mattered. The applause died down, and Theresa, dressed in the season's latest fashions, looked at her audience. "The ancient world at the time of the birth of Christ was a cesspool of iniquity,"[14] she said. She explained how women were the property of men, used to populate the planet or for the basest of pleasures. It was a society where theatres were "filled with the applause of indecent merriment of every variety." It was only after Jesus was crucified that Christians embraced "the law of Charity," she said. "Hospitals, foundling homes and ref-uges for the poor and aged dotted the land. They saw in the sick, the poor and the stranger the living image of the Saviour."[15]

Theresa Small's feminist hero was not a suffragette. She was "the sinless maid who mothered the Saviour," the virgin who elevated the status of women among men. The mother of Christ made men softer through her sacrifice, she said. Domestic virtue became a form of love, an ideal to aspire to, and it was still "the guarantee and safeguard of modern society," Theresa asserted. "When you ask me what has religion done for the world, I reply that it would take hours to answer," she said. "Conceive, if you can, all that is beautiful in the world today." She paused, and gazed around the ballroom. "Gaze upon it until its impression ravishes you, and I say, beautiful as it is, it is but a faint reflex of what the world owes to Religion." The applause was so loud it received a mention in St. Joseph's Academy's new literary journal. She was judged to be the best speaker, a credit to her old school.[16]

Theresa Small's life was an exercise in cognitive dissonance. Her parents had made their fortune in beer, which allowed Theresa to attend a school where she learned how to be smart and pious. Sin paid for salvation. Her husband ignored the Bible with a great flourish. The spoils of entertainment and the racetrack had paid for the Rosedale mansion—and her train tickets to the religious conference. She treasured the virtues of domesticity, but she had a staff that cooked her meals and cleaned her house.

As the Ontario governor on the executive, she sat through hours of meetings, doing her best to explain why it was necessary to approach Quebec alumnae in French. "It is a long story," she said.[17] "The French in our country are afraid of anything that the English people intend to do." When the other ladies debated what city would host the next conference, Theresa encouraged a quick decision—"Why not finish this meeting tonight?" she asked.[18] When the women decided whether they should spend $200 a year to support a blind orphan, Theresa was practical, even a little brusque: "I don't think the Federation should do that sort of thing," she said. "The individual Alumnae can do that."[19]

When war came to Toronto, many citizens treated the conflict as a chance to prove their loyalty to Britain. It all felt a little surreal in 1914. Germany, a country that had once been a cultural darling of the continent, had marched through Belgium as if international treaties meant nothing. The war's origins were complicated. Too much nationalism, too much patriotism, too much brinkmanship. But if Canada was being called to defend the motherland, Toronto would answer.

Many of Toronto's Catholics saw enlistment and patriotism as ways to prove themselves. French Canadians had been vilified for their low enlistment numbers, but in Toronto, "The Catholic Register boasted that its city's parishes had raised over three thousand men, enough to outfit three battalions."[20] They handed over parish halls, formed sock-knitting committees, and Archbishop Neil McNeil appealed for tolerance: as they faced the common enemy in Germany, the city's Protestants and Catholics needed to come together. Most of the men thought they'd be home in a few months, but that illusion was waning by Christmas. The Sisters of St. Joseph called it the "most awful of all wars in history," and guessed that it would last for at least three or four years. "Every day we pray for peace," they wrote.[21]

In the spring of 1915, the Germans released poison gas into the fields of Ypres, and it drifted towards the Canadian soldiers in a menacing yellow cloud, choking and killing men who couldn't escape. The Western Front became stagnant, and battles came with enormous death tolls. The telegrams from "somewhere in France" shattered lives: We regret to inform you that your son is missing in action. We regret to inform you that your husband was injured in a shrapnel blast. We regret to inform you that your father, gallant in his actions, died as a result of his injuries.

As the war dragged on, replacements were needed. D'Arcy Hinds, a legal clerk at Osgoode Hall, thought it would be a good idea to raise another Irish battalion in Toronto in 1916 to represent the "fighting brotherhood of undivided Ireland."[22] Most Irish didn't need a "specialty battalion that pandered to their Irishness," but Hinds thought it worth pursuing in the winter of 1916.[23] He asked Theresa Small for fundraising help. Theresa was involved in all kinds of charitable work but was most prominent as the regent of her local chapter of the Imperial Order of the Daughters of the Empire.

The IODE ladies hosted luncheons to raise money for Belgian relief and consumptive children. They were well connected and used their privileged status to lobby politicians with polite but firm telegrams.[24] The group was loyal to the idea of a British Canada. Their yearly magazine featured articles such as "Canadianize the Aliens," where the author noted that open-door immigration policies "tend to disintegrate" national life.²⁵ At one point during the war, the idea of expelling IODE ladies of German and Austrian origin was proposed, but it didn't get enough votes. (That was good news for Theresa. She was born in Canada, but her roots were Franco-German.)

As the leader of her chapter, Theresa ensured that her ladies sent 2,143 pairs of socks to the trenches. She was honoured with a fancy cake at a reception, where her portrait was revealed as an electric sign flickered to life, spelling "OUR REGENT."²⁶ She was a fundraising wizard, and industrial warfare required those skills. It cost an average of $20,000 to recruit a battalion of 1,160 men,²⁷ and Theresa was pleased to help. The battalion gave her an office, just down the block from the Grand, and she was at her desk every morning with a "spring in her step," managing a staff of ten with an accuracy and thoroughness "that any bank manager might envy."²⁸

Theresa's team enticed the men to war in all kinds of creative ways. She created a "guess how many beans" contest for new recruits, with a new car as the grand prize. For their first recruitment drive, they called all the downtown factories and asked them to ring every whistle at 10 a.m. to make a ruckus that would capture people's attention.²⁹ On the city's busiest corners, they parked cars, draped them in green, and had pretty "Irish colleens" handing out shamrocks to the men heading in for a shift, asking if they might want to clock in on the Western Front instead. 1916 was a difficult time to recruit. The war industry was humming along, and there were good jobs in Toronto that didn't involve the brutality of the trenches.³⁰ At the outset of the war, married men needed a permission note from their wives, but that stipulation was gone by 1916.[31] The Canadian government wasn't ready for conscription—but they desperately needed volunteers.

Theresa organized a fundraising concert at Massey Hall on St. Patrick's Day, and there was a big night at the Grand Opera House too, with a military play called *Watch Your Step*. Theresa gave the battalion $5,000 to help fund the recruitment drive, and a photographer came to capture the big moment, a crowd of soldiers radiating around her as she handed over the cheque, the extravagant plume of her hat blocking the face of at least one man in the back row. The men began to regard her as their fairy godmother. The local newspapers took notice, and her friends at St. Joseph's Academy proudly cut out the articles and glued them into a scrapbook. Their former pupil was flourishing in a world at war.

The same wasn't true for Ambrose. In 1914, he had hoped the "war excitement" would blow over, but the men were digging into the mud of Flanders for the long haul.[32] The travelling show had already been in decline before the war. In 1904, there had been more than four hundred companies travelling North America, but toward the end of the war, there were only forty.[33] The battles between the Shuberts and the Syndicate had created bloated circuits, and there weren't enough shows to go around. The audience wasn't willing to pay for mediocrity, especially with the rise of the moving picture.[34] It wasn't just Ambrose who was struggling. "As I thought, business in Toronto went to pieces," J.J. Shubert wrote to Lol Solman at the Royal Alex in the opening month of the war. "I'm afraid we are going to suffer a great deal with all our attractions in Canada."[35]

Some of the theatres played more films; others went with a cheaper local stock company. Patriotic war musicals and revue shows were reliable, but it was difficult to entice the best ones into Canada. "They are afraid to take any chances," Shubert wrote.[36] The war was challenging for the box office, and things weren't much better on the home front. In 1916, Theresa found out about Clara Smith. Clara wasn't a one-night stand who'd fallen for her husband's blue eyes and boxes of chocolate. She was a mistress with staying power.

Clara Smith looked a bit like Theresa, with a round face and curly brown hair. She was fiery. Jealous. Prone to calamity. A lover of Veuve Clicquot. His "ever-loving Clare," as she signed all her letters. They had started seeing each other in 1914, when Clara was nineteen and Ambrose was almost fifty. Clara loved the dresses, the gifts, and the comfort that Ambrose provided. He had arranged a pied-à-terre in Rosedale, ten minutes away from his mansion. Living there in 1916, she told Ambrose she would die for him, her "most idolized boy in the world."

Her love letters swirled with anxiety and her near constant apologies for being a "little jealous fool."[37] Clara was from the Grimsby area, and she ran with a fast crowd, which was how she met Ambrose. She was married to a soldier, but Ambrose helped her secure her divorce in 1917.[38] They had an intense, passionate relationship. One night, Clara smacked Ambrose during an argument, and the next day she sneaked into his office, posing as an advertising agent, to write him an apology letter: "I was crazy," she said, asking for forgiveness.[39]

It wasn't just fur coats and fancy dinners, and Theresa couldn't ignore it. She told Ambrose that Clara had to leave the city, and eventually, she got her way. But in the spring of 1917, before her 208th Battalion sailed across the Atlantic, the accusations of infidelity ricocheted back at Theresa. Ambrose accused her of having an affair with a high-ranking member of the battalion. Was there anything to his suspicion, or was it just a strategic act of revenge? The soldier in question was a few

Clara Smith sent this photo of herself to Ambrose Small. Clara and Ambrose were an item from 1914 through 1919, on-and-off.

years shy of forty, tall and handsome in a bookish way. He was married with a son, a pillar of his community, and beloved in the battalion. "In every sense of the word he is a soldier, a scholar, and a gentleman," the 208th wrote in their commemorative newspaper.[40]

Ambrose knew that the best melodramas relied on dramatic timing. When the battalion was about to leave for England in May 1917, he wrote a letter to Theresa's alleged lover, outlining the dates and times the pair had been seen together. One of Ambrose's cronies gave it to his cousin, who was an officer in the same battalion, telling him to deliver it when they were at least "one day on the high seas."[41] In May 1917, the soldier stood on the deck of the *Justicia*—a beautiful ocean liner outfitted for war—and read the accusatory dispatch. Then he ripped it up, and scattered the pieces in the ocean.[42]

SEVEN

THE MILLION-DOLLAR MAN

I n the summer of 1918, as the Allies pushed the Germans eastward, Ambrose Small's mistress moved south to Niagara-on-the-Lake. She had married again, but the groom was not Ambrose. She was Clara Jennings now, the wife of a travelling salesman. Douglas Jennings was two years older than she was, with blue eyes and fair hair. He was one of the first Canadian soldiers to ship out from Quebec City in 1914, but his war record was not marked so much by gallantry as it was by pay deductions for not following orders.[1] After several years with the medical corps in France, Douglas came home to Canada in May 1917, where he was discharged and signed up for a commission with the forestry and railway corps and eventually met Clara.[2]

They married in New York City in the spring of 1918, but Clara still dreamed of Ambrose. In her dreams, Ambrose was always cheating on her. "I was torn to pieces with jealousy, which I suppose I would have no right to be, but all the same I can't help it," she confided to her older lover.[3] She wrote to Ambrose from a hotel in Niagara-on-the-Lake, while swinging lazily in a hammock. With her husband apparently busy with his military duties, she tried to entice Ambrose to a picnic rendezvous. He could always return to Toronto by the afternoon boat, feeling the cool breeze off the lake. "Write me often sweetheart, and for my sake be a real good boy. Don't have anything to do with those women who are only out for all they can get," she wrote, "and if you ever feel that you can't be true to me any longer, for God's sake tell me and don't let me find it out from someone else because that would kill me."[4]

Clara asked Ambrose for little things to make her life more bearable—a new gingham dress for a "swell ball" in Buffalo, or maybe a new skirt to match the mauve sweater she was knitting. When she turned twenty-three, Ambrose sent a purse, which she considered "the most beautiful bag I have ever seen or hoped to own."[5] Ambrose told her he missed her that summer. He was "blue and lonesome" in the city.[6] Take your car for a spin, Clara advised, and "take your poor old Dad out more."[7]

The armistice flash came across the telegram wires at 3 a.m. on November 11, 1919. The church bells rang, the factory whistles screamed, and Toronto woke up to the ecstasy of peace in the middle of the night. By sunrise, the downtown streets were so packed that the streetcars couldn't make it through the crowds. Tickertape caught on the power lines and snapped in the cold November wind. Bonfires blazed. Men and women kissed and sang patriotic songs. The city went "joy crazy."

For Ambrose, the transition to peace meant that many of his "babies" and "pets" left the city. "How many have you had?" Clara asked when he complained of his post-war loneliness. "Sometimes I think that I did you the greatest favour I could have by going away, at least I saved you any more trouble at home on that score."[8] She was living in Minneapolis by 1919, where life was achingly boring. Once she paid the bills for the butcher, the electricity, and the coal, there was hardly any money left—she couldn't even afford a manicure or a shampoo. "Not like my Amby used to take care of me. I guess God didn't mean that Amby should be for me, so what's the use crying? I made my bed and I suppose I must lie in it, Hard as it is," she wrote.[9] She mockingly called her husband "His Nibs" in her letters. Whenever Douglas was away for a few weeks for a sales job, she invited Ambrose to visit. "I could kill myself when I think of what a fool I have been," she wrote. "I haven't the least particle of love for him and I still love you with all my heart and soul."[10]

As Ambrose was arranging the sale of his theatres, Clara had a "beautiful nervous breakdown" and took off for a hotel in Bronxville, New York.[11] She felt the lure of Broadway and the lights—her old life with Ambrose. "I just love a good time, and I wish you would come down and I will take you to all my favourite rendezvous, and have a wonderful time," she wrote.[12] As world leaders hammered out the details of Germany's surrender in the summer of 1919, the A.J. Small theatrical empire was also the subject of intense negotiation. Trans-Canada Theatres Ltd., backed by Montreal railway money, was on a shopping spree, buying and leasing theatrical properties across the country in their bid for national dominance in a coast-to-coast empire. They needed Ontario to complete the plan, and Ambrose had agreed to sell his holdings—the bricks-and-mortar theatres in Toronto, Hamilton, London, Peterborough, St. Thomas, and Kingston, in addition to his leases and booking arrangements throughout the province.

Clara worried about the "low rubbish" women in Montreal, where Ambrose had to spend a few weekends arranging the deal that fall. She was also nervous about his post-theatre freedom.[13] "I know you must have someone but please, please, don't forget little honey! Someday perhaps, if you want me, we can be together all the time," she wrote. "Let's pray for that time to come, when we can have each other legitimately."[14] She told Ambrose they should run away to the "end of the world," but at the very least, he should come to Minneapolis in December. "His Nibs" was going to be away on a sales trip. "I wish I could be with you," she wrote. "Would it not be great if I could just come down and cook you dinner like I did not long ago."[15]

William Shaughnessy, of Trans-Canada Theatres Ltd., trundled into the city on a train from Montreal with a $1 million cheque in his briefcase. He was a lawyer by trade, and his father, Baron Thomas Shaughnessy, was the former CPR president. On December 1, 1919, William was here to finally close the deal in person. Outside the train window, Toronto was a mess. A storm had torn through the city a couple of days ago. The mariners who were accustomed to the rhythms of the Great Lakes called these late autumn storms that blasted their ships with cold rain the "witches of November."[16] On land, the storm had torn crucifixes from church steeples and blown apart the flimsy tar-paper shacks that returned soldiers had built in the midst of a housing shortage.

Shaughnessy walked by the taxis and horses idling in front of Union Station. A new train station had been built down the road, but the war (and the typical bickering over who was going to pay) had delayed its opening. The new station was surrounded by construction hoarding enticing him to drink a refreshing Coca-Cola and chew Stag Tobacco, which was "Ever-lasting-ly Good." Further ahead on Front Street, cars idled in front of the Queen's Hotel.* The charming hotel was a throwback to a simpler time, and was the place where all the prime ministers and presidents stayed when they came to town. But its days were numbered; a bigger hotel was planned to match the new train station.

Shaughnessy likely walked up Bay Street—a gauntlet of wealth—surrounded by banks, insurance companies, and law firms.[17] A lattice of streetcar wires sparked overhead, but the people in winter tweed hardly noticed. A police officer was hollering as he directed the cars, horses, and streetcars. Shaughnessy was meeting Small at the law office of Osler, Hoskin & Harcourt, in the upper reaches of the Dominion Bank building. The building was one of three skyscrapers at the corner of King and Yonge,

---

*   Turn-of-the-century journalist Paul Bilkey writes in his memoir that the hotel manager hovered "like a hen" over the guests, helping them out of the horse-drawn coaches, ensuring that their every need was met with grace and decorum.

home to the corporate offices of many of the city's new breed of money tycoons.[18]* The Osler law firm had taken care of the real estate portion of the deal for Trans-Canada, and Shaughnessy stepped into the wooden elevator with the morning crowd, everybody's winter wetness soaking into the carpet.

Ambrose arrived at the library of their eighth-floor offices at 10 a.m., but Theresa wasn't with him. The lawyers, familiar with Ontario's Dower Act, knew that was a problem. The act was meant to protect women from neglectful husbands by automatically carving out one third of a man's real estate for his wife after his death, regardless of the specifications in his will. There were loopholes if you wanted to leave your wife penniless, since it was only real estate that was covered and not cash, stocks, or bonds.[19] But the Dower Act protected women like Theresa when their husbands tried to sell the family real estate.[20] The wife had to give her blessing, and before the sale could go ahead, Theresa had to sign away her dower rights in the properties.[21]

In this moment, Theresa held all the power, and that wasn't ideal for Ambrose—since his wife had just come across an incriminating love letter from his mistress when he was in Montreal. The letter was strangely intimate. Clara complained about rotting teeth that had been removed in a gruesome bit of

---

*   The tycoons were starting to lead the city, J.M.S. Careless writes in his history of Toronto, taking over from the merchant princes. Toronto's largest employer was still the manufacturing sector. Manufacturing jobs employed 65,000 before the First World War, compared to the 40,000 people in commerce and finance, 20,000 in building trades, and 18,000 in domestic work.

modern dentistry. "I believe that a good percentage of sickness today is due to bad teeth, so if I were you I would get your teeth fixed up, if there is any dead ones have them out as they are sure to be infected sooner or later," she wrote to Ambrose. "I guess you are too busy to even think of your poor little old sweetheart away out here. I do get very homesick and blue when I think of you away in Toronto. I want to see you so badly I could just run away."[22] Ambrose told the lawyers that his wife was suffering from a spell of "nervous prostration," and he and his lawyer Edward Flock left the office hoping to cajole Theresa downtown.

That afternoon, the Smalls were back in the office. At first, Theresa refused to sign the paperwork, but after she and Ambrose left the room for a short conference in private, she relented.[23] Whatever terms they had agreed to, whatever assurance Ambrose had given his wife, it had done the trick. She signed away her dower rights. Shaughnessy pulled the $1 million cheque from his briefcase and gave it to Ambrose. Best to give this to your wife for safe-keeping, he joked, and the men all gave knowing chuckles as Ambrose handed it over to his better half.[24] Shaughnessy asked Theresa about her charity work and everybody left the office in a better mood, waiting for the next chapter of their lives to unfold. For the Trans-Canada men it was going to be a nationalist theatrical adventure. The Smalls had always been rich. Now they were millionaires.

On December 2, 1919, Ambrose Small woke up in his second-floor bedroom and had a look into the backyard. A light snow was falling. He'd planned to drive his Cadillac to the theatre, but he hadn't put the winter chains on the tires. He usually took the Church streetcar line that rolled through Rosedale, but he was running late, and so he hustled off in the direction of Bloor Street with his umbrella, hoping to catch the faster Yonge streetcar.[25]

Small hopped off at the Adelaide Street intersection and walked by the candy shop and barber that rented his storefronts. The shops on the western half of the building, where his family had taken a chance in 1880, were vacant. The saloon business was tough during Prohibition. If you were well connected, it was easy to get your hands on good alcohol, but it was still illegal to drink in public. You had to go to an underground bar, or have a friend like Mr. Lamb, who ran the hotel next door to the theatre and kept champagne on hand for late-night friends like Ambrose.

The Grand Opera House had been his first love, his life, and Ambrose couldn't leave it behind. There were still a few details to square away, and he had finagled a deal with Trans-Canada: he would keep this office, halfway up the first-floor stairs. The Dumbells were on the marquee tonight, in the middle of a two-week engagement with their *Biff! Bing! Bang!* show, with tickets selling from twenty-five cents to one dollar. The Dumbells were a group of soldiers who had been a smash hit on the Western Front, performing skits and songs, often in drag, about life in the trenches with a bittersweet, comic tone that played well with men who needed a laugh—like "Oh, It's a Lovely War," and "Those Wild, Wild Women Are Making a Wild Man of Me."[26] They had taken the edge off the war, and they helped take the edge off the memories. Ambrose had been the one who had told them they needed to invest in a bigger cast if they wanted to tour Canada.[27] Their reworked show premiered at his London theatre in 1919. It was a sellout, and Small called from Toronto during the first act and stayed on the phone for the entire show, listening to the thunderous applause.[28]

As the theatre staff prepared for that evening's performance, Ambrose popped out for a shave around 1 p.m.[29] Everyone in the barbershop knew about the deal because he mentioned there might be a case of whisky in it for them to celebrate.[30] "I have the million right here," Small said, patting his coat pocket as the barber expertly ran the sharp blade against the stubble on his neck. The rest of the afternoon passed pleasantly enough. There was lunch with his lawyer and Theresa, and then he walked Theresa to the nearby orphans home, promising he would be home for dinner. At some point that day, Ambrose walked into the Dominion Bank and deposited his $1 million cheque in his personal savings account. Had he told Theresa he would put the money in their joint account so they both could access the funds? Was she meant to receive other money? Nobody knew except the Smalls, but Ambrose had grown rich off these kinds of tricks—promising one thing, doing another.[31]

When lawyer Edward Flock dropped by the Grand Opera House at 5 p.m. to pick up his money for helping Ambrose to close the deal, Ambrose was in a good mood, "just like a boy out of school."[32] Ambrose invited Flock for dinner at his home in Rosedale—the two of them could get a taxi together, he suggested—but Flock had to catch the 6 p.m. train back to London.

Flock gave his regrets and left Ambrose at 5:30 p.m., climbing down the creaking stairs into the lobby and then into the cold.[33] It would be the last confirmed sighting of Ambrose Small.

———

When Ambrose didn't come home for dinner that night, a worried Theresa left Rosedale to find him. She darted about the city like a pinball, travelling on foot and by streetcar, stopping by the homes of her sisters, making telephone calls to her husband's associates, trying to figure out where Ambrose was, if anybody had heard from him.

Meanwhile, Alfred Elson, the caretaker of a girls school on Bloor Street, was enjoying the crisp night as he flooded the lawn for the skating rink. Toronto's skating rinks were popular spots in the winter: You met your friends, you wore a fashionable winter outfit, you lined up a few laps with a handsome boy. For a few days now, it had been cold enough for a scarf, so Elson stood on the plateau above the Rosedale Ravine and turned on the hose.

It was a bright night, and a dusting of snow glittered on the ground. Downtown, *Hamlet* cast a spell over the crowd at the Royal Alex, Charlie Chaplin's plasticine face was sending audiences into hysterics at the moving picture houses, and *Follies of Pleasure* was titillating the crowd that went in for that kind of thing at the Star Theatre.[34] From the edge of Bloor Street, where the city dipped abruptly into a forested ravine, Elson saw a car driving along the road below, on the way to the dump.[35] The car stopped under a lamppost and four men dragged a rather cumbersome lump from the car. Elson was curious, but a fence blocked most of his view. When they returned to the car empty-handed, he went back to flooding his rink.

EIGHT

THE DETECTIVE

TORONTO, DECEMBER 1919

When people went missing, their loved ones wrote to the police: My husband hasn't been himself since the war. My son ran away from home. My wife ran off years ago to be with another man and I want to marry again, but I need to divorce her first. They attached photos if they had them and described the details ingrained in their minds. Fred had a funny walk; Hollis had a round pimply face; Viljo the Finn had the typical Nordic complexion but had a few bullets from an earlier scrap. The police printed off photo postcards and mailed the information to detachments across the province, hoping to get lucky with a sighting. Sometimes it worked: a husband found dead, a wife in the arms of a new lover. Many of the cases were unresolved, the photos of happier times filed away in manila envelopes at OPP headquarters.[1]

On December 8, Small's lawyer Edward Flock returned to Toronto to finalize the last few details of the turnover. When he arrived to find Ambrose's office locked, he called Theresa. "She inquired if Mr. Small had not come down with me from London," he said. "This was the first I had known that he had disappeared."[2]

Theresa Small did not file a missing person report. Although she had spent the evening of December 2 in a panic, she was telling friends and family that Ambrose would turn up. They understood. No point getting the police involved if this was another trip to the racetrack, or a week away with Clara or one of the other "babies." Theresa put on her georgette crêpe dress and diamond earrings and went to the train station on December 9.[3] She had made a commitment to host a renowned French author for a series of patriotic talks, and for the next few days, she squired her guest around town for the official ceremonies and gala dances, and the papers wrote about Theresa's mellifluous French. There was no word on her missing husband.

"Smiling Jimmy" Cowan, the former newspaperman turned manager of the Grand, was anxious. It wasn't like Ambrose not to send a telegram. Cowan was a good employee but not a close friend. He was "kept in the dark" about Small's life,[4] but he had a general sense of what went on with his boss regarding gambling and women, and this didn't feel right. He wrote a letter to Jack Doughty in Montreal. If anyone knew Ambrose's schedule— whether there were any last-minute trips, perhaps—it would be Jack. "If I remember right, last time I saw Mr. Small it would be in the neighbourhood of 5 p.m. Tuesday [December 2]," Doughty wrote back. "I know I waited until after six before going home, and it was quite a while before I left. Took 10:30 C.P.R. Tuesday night—an upper berth—and a darn cold one—wish I had stayed in Toronto. . . . Best of luck and good wishes to yourself and kiddies. Anything further let me know."[5]

Cowan shared his worries with Thomas Flynn, a thin older man who advised Ambrose on his bets and extramarital affairs. Flynn was a slippery character who knew all the hiding places, but Ambrose wasn't in any of them. In the middle of December, Cowan and Flynn walked to City Hall. It was cold, with a biting west wind. Toronto's municipal building was a large sandstone castle with thick support walls and human faces carved into the exterior. Finished in 1899, it had become the gathering spot for

Thomas Flynn, Small's confidant and betting commissioner, in 1923.

historic moments. In 1918, thousands had danced and sung late into the night when the war ended. The building was just as lovely on the inside, with mosaic tile marble floors, municipally appropriate artwork, and gleaming wood banisters. Mayor Tommy Church had an office here, and most of the important police departments were here, including the morality squad, the detectives, and the chief himself—Lieutenant-Colonel Henry Grasett.

Grasett had been in charge of the Toronto Police for thirty-four years, and he'd seen tremendous technological change. When he assumed his post in 1886, the city had recently installed electric arc streetlights, which lit the dark corners better than gas had.[6] Call boxes came next, placed at strategic locations throughout the city so the beat cop could connect back to the station rather than passing on a message via a stranger. Bicycle patrols were introduced in 1894, fingerprinting by 1906, and the rise of the automobile brought the first parking tickets in 1907.[7] Motorcycles came in 1911, and by 1914, traffic was so bad that police officers were "absorbed" into intersections, holding semaphores and glaring at motorists who dared speed in their presence.[8]

"There is no reason to believe that the morals of the people are improving," Grasett wrote in 1918.[9] Wife desertion was on the rise, and with more soldiers in town, Toronto had its fair share of "street walkers," fortune tellers, gambling dens, indecent politicians, illegal taverns, incompetent drivers, and businesses that insisted on ignoring the Lord's Day Act—"foreigners who take a chance when they can," Grasett wrote.[10] The city's burgeoning diversity was something of a hassle for police, who were a fairly homogenous group—Irish, Scots, English, and Canadians of British descent. The brass viewed the "Britishness" of the force as a "source of prestige."[11] "It may become necessary to confine street orations to the English language, as the Police do not understand what is said in a foreign tongue," Grasett wrote during the war.[12] ("Apart from a handful of Italian or German-speaking officers and police court interpreters, the police commissioners displayed little interest in broadening the department's ethnic base," historian Greg Marquis writes.[13])

There were still moments that made Toronto feel like a small town—like the citizen who wrote a nice thank-you note to police for recovering his stolen chickens—but in the year after the war, ten citizens were run over by cars, two were killed by streetcars, six died in "drunken quarrels," and seven were murdered in cold blood. (That was a big surge from the usual murder count, which hovered around two.)[14] Five people had been arrested for the murders, but the other two "had escaped for the time being," Grasett wrote in his year-end summary.[15] He chalked up the increase to a world still shuddering from the war. He knew violence made people nervous. He'd written enough permission slips for accountants who wanted to carry a revolver to guard against the holdup artists that were the new menace about town.

When Cowan and Flynn walked into the detective department, Detective Austin Mitchell was assigned to the case.[16] Mitchell had the classic Toronto story. He'd been born in the rural ribbon above the city and moved south to make his living, joining the

Detective Austin Mitchell

force in 1899. He patrolled the city on horseback and motorcy-
cle and was promoted to detective in 1910. Detectives knew the
city bylaws and the Criminal Code, but there was not much
professional training beyond that.[17] Typically, Mitchell and a
partner walked around the places where intriguing things usually happened—the trains, stores, theatres, streetcars, hotels,
poolrooms, lodging houses, and pawnshops.[18] Sometimes they
were pulled off the beat for an investigation. (A few years earlier, Mitchell had brought down a ring of doctors and veterinar-
ians who were writing prescriptions for cocaine.[19])

By the time Ambrose Small vanished, the world was enam-
oured with the idea of the detective—Arthur Conan Doyle had
made the elite investigator a noble figure when he dreamed up

Sherlock Holmes in the 1890s. But the profession was still rela-
tively new and misunderstood. Before Canada existed as a country, the British colonial government had forced every incorporated
town to appoint a paid chief constable in 1859 to protect citizens
from the villains who cantered into town on horseback.[20] In the
beginning, detectives worked outside the system as sleuths for
hire. Ontario appointed its first government detective in the
1870s[21] to look into tavern licences, death, and arson, but private
detectives—like the Pinkertons—were still very popular.

One of the provincial government detectives, John Murray,
was the closest Ontario ever came to having its own Sherlock
Holmes. Based in Toronto, he studied extradition laws, poisons,
weapons, and banking rules, and had a wide circle of acquain-
tances, including several notable crooks.[22] Photography was a
new craze, and Murray stared at criminal mugshots to memorize
their details the way a small boy would commit a hockey card to
memory. He was the sort who welcomed new ideas and in 1876,
he asked a professor to analyze blood and bone to help him solve
a murder case in Caledon, a watershed moment for science in
Ontario policing.[23] A farmer claimed his wife died in the blaze,
but Murray suspected he was lying, and sure enough, the tests
revealed another story.[24] Murray liked to remind people that
there was no magic in his chosen career. It was grounded in hard
work and logic. "A detective walking along the street does not
suddenly hear a mysterious voice whisper: 'Banker John Jones
has just been robbed of $1,000,000,'" he wrote. "He does not
turn the corner and come upon a perfect stranger, and then,
because the stranger has a twisted cigar in his mouth, suddenly

pounce upon him and exclaim, 'Aha, villain that you are! Give
back to Banker Jones the $1,000,000 you stole ten minutes ago.'"[25]

As Ontario grew, there was a patchwork of police forces
funded by local taxpayers. Toronto's was one of the most modern. The force borrowed the idea of regular hours and assign-
ments from Boston, and the military drills were inspired by
the Royal Irish constabulary.[26] After a trip to England in 1876,
Toronto's police chief insisted that the city offer twenty-four-
hour police service like he'd seen abroad. Toronto criminals
no longer enjoyed a free pass for assorted depredations between
4 a.m. and 9 a.m.[27]

Murray didn't work directly for the Toronto Police, but he
had great hopes for his profession. "The detective business of
the future will be far ahead of the detective business of the
past," he wrote before his death in 1906. "I hope that the future
will see it raised to the high place of a profession."

"The real story of policework in criminal detection in
the twentieth century took place in the courts, not in the labs,"
historian John Weaver notes.[28] (By 1919, policing had come a
long way, but the scientific era had not dawned.) Although
Austin Mitchell had proved his investigative chops with the
drug ring, he was better known for getting his man in the physical sense. He caught a shoplifter in Eaton's department store,[29]
apprehended a bicycle thief in a second-hand shop,[30] ran down
a couple selling a diamond ring on Queen Street,[31] tracked
down a murderer crouching behind his bed hours after he had
stabbed a young boy,[32] and sniffed out the rapscallion who stole
twenty cartons of peanut candy from a confectioner through a

mail scheme.[33] Mitchell usually solved cases because he was on the scene as part of his patrols. (Some of his most convenient arrests came from lurking in pawn shops, but that didn't mean they were easy—one time a man bit his hand when Mitchell tried to handcuff him.[34]) The Ambrose Small case was already two weeks stale, and the men standing in front of him weren't even sure that Ambrose was missing.

Thomas Flynn told Mitchell that Ambrose might be down in Havana with Clara Smith, a girl he was "very sweet on." Alluding to Ambrose and Theresa's marital troubles, Flynn said, "He's mad at the old woman, but he'll be back."[35] Cowan wasn't so sure. He'd been watching the bank accounts. No money had come out.[36] They asked Mitchell to be discreet. Ambrose's wife hadn't reported him missing, and they didn't have her permission to tell the police. As soon as the two men left, Mitchell and another detective went to visit Theresa in Rosedale, where they were served afternoon tea.[37]

Theresa told the police that she believed her husband would be home soon. She told Mitchell about the last time she had seen him. After a lunch on December 2 with lawyer Edward Flock, they said goodbye at the front door of the orphans home on Bond Street around 3:30 p.m., and Ambrose promised to be home for dinner.[38] The sky was beginning to fade to early winter dusk, and Ambrose told Theresa he planned to stop by the Cadillac Motor Car Company to check on a limousine he had on order for her.[39] Mitchell watched her closely. "She appeared to be very much worried and appeared to be withholding something she did not like to tell," he wrote.[40] Mitchell asked her if that was the case. "You are cruel in your questioning and very severe," she said.[41]

The next day, Mitchell returned with a different partner and Theresa was in a better mood. She admitted she had been keeping something back and handed him a letter from Clara. Explaining that Ambrose had been "paying his attentions" to Clara in the past, Theresa said she had forgiven Ambrose but then she had intercepted a fresh letter from Clara while Ambrose was in Montreal at the end of November. When Ambrose returned, she confronted him, saying some "unkind" things, "for which she was very sorry."[42] Theresa didn't want to put a notice in the paper, because Ambrose would be furious when he came back.[43] He was probably with Clara now.

Mitchell continued to visit Rosedale. One week before Christmas, Theresa told him about the night Ambrose didn't

Ambrose and Theresa Small's home in Rosedale.

come home. She said she arrived in Rosedale at 6 p.m. to find her sister, Josephine Small, at the house, along with the maid. Josephine was ready to leave, so Theresa accompanied her for part of the streetcar journey, hopping off at Yonge and Bloor, where another sister, Madeleine Holmes, lived in the old Kormann home. Theresa said she popped inside for a quick visit but was back in Rosedale for 6:30 p.m. She waited for Ambrose, but he never showed. She left Glen Road at 9 p.m. to see if anybody had heard from him. She returned to her sister Madeleine's for a "few minutes," and then it was over to Josephine's on Kendal Avenue at 9:30 p.m. Theresa called home to see if the maid had any news. Then she called the Grand Opera House. Nobody had any news.[44] She went home.

Theresa and Mitchell had a "long conversation" about what might have happened to Ambrose. "She was very much worried," Mitchell noted, and that's when she handed over a gold pocket watch. It was from the Toronto jeweller Ryrie Brothers, engraved with her husband's initials. Theresa said the maid had found it underneath his pillow when she made the bed on the morning of December 2, the last day Ambrose was seen alive.[45] Mitchell searched the house for clues, walking up the grand staircase where a lavender stained-glass window bathed the wood in a delicate glow. He pored over Ambrose's wardrobe: two Prince Albert coats, a morning coat, a vest, a dress suit, several pairs of trousers, a blue serge suit, a couple of light overcoats. There was nothing amiss. Even the great detective John Murray would have been stumped.

———

Austin Mitchell wasn't the only one searching for Ambrose. The men of Trans-Canada Theatres Ltd. needed to talk with him. They had a few "sure things" lined up for their first year, including the distinguished British actor Tyrone Power and a cross-country tour of the Dumbells, but they had many questions for Ambrose Small. How much did he charge in rent for the street-front businesses at the Grand? How much money came in from the candy machines? What were the rates on the curtain advertising? How much did he pay for property tax, water, and insurance? Where were his accounting books?[46] They sent all of these questions to Edward Flock, but Small's lawyer had no answers.

The Toronto Police had searched Small's office before Christmas. They'd found the broken chair and busted telephone, but there was no paperwork in the desk. Flock imagined all kinds of terrible ends. Maybe Ambrose was beaten and mugged when he stepped off the streetcar on his way home to Rosedale. Maybe he was dragged to the bottom of the ravine. Flock didn't think the Toronto Police were capable of handling a complicated case like this. He thought the Boy Scouts should scour the snow-covered slopes of the Rosedale Ravine—they'd do a better job.[47]

Christmas was coming, and the reporters were circling. The familiar refrain of "he'll be back any day now" was wearing thin. When New Year's Eve came, Ambrose didn't raise a glass of champagne to ring in the new decade. When the city re-elected mayor Tommy Church on New Year's Day, Ambrose did not cast a ballot. At the Precious Blood convent on St. Joseph Street, there was a curious message posted on the wall, written in red ink. "SPECIAL REQUEST," it read. "Requesting prayers for the Repose of the Soul of Ambrose J. Small."[48] A woman named Mary Quigley saw the note, thought it strange, but shrugged it off. She didn't know theatre magnate Ambrose Small personally. As far as she knew, he wasn't dead. Ambrose Small wasn't even missing.

NINE

THE INVESTIGATION BEGINS

TORONTO, JANUARY 1920

On January 3, 1920, Ambrose Small glowered on the front page of the *Toronto World*: "Startling Disappearance of Toronto Millionaire Causes Grave Apprehension." The news ricocheted across the continent. "New York and Montreal are searched in vain for A.J. Small," said the *New York Tribune*. "Theater King Vanishes When Paid a Million," noted the *Chicago Tribune*.

American reporters explained the caper in their best florid language. The night he disappeared wasn't just cold, it was crystalline and bitter, Small wasn't the typical downtrodden sort who went missing—he was saturnine and vulpine, an "imperious lordlet" at the height of his power.[1] It was one of the "greatest enigmas of the age," as "if a Shubert or an Erlanger had suddenly walked out into Broadway one brisk evening at lamplighting time and been seen no more."[2] Some reports said Ambrose was last seen in his office, while other stories painted a vivid scene of Ambrose buying a newspaper under the "yellow glare of the street lamp," buttoning his coat "against the gelid obtrusions of the winter night," and vanishing into the mystical fog of Adelaide Street.[3]

Small's lawyer, Edward Flock, wasn't used to this kind of popularity. The phone in his London apartment kept ringing, and Flock puzzled out his theories to reporters. "I do not say that it is deliberate murder . . . It seems to me that he was knocked on the head to make him unconscious and that the blow was too heavy," he told one reporter from Buffalo. "In that case the first thing to be done would be to hide the body."[4] One reporter asked if Small might have been killed by radicals, given the spread of labour unrest. The big strike in Winnipeg in 1919 had been the work of "extremists," the *Star* had said, but there had been strikes in Calgary, Edmonton, Toronto, and Montreal too. Steelworkers, coal workers, and actors had all walked off the job in the United States in 1919. The actors strike had hurt Ambrose, but none of his theatre employees were involved in labour trouble. Ambrose had been good to his employees, Flock said, even if his employees might not share the assessment.

Austin Mitchell set up a command centre in Ambrose Small's old office at the Grand Opera House.[5] Police sent his particulars to the newspapers. Ambrose, they said, was fifty-three years old; five feet, nine inches tall; and a trim 150 to 160 pounds. He had blue eyes and a reddish complexion, with brown hair receding at the temples and a moustache facing its first incursions of grey. He was quick in his movements, they said, evoking a scared, cornered animal. To help loosen lips, there was a five-hundred-dollar reward. A cheap return on an expensive man, the reporters grumbled, but Mitchell was flooded with tips and offers of help from citizens and private detectives.[6]

Fred Lamb, who ran Lamb's Hotel at the southwest corner of Yonge and Adelaide Streets, said Ambrose had come in for a drink one evening in early December, but he wasn't sure of the exact date. Neither was the newsboy who remembered selling Small the New York papers between 7 p.m. and 7:30 p.m. before Ambrose crossed Yonge Street in the direction of Church Street.[7] "He seemed to be in a big hurry," the newsboy said, certain it was December 2—but he couldn't be sure, and later recanted the story.

Mitchell wanted to get a sense of Small's movements from his personal secretary, Jack Doughty, but Doughty was a difficult man to get a hold of. Now living in Montreal, he was working with a "real bunch of fellows" at Trans-Canada, even if they didn't really understand "the game they are up against," as he wrote that December.[8] His last visit to Toronto was just before New Year's Eve, when he'd been fetching some paperwork for his new employer. He told his boss that he was too sick for the return trip, and nobody had heard from him since.[9] Doughty hadn't been happy in the new job. He had sent a letter to his old manager Jimmy Cowan, saying as much: "Dear Jim: Am fed up with Trans-Canada and tired of being the goat. Am offered a fair job and am going to tackle it. Will write you how it turns out. It is country stuff—so perhaps I can forget show business for a while. Best of Luck, J. Doughty."[10]

Cowan showed Mitchell the letter, and told him there had been something else that was strange in hindsight. He wasn't certain of the date, but figured it had been December 2. Cowan heard a noise on the private stairs leading from Ambrose's office to the side lane around 6:15 p.m. He popped outside to see what was going on.

"Is that you, Jack?" he called out.

"Yes, Jim." Doughty responded.

Doughty's car was idling in the lane, and there was a "young fellow" beside it—Douglas Doughty, Jack's nephew.[11] Cowan went back inside.[12] He figured Doughty was just taking a few things from the office for his move to Montreal.

On January 10, Clara Smith walked into City Hall, her high heels tapping across the marble floor, fresh from Minneapolis. Thomas Flynn had picked her up at the train station to escort her to Mitchell's office. She had been Small's main mistress since the war, and Mitchell hoped she'd be the one to break the case open. Maybe she'd say that Ambrose had been with her all along in a romantic cabin secluded in the woods. But Clara hadn't seen Ambrose in person since October, when she came to Toronto for a dalliance. They had been writing to each throughout November, and the last letter she received at general delivery Minneapolis was dated November 28, 1919. Small had written from Montreal to say that the deal had gone through.

Clara was worried, but she echoed Flynn: Amby was probably at the racetrack, maybe in Havana. She talked wistfully about how good he'd been to her. Her hands sparkled with jewels and she ran them over her seal coat, touching the soft sable collar. She told Mitchell that her relationship with Ambrose had landed him in the dog house with his wife.[13] Ambrose had an apartment in Toronto for Clara, and when Theresa found out, she was furious. Her anger hadn't stopped Ambrose and Clara from seeing each other. (Her more recent marriage and move to Minneapolis was a bigger obstacle, but even that hadn't kept them apart.) Maybe, Clara said, Theresa knew something about where her husband had gone. Clara "appeared to be very much upset at Small's disappearance and seemingly did not want to talk very much, but expressed a desire to try and help locate Small," Mitchell wrote. "Before this I had an opinion that she might know something of Small's disappearance."[14]

Mitchell had other leads to follow. Now that Jack Doughty was missing in action, troubling anecdotes were trickling out. The talk in the theatre crowd was that as Small's wealth grew, a resentful Doughty had talked about getting his share of the riches throughout 1918 and 1919. George "Bud" Lennon, who worked in the burgeoning field of film distribution, remembered Doughty dropping by his Richmond Street office in 1919. Doughty wasn't happy at the Grand Opera House and he "wanted to know if it was possible to kidnap a man" and how to get money in such a situation. "I explained to him at the time that he could not do this himself," Lennon said, "and he would have to get someone else to do the job for him, and that they might make a miscue, and then he would be up on a murder charge."[15] Doughty hadn't mentioned Ambrose, but Lennon said he knew who he was talking about.[16] He told Doughty to find another job. Don't be "a damn fool," he cautioned.[17]

Frederick Osborne, who had been a caretaker at the theatre, remembered that in August 1918, Doughty approached him "five or six times" and offered him $20,000 if he'd agree to join him and another mysterious fellow in a "deal" he'd been working up.[18] The idea was to get Ambrose out of Toronto with a fake telegram—some kind of emergency—and then, while he was away, Doughty would get a hold of cheques, write out a few, and Osborne would help him cash them. "He asked me to send my wife and children away so that they would not know anything about it," Osborne revealed. "He told me he could quiet Mrs. Small and Cowan, also the Boss's two sisters." This was before the big sale, and Doughty figured Ambrose had nearly $400,000 in the bank, and Doughty's share would be $75,000, Osborne said. "He further told me that Mr. Small was a damn rogue who had got his money dishonest by doing people down and it was no crime for us to have a share of it," Osborne said.[19]

Ernie Reid later told Mitchell a similar tale. The chocolate supplier travelled across the province for his work, and in 1919 he was at the Peterborough Grand Opera House, a theatre that was a part of the A.J. Small network through a rental agreement. As he stocked the concessions, Reid heard some interesting gossip from the janitor. The theatre was about to be sold out under Ambrose's nose. Reid considered himself an ally of Ambrose, so he called him straight away. Doughty answered the phone and passed it to Ambrose, who intervened and bought the theatre for $40,000.[20] Reid said that Doughty sent for him a few weeks later and told him, "You are not going to get a damn thing out of this." Reid figured there would be some token of thanks coming his way, but said that Doughty scoffed at the thought of a grateful Ambrose Small. Jack was on his way to redeem some of the interest coupons of Ambrose Small's Victory Bonds, and he allegedly asked Reid, "Couldn't two smart men figure out some plan to get some of these?"[21] He told him to think it over for a few days, but Reid never followed up.

George Kennedy ran into Doughty walking along Bay Street at the end of November, when the sale was almost completed: "John said to me, 'Would it not be nice if A.J. would come over with $1,000 for each year's service, that would come to $18,000.'" According to Kennedy, Doughty then said: "If he doesn't, I will get even with him."[22]

No one had been worried enough to warn Ambrose. It seemed like foolish chatter. Doughty was a good fellow, a generous sort. "In fact, when I was married he loaned me money," the head usher William Wampole told Mitchell.[23] But Wampole said that Doughty had a tendency to go on a tear about Ambrose. "Is not he a lousy cheap bastard?" he would say, and, "Is there no way we could get to the son of a bitch?"

But "I never thought he ever meant anything," Wampole said. "I would have told the boss."[24]

———

Before he left town, Jack Doughty and his boys had lived with his older sister's family in a roomy brick home at 8 Kingswood Road, on the eastern fringe of the city. It was nearly an hour from downtown on the Queen streetcar, in a newly annexed part of Toronto where flowers and strawberries still grew wild and a handful of waterfront amusement parks thrilled every summer with log chutes and Ferris wheels.

Eliza was married to a carpenter named Thomas Lovatt, and they had two boys of their own. At first, they lived on River Street, surrounded by Eliza's family. But Thomas began building his home in the still distant neighbourhood of Balmy Beach around 1911, dreaming of a peaceful respite from downtown. He had perhaps done too good a job. His wife's siblings—Jean, Barbara, Will, and Jack—all lived there for months, if not years, at a time, and those with children brought the youngsters too. "The constant presence of Doughtys caused friction in Tom and Eliza's marriage," Eliza's granddaughter wrote in her memoir. "People regularly asked why the siblings chose to be at their sisters' when they each owned several homes on River Street. . . . Some speculated that they simply liked life in the Beaches with its lake breezes better than life downtown."[25]

Working on a tip that Jack may have been swallowed by the same mystery that claimed Ambrose Small, a reporter rode the Queen streetcar to the end of the line to visit the Lovatts. "How do you know that he is missing?" Eliza shot back when the reporter asked after her brother. "I have been pestered to the verge of insanity over this affair now, and I refuse to discuss it."[26] When Detective Mitchell came calling, Eliza said that Jack had left

Toronto on December 29, carrying his black suitcase.[27] He had a bad cold and wasn't enjoying Montreal very much, she recalled. Eliza tried to encourage him to stay until he felt better, but he insisted on leaving. She stood on her front porch and watched him walk toward Queen Street under the snow-covered trees.

Weren't the Doughty siblings worried? Mitchell asked. Surely it was time to put up a few missing posters? Eliza and the rest of the Doughtys said they weren't concerned because their brother hadn't done anything wrong.[28] If anything, he might have left town on account of his second wife, with whom he'd had some marital trouble.[29] Jack and Connie married in 1917, but the relationship had soured. (Mitchell had never heard of this second wife, but when he eventually spoke with her, Connie had no clue where her husband was. She was eager that police find him, though, so she could divorce him.)

It wasn't clear if the Doughty siblings knew where their brother was, but they'd later explain to a courtroom that they were keeping something from Mitchell.[30] In early December, minutes before Jack left for his job in Montreal, he had handed his sister Jean a package on the train platform, telling her to drop it off in his bank vault. The package contained $105,000 of Victory Bonds belonging to Ambrose Small. It had been too large for the vault, so Jean stored it in her dresser, and later placed it under some loose floorboards in the attic.[31] She was nervous every time the police came around, so in the spring of 1920, her older brother Will undertook a small renovation project and hid the Victory Bonds in the attic wall.[32]

TEN

ABSENTEE

TORONTO, SPRING 1920

Ambrose Small's unexplained absence created a series of problems for investigators. There had been rumours that some of his money was missing, but nobody knew for sure if this was true. The only person authorized to open his bank vault, aside from Ambrose, was Jack Doughty, who was also "lost in some unguessed part of the living or the dead."[1] In April 1920, the attorney general of Ontario introduced a workaround with the provincial Absentee Act.[2] Under the new act, estates of missing people would be managed by trust corporations until the person reappeared or was declared dead: "While the bill is a general one, the occasion of it is the disappearance of Ambrose Small, Toronto millionaire," the newspapers said.[3]

Ambrose Small was declared an absentee, and the Capital Trust Corporation and Theresa Small were appointed to manage his property, valued at $2.1 million.[4] Any withdrawals had to be approved by both parties and rubber stamped by a judicial official at Osgoode Hall.[5]

Capital Trust would earn a fee for their service. The firm was run by Catholics, and people took note. "This circumstance has caused certain Orange newspapers to attack the wife and her associates for putting the special act through the Provincial Parliament," an American newspaper explained.[6] "These incontinent papers, whose attitude reveals the religious bitterness felt in Ontario . . . have been trying to suggest that there was indecent haste shown in getting control of Small's money."

Granted this moderated access to her husband's account, Theresa upped the reward, offering $50,000 for Ambrose alive, $15,000 for his corpse. It was akin to a regional sweepstakes.

Private detectives and amateur sleuths hunted for Ambrose in back alleys and ravines. There was a bloated corpse floating in a lake near Sarnia, a rotting body in a Toronto shed, and a lookalike discovered in a Parisian morgue. "Send a mirror used by your husband, and also one used by yourself," an American schemer wrote to Theresa, requesting a cash infusion to begin his sorcery.[7] An astrologist sent a map of the stars. A medium shuffled his tarot cards, cut the deck only to find the death card: "I have no doubt whatever that Mr. Small is dead," the medium wrote to Small's lawyer. "It looked like a robbery and murder case."[8] A clairvoyant suggested that a photo of Ambrose be burned with powder that only she could provide. The rising smoke would point police in the right direction.[9] Amnesiacs in hospital beds became strategic investments. There were two men in Iowa who figured they hit the jackpot when they found a poor soul who had lost his legs to a train. He looked quite a bit like Ambrose Small and he liked to sketch bars of music— just the thing a theatre magnate might do in a haze of memory loss. They jealously guarded their "Mentally Incapacitated Human Wreck" for months at a private home in Iowa, until the police dashed their dreams by declaring, "STORY IS NOT CREDITED,"[10] in the headlines.

Detective Mitchell was rooting through abandoned trunks, deciphering maps of the celestial heavens, and digging holes across the city on the advice of a guy who knew a guy. He went to New York to suss out an alleged kidnapping gang, dismissed it as a ruse—and went back to sifting through the ashes in the furnace room of the Grand Opera House.

A prisoner at a Wisconsin asylum had sent a few letters to Toronto, claiming to be an old friend of Ambrose. He promised he would help solve the crime, so long as they found him a good lawyer. "Why dont you ask Mrs. Small why she watied 2 weaks before she notified the police that her Husban was Gone [sic]," the man wrote in curly capital letters.[11] "I can tell you the last words he said to his wife on the 2 Day of December 1919 and prove it," he pledged.[12] Mitchell travelled to Wisconsin, but the man's claims were "worthless."[13] The attorney general's office filed the dispatch in their "Letters from Cranks" envelope, alongside correspondence from a nurse who claimed the government owed her $1 million, and a woman who wrote a nineteen-page letter about the people she met on her walks and the horses that nearly ran her over because the sidewalks weren't big enough.[14]

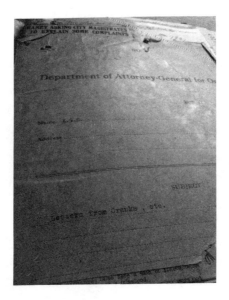

The Letters from Cranks file.

Theresa Small was becoming accustomed to the whispers and stares. She resigned as regent of her IODE branch, "owing to the sorrow that had come into her life."[15] The group asked Theresa to reconsider, but appointed a new regent, and gave her a jewel-encrusted badge as a token of thanks.[16] A few people had suggested to Mitchell that she wasn't as innocent as she seemed, but he had searched the Small property, digging to a depth of five and a half feet in the backyard, as suggested by an anonymous letter. Theresa had been pleasant and helpful with each search.[17] Mitchell considered the anonymous tips "far-fetched," malicious and the work of one of her enemies.

———

In early May 1920, a safebreaker held his ear to the cool metal of Box 1654 in the basement of the Dominion Bank, as Det. Mitchell stood by, search warrant in hand, eagerly awaiting the secrets inside Ambrose Small's private vault. The police believed there were "reasonable grounds to suspect" that something was missing that might show that "one Ambrose J. Small is secretly confined or imprisoned in Canada, against his will."[18] Inside the box, there was a bundle of deeds, mortgage documents, letters, and bank books. Everything was as it should be, except for the Victory Bonds.[19] Those were missing.

Victory Bonds helped finance the Canadian war effort, and the government encouraged people to buy them with a campaign featuring images of hardy soldiers smiling as they left home: "Come on! Let's finish the Job," the posters implored. Ambrose had bought around $300,000 worth of Victory Bonds during the war.[20] They were bearer bonds, which meant that while the government borrowed his money to fund the war effort, Small earned interest several times a year. Doughty was the man who came to the vault to clip the coupons and redeem the interest for his boss. Police had a look at the logbook. The ledger showed that Doughty had accessed the box three times from December 1 to December 2. There were two trips on the afternoon of December 1, that exhausting day when Ambrose and Theresa finally signed the paperwork after a tense standoff over her dower rights, and another three-minute visit the next morning.[21] It looked as though $105,000 of the Victory Bonds were unaccounted for.[22]

Two weeks later, Mitchell arrived at Kingswood Road with a shovel.[23] He told Eliza Lovatt that he was looking for the bonds, but he was actually looking for a body. (The latest tip was that Ambrose had been buried in the backyard.[24]) "You can dig the entire yard up," Eliza told him.[25] Mitchell squinted at her grass like he was looking for a missing wedding ring. He dug in two spots but didn't find anything.[26] "There is no doubt that this woman knows something about what has taken him away and what her brother Jack has done, and in all probability knows where he is," Mitchell wrote. "She cannot believe Jack would do anything wrong, and if he had and she knew where he was she would not tell."[27]

Jack had been missing for five months, and newspaper readers didn't know what to make of it. The police clarified the narrative in June when they issued two warrants for his arrest: one for conspiring to kidnap Ambrose Small, and the other for theft.[28] "Those who have faith in Doughty point out that he was a genial and soft man, quite incapable of any deed of violence," an American journalist wrote.[29] He *did* look genial in the wanted poster, his curly brown hair whipped up on his head like a cresting wave. He was described as forty-three years old, with a stout build, medium complexion, clean shaven, a "very neat" dresser.[30] There was a $5,000 reward for his capture—which would soon increase to $15,000, authorized by Theresa Small and the Capital Trust Corporation. And just like that, genial middle-aged men became the latest jackpot.

ELEVEN

THE BALLAD OF
CHARLES BENJAMIN COOPER

OREGON CITY

I n the winter of 1920, Jack Doughty travelled west until he
hit the Pacific Ocean. He got off the train in Seattle, but the
dampness soaked into his bones, so he went a few hours
south to Portland, Oregon, a city so renowned for its logging
that it was called "Stumptown" by the locals.

A century later, logging doesn't have the same hold that it
once did. Portland is better known for eccentricity, which is
confirmed by the woman in a velvet top hat, holding a basket
of kittens and a sign inviting people to "Come pet my weird
dogs." The closer I walk to the train station, the more tran-
sient life becomes. People camp on the sidewalk. They're carrying their lives with them, just like Jack Doughty did when he
showed up in 1920, black suitcase in hand.

The Portland train station has the feel of a country club,
with palm trees on the front lawn, art deco chandeliers inside

the waiting room, and ceilings that are tiled with flowers. The benches are smooth as church pews, but the signs are not welcoming: no public restrooms, no pets, no loitering. I feel conspicuous, so I ask the staff about the history of the place, and they guess at what is original, like this is a game show. They have never heard of Jack Doughty or Ambrose Small, but they're curious when I tell the story. He didn't stay in the city long. He went a little further south, to Oregon City, the place where the towering trees of the Pacific Northwest went to die. Doughty thought he might get a job in one of the mills along the Willamette River, where the pines were ground into pulp and reborn as newspapers and toilet paper.

I buy a ticket to Oregon City and wait in the lobby as the sun streams in through the old windows. The train comes from Seattle and we are led out to the platform like a kindergarten class. It's a hot day, and the tracks smell like an amusement park—that wonderful hot iron smell of roller coasters in the sun. The whistle blasts, and the train creaks along Portland's industrial waterfront. "Don't work too hard," a passenger drinking a Budweiser tells the steward checking our tickets, and she says she won't. It's a half-hour ride, and my seat pops like a juice bottle lid. The trees and underbrush cocoon us from the farmland, golf courses, and suburbs outside the windows, but when Doughty made the journey in February, he would have had a better view of the hills in the distance, topped with trees.

"Oregon City, coming up!"

———

The Willamette Falls have drawn people in since "time imme-morial," according to the plaque near the rusty mill buildings where Jack Doughty worked. The old Indigenous story goes that the waterfall was created when a meadowlark teamed up with a coyote and the two creatures held a rope made of hazel shoots from their posts on opposite sides of the river: "Then Coyote called on his powers and turned the rope into a rock. The river poured over the rock."[1]

The land was rugged and forested, and as Europeans made inroads across North America, it was an important cog in the fur trade. When Oregon became a "territory" of the United States in 1848, the frontier settlement on the banks of the Willamette River was the seat of power, called Oregon City. Indigenous people who had survived the diseases and trauma wrought by the Europeans were sent to reservations despite

Willamette Falls and Old Hawley Mill.

government assurances and treaties.[2] In 1850, the American government passed the Donation Land Claim Act, which gave "every white settler" and "American half-breed Indian" the right to 320 acres of land.[3] (The price went up to $1.25 an acre in 1854.)

Free land sent thousands of pioneers across the plains, dreaming of the lush valleys and farmland that awaited them. They spent hard months walking the Oregon Trail, then hitched their wagons at Abernethy Green, a swath of land north of the city where they would camp while they replenished supplies in Oregon City. Many settled elsewhere, but some stayed right where they were. The Willamette River, which had long been a source of food for the Indigenous peoples, helped provide a new kind of sustenance: hydroelectricity and mills. Oregon City had a way of collecting people, and in February 1920, Jack Doughty was one of the thousands to find a fresh start.

A steep basalt cliff divides the city into two distinct parts: the old downtown is at the river level; the rest of the town, with most of the houses, is up top. The city built a municipal elevator between the two tiers in 1915. Powered by early hydroelectricity, it had a tendency to lower the water pressure of the entire community as it made the "harrowing" three- to five-minute elevation to the top of the town.[4] There were also staircases that zigzagged across the cliff face.

Life felt healthy in Oregon City. The air was forest fresh, and deep breaths felt like opening up the windows after a long winter. There were occasional belches of sulphur from the mills, but that meant there were jobs. Doughty got a job at the Hawley

Pulp and Paper mill as Charles Benjamin Cooper, a name he found classy and respectable.[5] J.P. Strain and his wife found their new boarder to be "the nearest type to a perfect gentleman" they'd ever had at their quaint home atop the cliff, where a setting sun was carved into the peak of the roof.[6] Charles Cooper was different from the other men at the mill. He saved his money, opened a savings account, and occasionally played a game of pool or saw a show in Portland. As far as the Strains knew, he'd come west after a domestic spat, but they didn't pry. Lots of people showed up in the West looking for a second chance.

Between the house and the cliff, there was a small outcrop of basalt rocks, a good place to smoke a cigar and stare at the blue-green-blue of the horizon, beyond the rust and brown of the mill below. Cooper was a good employee and was soon making $4.30 a day, trundling sulphite by truck.[7] His bosses were surprised to see shorthand on his time cards, but he explained he'd been a secretary for an "Eastern man" before he moved west for his health.[8] They took him for another "blamed fool" who drifted from town to town, but at least he was reliable. Physical work was a nice change of pace for Doughty, who was so focused on his new job that he didn't notice a man sizing up the contours of his face, wondering if it was worth a $15,000 reward.

In early November 1920, a private eye saw a thickly built man walking around Portland. There was something about him that looked familiar to Ed Richardson, and he followed the mystery man to Oregon City so he could see where he lived. When he returned to Portland, he found the wanted poster for Jack Doughty—it seemed to be the same fellow.

Richardson returned to the mill with Portland police officer Ed Fortune and shadowed Doughty from a good distance away.[9] It was hard to get a look at his face, because he wore a slouchy hat. The *Star* said the identity confirmation came on a Sunday, when Doughty came in without a hat. An American wire service was more dramatic: "Something made him lift his hat and slowly scratch the back of his head. It was long enough for the watching constable to be sure of his quarry."[10]

When Austin Mitchell got the telegram from the Portland Police he threw it in the trash. He had travelled to New York and Wisconsin, and both trips had been useless. "Then I thought

The house where Jack Doughty boarded in Oregon City, according to census records and newspaper stories in 1920.

it over for a while, pulled it out of the waste basket and decided to take a chance," he told reporters later.[11] The police would only pay for investigations within the province. If someone desired "justice" in somewhere faraway like Oregon, they had to put up a bond to guarantee that they would pay the entire shot for bringing the alleged criminal to the Ontario border.[12] The Small estate bought Mitchell his train tickets to Portland and he quietly left town to investigate the latest long shot.

He arrived in late November and travelled to Oregon City with Constable Fortune. Mitchell didn't want to waste any time. He'd already been on "a hundred trips" looking for Ambrose, and he was still doubtful about this tip.[13] It was Monday, November 22, 1920, and the two men walked along the basalt cliff and stood on the porch of the Strain home. As Fortune knocked, Mitchell hung back a little, curious to see how this would go down.

When Doughty answered the door, Fortune flashed his badge. "You're wanted," he said. "Come along."

"What am I wanted for?" Doughty calmly responded. "If you want anything with me, you'd better come inside and talk it over."[14]

When Fortune stepped inside the house, Austin Mitchell walked in behind him. Doughty and Mitchell marvelled at the sight of each other.[15] "Those bonds are all right," Doughty said as Mitchell passed him the wanted poster with his face on it. They walked down to the lower city and into the Elks Lodge. Doughty wouldn't make Mitchell extradite him. He told Mitchell the Victory Bonds were in Toronto, and he would go home willingly and hand them over.[16]

The Portland train station where Doughty and Mitchell began their journey back to Toronto.

The day after the arrest, the reporters found Mitchell and Doughty wandering around Portland like a pair of tourists. Mitchell was enjoying the spotlight, but he wouldn't share any details about Doughty's possible involvement, or give any hints about their route home.

"Is Ambrose alive?" one of the reporters shouted.

"How'd you do it, Jack?"

"How was Small when you last saw him?"

"That would be answering a question and you know I said in the beginning that I couldn't answer any questions at all," Doughty said.[17]

The reporters jotted details in their notepads: Doughty was "far from the flapper type."[18] Respectable in a dark blue suit, probably tailored. Strong, healthy, charming, with the ruddy complexion of a man who spent his life outdoors. "I have never seen him since the evening he disappeared," Doughty said. "I wish I could give you a good story, I know how you value that kind of thing."[19]

Back at the *Toronto Star* newsroom, the editors called a meeting. The paper was known for its strong social justice bent, but it was also "the last home of razzle dazzle journalism."[20] Editor Joseph Atkinson and his number two, son-in-law Harry Hindmarsh, loved to throw "battalions" of reporters at stories so they could own every angle of the file. They lined up free-lancers at all the possible train stations through the Midwest and sent one staffer to Winnipeg and another to Minnesota, hoping one of the men would be lucky enough to catch up with Toronto's most famous duo.

"Just because a man may have made an error is no reason why he should be trampled down," Mitchell said before they left Portland. "I am not saying anything about Doughty's alleged connection with this affair, but I know he has always been a straight shooter and I want to see him get a square deal."[21]

Inside their clifftop home, the Strains cleaned up Doughty's room. They couldn't believe Charles Benjamin Cooper was mixed up in the Ambrose Small disappearance. "We only hope it is all a mistake and that he will be cleared," Mrs. Strain said.[22]

———

The press didn't know what to make of the pair. The jailer and his charge behaved like old friends, a "fair imitation of the

Damon and Pythias act."[23] They smoked and chewed tobacco, stretched their legs on the platform, and teased the American reporters about their inferior cities as they travelled east. "If I live, Jack shall have a fair trial," Mitchell said in Spokane. Their travel was recounted with the same vigour devoted to a royal tour. "Is the autobiography of John Doughty to be the season's best seller?" the *Globe* wondered.

Theresa Small and her niece Madeleine (who was also Ambrose's half-sister) returned to Toronto from New York, where they had been visiting family. Theresa knew Mitchell was going to Oregon, and she had been waiting to see if the tip was good. "Mrs. Small, who is apparently in a highly nervous condition, did not care to discuss the case at any length tonight," the *World* reported.[24] The city roiled with anticipation. What would Jack Doughty have to say for himself?

On the train, Doughty was deliberate in his answers, taking long puffs on his cigar in between questions, leaning out the door to blow the smoke out of the compartment.[25] Outside the window, the fields were as frosty as his tone whenever a reporter brought up Ambrose.

"Now look here," Doughty said, when a reporter broached the subject. "I have treated you courteously and all that but don't ask me anything on this case."

"Why did you leave Toronto?" the reporter pressed.

"I've known this man for years. He comes of a fine family and has some mighty fine sisters," Mitchell cut in, trying to ease the tension.[26] The Doughty sisters—Eliza, Jean, and Barbara—were indeed very nice people. What that had to do with Doughty's guilt or innocence was unclear.

———

The early American settlers called St. Paul, Minnesota, "The Last City of the East" because it was the spot where the Northwest began, where you pulled your boat from the Mississippi River and continued the overland journey west.[27]* *Star* reporter Gordon Hogarth arrived on a busy Friday morning as travellers walked through the terminal with their heads pulled close to their bodies for warmth, like pigeons in winter. When the cross-continental train arrived that night, Doughty was as friendly as ever. "I suppose you have come all this way to get some news, so we cannot disappoint you," he told Hogarth. They walked briskly toward their hotel, and Mitchell told stories from the road, amused by all the attention from the press. He told Hogarth he was the eighty-first journalist they'd met. "Just about the third," Doughty corrected him, with the timing of an old hand in a comedy duo: "The rest weren't even gentlemen."[28]

They checked into the luxurious Saint Paul Hotel, the choice of railway barons, inventors, and the private secretary of A.J. Small, who was so good natured he invited Hogarth into the room to listen to his tale of nothing much at all.[29] Reporters

———

* The "West" was said to begin in Minneapolis, the twin city of St. Paul on the west bank of the Mississippi River.

who had met Doughty were struck by his "uncanny adroitness" and pose of "artificial apathy," and observed, "Unless the crown attorney can tear away this alleged mask there is little possibility that the find of Doughty has contributed in any way to the solution of the Small mystery."[30]

Doughty gave his official statement when they crossed the border at Windsor and left the train for a local hotel.[31] He told Mitchell he last saw Ambrose Small around 5 p.m. on December 2. Jack said he left the theatre about an hour later, around 6:10 p.m., when two of his nephews picked him up in his car. They drove back to the Beaches for dinner and last-minute packing, arriving home about 6:45 p.m. Shortly after 9 p.m., the family piled into his car to drop him off at Union Station for his train to Montreal. They stopped at the Grand Opera House on the way because Doughty had unfinished work—a few "letters in connections with Mr. Small's tenants." He went inside the office but didn't see his boss. "I believe both James Cowan and Percy Small seen me going in and coming out. . . . I believe I waved my hand at Mr. Cowan. . . ."[32]

Doughty explained that he had taken the Victory Bonds out of the vault in a play for a bonus. "I felt if I handed them back to him personally, as I intended to do before leaving Montreal . . . there was a possibility of him presenting me with some of them in recognition of my long service in his employ, as I know him to be rather eccentric."[33] But he never got around to it, and he passed the bonds to his sister on the train platform that night before he left for Montreal. As the weeks passed, "I simply could not stand it any longer," he told Mitchell. "I made my mind up on the spur of the moment and got out of the country as far as I could get until the matter of Mr. Small's disappearance was cleared up, the longer I was away the worse it seemed to me as I felt it would be far better to have handed in these bonds when I first heard of Mr. Small's disappearance," he said. "Now this is the absolute reason of my leaving Toronto, for parts unknown, I had nothing to do with Mr. Small's disappearance, directly, or indirectly, neither do I know as to what has happened to him, If I did I would only be glad to tell you."[34]

With the statement behind them, Doughty and Mitchell popped out for a meal in downtown Windsor. "Doughty has been a model prisoner," Mitchell told the reporters who found them. "He has been pleasant company throughout the journey." Mitchell clearly relished the moment. "I have always known that we would get Doughty, and his capture I attribute entirely to persistence, which never admitted of defeat, no matter how black the situation appeared."

The reporter asked what came next.

"The solution of Small's disappearance," Mitchell replied.[35]

TWELVE

HOMECOMING

Doughty's resolve crumbled as the train approached Toronto. He knew most of the reporters as well as he knew the scenery flashing by his window. They told him that his sister Eliza was recovering from pneumonia, the same sickness that had killed his first wife. Doughty ran his hands over his face, and the journalists saw the tears he was trying to hide.[1] When the brakes gave their high-pitched wheeze at Union Station at 8:30 a.m., he steeled himself against the hundreds of people waiting on the platform. The police escorted him to a waiting car, but he didn't rush. Like a visiting dignitary, he shook hands with officials as photographers chased him and children screamed his name.[2] At City Hall, he posed for a photograph with his captors, even obliging the photographer's request to remove his hat.

"How'd you like to face that?" he said to a reporter, nodding to the phalanx of boxy cameras, before he disappeared inside.[3] Toronto Police headquarters was jammed with desks and the recovered bicycles that nobody ever picked up. There was a wall of posters—the missing and the wanted—including Ambrose Small, staring into the middle distance.[4]

Doughty had expected the Victory Bonds would be in his bank vault, but his brother Will showed up at City Hall to tell him they were at the family home. The police drove Jack to 8 Kingswood Road, and he hugged his boys and ate a proper breakfast in the kitchen while the police took a hammer to the attic wall.[5] His family told him they had already lined up a lawyer to defend their brother from his formal charges, to be heard that afternoon.

Clara Brett Martin was the first female lawyer in the British Empire. When she first applied to law school in 1891, she was rejected because a woman didn't meet the legal definition of a person. Finally admitted in 1893, she found that her classmates were not very welcoming. "The thousand ways that men can make a woman suffer who stands among them alone," she said.[6] Martin lived with her sister and didn't chum around with the other lawyers at their golf courses and private clubs. She bicycled around the city, hired female law students, and helped establish a women's court in Toronto in 1913.[*] Some thought her a "queer duck" and "eccentric."[7] But she was talented and had already convinced the police magistrate to let Jack have a little more

---

[*] Clara Brett Martin was lauded as a feminist pioneer in 1989 when the offices of Ontario's attorney general were named for her, but the following year some of her correspondence was discovered by a law professor and included anti-Semitic remarks. Her name was eventually removed from the building.

time to make his plea. Her client still had to make a formal appearance in court, so Jack had to return to City Hall.

Toronto's police court had a rotating cast of police magistrates, and George Denison, who happened to be working that day, was something of a local celebrity.[8] At eighty, he was old enough to have defended Upper Canada against the Fenians in the 1860s.[9] He was a diehard British loyalist who wanted to be a decorated career soldier, but his greatest military feat had been his book about the history of cavalry techniques.[10] He had been appointed to police court in 1877, and for the last four decades, there had been nobody like him. He worked quickly, and many of his rulings were based on intuition. He favoured people like him: the upper classes and retired soldiers.[11]

The courtroom was rammed as Denison presented the usual cast of drunks with a ten-dollar fine or ten days in jail. When Doughty stood for the charges, the room went silent. The charges, Denison declared, were "That John Doughty, on December 2, 1919, did steal Victory bonds to the value of $100,000, the property of Ambrose J. Small" and "That John Doughty in the years 1918 and 1919 did conspire, confederate and agree with others to kidnap one Ambrose Small."[12] Since Martin had arranged for her client to plead to the charges at a later date, this was a formality. Doughty bowed and was escorted back to the detective department, where he scarfed down a sandwich, chocolate éclair, jelly donut, and coffee.[13] Afterward, the police took him to the pre-Confederation hellhole on the sluggish Don River. The Don Jail looked like a castle, but it was squalid and overcrowded. Doughty had privacy in his pretrial

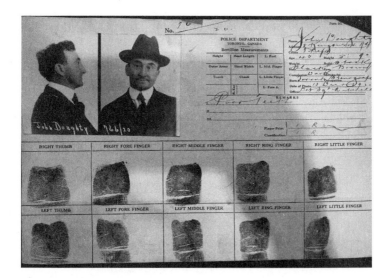

Jack Doughty was arrested in Oregon City and travelled back to Toronto on a cross-country train ride with Det. Austin Mitchell before he was booked in Toronto.

solitary confinement: twenty-three hours a day in his cell, with one hour of cold exercise in the courtyard.[14]

December passed slowly. Every morning was marked by bread, molasses, and oatmeal.[15] Doughty's old co-workers in Oregon City wrote letters, and his sisters brought homecooked meals.[16] His friends tried to spring him for Christmas, but the courts said no. When he eventually entered his two "not guilty" pleas, Denison figured that it was best to send both cases forward to the general sessions court that spring. "I do not think [Ambrose Small] has gone away just for a change of air, or anything of that kind," he said in his ruling. "He apparently did not take any of his money away. He left over a million dollars behind. Apparently he did not take anything. That would quite agree with the assumption that he was kidnapped, or, as I say, murdered."[17]

THIRTEEN

JACK DOUGHTY ON TRIAL

The skyscrapers caught the warm yellow sunlight as Eliza, Jean, and Will Doughty walked along Queen Street with lawyer Clara Brett Martin for the first day of Jack's theft trial in March 1921. Their brother had been locked up in the Don for months, and anticipation had been building. The case would be heard at a courtroom at City Hall, and the atmosphere was "reminiscent of Hanging Day in a western Cowtown," journalist Fred McClement would later write.[1] The photographers stood on the steps of the Romanesque building like sentries. The Doughtys were tired of the circus, and as the flash crackled, Will jumped in front of his sisters, giving the photographers an even better shot.[2]

Inside, a crowd of reporters, family members, and looky-loos read the newspaper while the jury was selected. The news was bleak: the Germans were balking at the latest reparation payment, and it might all lead to another war, the ruin of Europe. "Why is John Doughty in jail?" a woman yelled, capturing everyone's attention. "I found Ambrose Small a year ago, and I'll make sure he's released. Even if it costs me $1 million!"[3] As one reporter noted, the woman appeared "to be somewhat demented."[4]

In addition to Clara Brett Martin, the Doughtys had splurged on Isidore Hellmuth to lead their brother's defence. Now in his fifties, Hellmuth was Cambridge-educated and had been Canada's first national tennis champion.[5] In legal circles in Toronto, he was known as one of the "big three" litigators.[6] Hellmuth was well matched with Richard "Dick" Greer, who was arguing the case for the Crown.[7] Greer wore owlish glasses, and had been a semi-professional shortstop and a mountain climber, and had raised a sportsmans battalion for the war. Most Toronto lawyers were political men, and Greer was a Tory. But he despised blind party loyalty and had the reputation of being a maverick and a fighter, which made him an "outstanding trial lawyer."[8]

Doughty arrived in the dock looking thinner than usual in his grey suit. He looked around the court, nodding to his sisters and friends. The Crown called a Victory Bond salesman, the vault manager at the bank, and the men who said that Jack tried to entice them into a scheme to take a sliver of Ambrose Small's riches.

A new character in the saga was Fred Daville, whom Greer called to the stand, surprising the defence because he was a witness for the kidnapping case. Daville printed the programs for the Grand Opera House. He said that in early 1919 he and Doughty were complaining about Ambrose, and Doughty suggested there were other ways to "get even."[9]

"I said the only other way I could think of was to kill him," Daville told the court.[10]

Hellmuth objected. Why was Daville even here? He wasn't a witness for the theft charge. "It is an attempt to prejudice this man in a most unjustifiable way," Hellmuth said. "I never heard of such a thing!"[11]

Daville was allowed to continue since his story had a theft angle. He said that Doughty outlined a plan to get $250,000 from Small by kidnapping him and forcing him to write letters to the manager of the Grand, Jimmy Cowan, asking for big piles of money.[12] The letters would make it clear that Doughty was the trusted intermediary to deliver the ransom money on Small's behalf. After Doughty received the cash, he would split it with Daville fifty-fifty, he said.[13]

Hellmuth could barely contain his rage. He rifled through the earlier transcripts of police court and read Daville's testimony aloud. There was no mention about "killing" Ambrose Small or a specific ransom.[14] Why had the witness remembered these crucial details all of a sudden?

"Since the police court I have taken my memory back," Daville said.

"You won't get away with it. What policeman have you been speaking to—Mitchell, or any of them?"[15]

Nobody had time to dwell on Hellmuth's dig at Mitchell, because Theresa Small was the next witness, wearing a black dress and a stylish veil that telegraphed her loss to the world.[16] Theresa removed her veil and spoke in a voice that was barely above a whisper as she described her husband's final days and the aftermath of his disappearance.

She said that she met with Jack Doughty on December 29, 1919. Ambrose had been missing nearly a month by then, and she had heard that Jack was in Toronto on business for Trans-Canada Theatres, so she summoned him for a meeting in Rosedale. She wanted more details about the last time he saw Ambrose—had he seemed like a man who might suddenly lose his mind and memory?[17] Doughty told her that Ambrose was nervous on December 2—that he paced the office, dictating three letters.[18] Doughty left Theresa's home at lunchtime and she did not see him again until he was in police court for the preliminary trial.[19]

In his cross-examination, Hellmuth tried to extract financial information from Theresa. Ambrose had sold his chain of theatres for $1.75 million, and as his wife, Theresa had dower rights to his real estate. Hellmuth figured that Theresa wouldn't sign away her dower rights for nothing. What was she promised in return?

"Must I tell all there is—the little business between my husband and myself?" she asked. She was a difficult witness. Hellmuth's volleys were straightforward; her returns were a shrug of her shoulders, a loss of memory on the subject, a vague answer. "He signed over a certain part of the transaction— certain," she said.[20]

The court heard that, in celebration of the deal closing, Ambrose sent Doughty to the vault on December 1 to withdraw

$100,000 of Victory Bonds for Theresa. (This was separate from the Victory Bonds that Jack was currently on trial for stealing.) Theresa called Jack a "messenger"—a dismissive assessment of close to two decades of service—but allowed, under repeated questioning, that Doughty had full power of attorney for the vault, something she did not have herself. Hellmuth wondered if the $100,000 of Victory Bonds was meant to be her only payment for signing away her dower rights.[21] No, Theresa replied. It was money she could give to charity, to celebrate the deal going through.[22]

"You barred your dower, and the $100,000 had no connection with the barring of the dower."

"No."

"You are quite certain of that."

"Quite certain."[23]

Hellmuth kept circling the deal—and what Theresa was promised—but he didn't get anywhere. The reporters didn't know what to make of it. The *Star* thought Theresa seemed to be under great mental strain,[24] but the *Toronto World* said she had "all her wits about her."[25]

———

The star attraction for the second day of the trial was Jean Doughty, and the courtroom was packed like Christmas midnight mass.[26] Jean told the same story that Jack had told Detective Mitchell. Before her brother had boarded the train, he'd handed her a parcel. It belonged to Ambrose Small and she was to hold on to it for a few days and, if she didn't hear from Jack, put it in his safety deposit box at the bank.[27]

When the police issued the warrant for her brother in May 1920, she testified, the family debated whether they should give the bonds to the attorney general or to Theresa Small. Eliza Lovatt tried to call on Mrs. Small, but Theresa refused to see her.[28] The bonds were a terrible burden, Jean said, but her family had only acted as a storage facility: "The bonds were never stolen."[29]

Hellmuth didn't call any witnesses. Instead, he asked Judge Denton to throw out the case. Doughty had full power of attorney and every right to remove the Victory Bonds. He hadn't cashed any of them. His actions were akin to "transferring a man's horse to another stable."[30] It wasn't convincing enough to dismiss the case. Judge Denton thought it best to let the jury decide.[31]

In his closing arguments, Crown Attorney Greer called Doughty's story a carefully fabricated lie from a man with "treachery and blackness in his heart."[32] The theatre men who recalled Doughty's plans had no reason to lie. The scheme had been in Doughty's "wicked mind" for a year or more.[33] Greer imagined the scene on December 2, 1919: Doughty in the bowels of the Dominion Bank, stealing the bonds in a "three-minute grab." If this was his attempt to ask for a bonus, why didn't he execute it? He had all day to approach Ambrose. Instead, he handed the bonds to his sister on a train platform. "Was this proper protection for important papers of his employer, or the frantic act of a dishonest man?" Greer asked.[34] If Doughty had been "clean in his heart," he would have given the bonds back, but he put his family—who had a "laudable sense of loyalty, but a disastrous sense of morality"—in an impossible situation. And then Jack Doughty ran. He ran 3,200 miles, changed his name, and was not caught until close to fifteen thousand posters had been sent to all corners of the world. "That conscience God had given us to act like a compass in the darkness of the night—this conscience makes cowards of us all, [and it] made a coward of John Doughty, and sent him out as a fugitive from justice," Greer declared.[35]

In his closing speech, Hellmuth said that Doughty's plan to use the bonds to squeeze a bonus out of Small was stupid, but not malicious. "This is the indictment of a family," Hellmuth claimed. "The police are out for a head and they feel they will get the contempt of the community unless they can get John Doughty's head." Doughty had been at Small's side for eighteen years. He had had countless opportunities to steal, but he had never done so.[36]

"John Doughty knows no more of Small's whereabouts than do you or I."[37]

The jury returned with a guilty verdict one hour later, the amount of time it took most theatre companies to make it to first intermission. Doughty's expression hardly changed, save for a slight twitching around his mouth. He shook hands with his lawyer, and then he was taken back to the Don in hand-cuffs, the kidnapping charge still hanging over his head.[38] The *Star* rushed a story into their evening edition with a photo of

THE MISSING MILLIONAIRE   143

Ambrose Small's sisters, taken earlier that day as they left home. The *Toronto World* had more time to plan for their morning edition. They wrangled the twelve jurors onto the courthouse steps for a sombre group shot. These were the men who had heard nothing from Jack Doughty, but plenty about him. "It will be agreed that the appearance of the jury suggests a high average of intelligence," the paper noted.[39]

Doughty's legal team appealed, arguing that the evidence of Fred Daville should not have been allowed. As he waited on his appeal at the rat-infested Don Jail, Doughty tried to talk sense into the young men weighed down by heavy charges like armed robbery, attempted murder, and theft.[40] He was in the midst of a divorce battle with his second wife. He was already out a few thousand for the criminal trial, and then the courts awarded Connie $10 a week for support and a $155 lump sum.[41] He had always been a good saver. It was a part of who he was, and now his money was slipping away.[42]

By early May, there was more bad news. While the theft trial was deemed not "entirely satisfactory," an appeal court ruled that it would be "almost inconceivable" for a jury to acquit Doughty.[43] Sentencing went as badly as it could. The maximum sentence was seven years, and Doughty got six.

"Your lordship is that final?" Doughty asked.

"Final as far as I am concerned," Judge Denton replied.[44]

The conspiracy to kidnap charge was never heard. The scuttlebutt at the courthouse was that since Doughty was denied a retrial on the theft charge, the crown would accept a not guilty plea on the conspiracy to kidnap charge, with no trial.[45] The kidnap charge would linger on the books for a while but would eventually fade away.

Doughty left Toronto before the sun was up on a pleasant May morning.[46] A *Star* reporter had been tipped off about the journey to Kingston and he found Doughty friendly as ever in the parlour car of the train, trying to guess the reporter's age like a carnival barker. He squinted at his face, his hands, and his neck.[47]

"I bet I am about fifteen years older than you," Doughty— then forty-three—said to the reporter, who was twenty-eight years old.[48]

Spot on.

The train clattered through the inner city, as kitchen lights flickered on and milk bottles were brought in from the front stoop. Doughty reviewed his stay at the Don Jail like a travel writer. Solitary confinement had been "hell" and the food was certainly nothing to rave about, but the treatment was fair, aside from the rats. He pulled out his rat-bitten pockets of his coat as proof.

"You get real meals at Kingston," his police escort said.

"How many months do I get off for good conduct?" Doughty asked.

"Three months a year?" the reporter guessed.[49]

Kingston Penitentiary was home to the country's most notorious criminals, and Doughty was one of the bigger celebrities of 1921. He was Inmate 750, processed after Willy the horse thief, Jimmy the seducer, and Eugene, a servant from Quebec who concealed a birth.[50] In the prison register, Doughty was reduced to basic details: a moderate-drinking Presbyterian with brown eyes and dark brown hair.[51] He traded his dark suit and wide-brimmed brown fedora for a regulation blue coat, blue pants, and a blue-striped shirt—an outfit that would have served him well in the chorus line of the Cole Porter musical *Anything Goes*, which was still a decade away from conception. Doughty was issued a comb, toothbrush, and sewing kit. His cell was a five-by-ten-foot box—no bigger than two coffins set side by side. It was crammed with a brass sink, toilet, desk, and a bed that folded into the wall. A lightbulb that he had no control over hung from the ceiling.[52]

Back in Toronto, Doughty's siblings were frustrated. They had visited their brother at the Don Jail a few days before, but nobody had hinted at this sudden departure. More than anything, they felt the verdict had been unfair, their brother a fall guy.[53] The family's lawyer had received a letter a month back, in fact. "Are you aware of the fact that Mrs. Small, the wife of Ambrose Small, is a 'German' pure and simple?" it began. "I don't believe anything has ever happened to Small and I think if Germany were thoroughly searched you would find him over there, hatching up dear knows what now." The letter was signed, "One who knows."[54]

FOURTEEN

THE FORGOTTEN SISTERS AND
THE NOTORIOUS AGITATOR

By 1921, Gertrude and Florence Small were habitual frowners. In truth, there was little to smile about: Ambrose had supported them with an allowance, had bought furniture for their apartment, and now he was gone. The police investigation had stalled and Theresa refused to give them any money. Gertrude was in her mid-thirties and Florence had just hit forty, and both were single and jobless in a world where marriage was still the best way for a woman to ensure security. There is a painting of the sisters before their life diverged from its more comfortable path. They are young and hopeful, their brown curls piled on their heads, with ambiguous smiles that lean more towards happiness than sadness. Their prospects had diminished in the years since, and nobody seemed to care.

Gertrude Small had written to Ontario's attorney general in 1920, asking him to take a better look at her brother's case. Citizens were always writing to William Raney. Some complained about nudie postcards, others asked for an exception to the prov-ince's temperance act for their well-placed friends.[1] In the rural districts of the province, it was poison that kept the farmers up at night. One man even asked the attorney general to analyze the potatoes taken from his cow's stomach. The entire province roiled with intrigue, and Gertrude's modest request was noted in the office ledger: "Regarding disappearance of A.J. Small. Asks that steps be taken to find him."[2] When the sisters had a meet-ing with the attorney general and his staff, the officials were "more inclined to believe that Mr. Small had been drugged and kidnapped and was being held for ransom," the Toronto World wrote.[3] The Ontario Provincial Police were called in to help the Toronto Police, at the request of the attorney general, in 1920.[4] OPP commissioner Joseph Rogers and lawyer Richard Greer, acting as a special counsel, interviewed Small's friend Thomas Flynn, theatre manager James Cowan, and the Small family maid, among others, at a series of hearings at Queen's Park. "Not only was it thoroughly investigated by the Toronto City Police but by the Ontario Provincial Police as well," an undated note in the Toronto Police file says.[5]

The dead ends and lacklustre investigation meant that the Small sisters were desperate by the time Patrick Sullivan rolled into town in 1921. He was nearly six feet tall, stout, mid-thirties, but looked older with his greying, balding hair.[6] He told anyone who would listen that he had been an undercover investigator with the Alberta Provincial Police but abandoned the force in disgust at the "unchecked carnival of crime" in the prairies. He said he had a nose for corruption and sensed a "rancid stink"

Florence and Gertrude Small, the younger sisters of Ambrose Small

emanating from the halls of the Toronto Police Department when it came to the Ambrose Small case.

Sullivan was living at the Iroquois Hotel, at the corner of King and York Streets, and had been talking so loudly about Ambrose that word got back to Toronto's new chief constable, Samuel Dickson, who wrote to the Alberta Provincial Police to find out more about his storied career in the West.[7] "I have no hesitation whatsoever in stating that he is a very dangerous man, a trouble breeder and agitator of the worst kind," APP commissioner Alfred Cuddy replied. "To go thoroughly over Sullivan's record since he joined this Force would take about a week."[8]

Cuddy had it all on file: born in Ireland, Sullivan had been a cop in Dublin, but bosses found him a touch "unsettled" and "generally opposed to authority and discipline."[9] He enlisted for military service during the war, fighting for the British and later for the Canadian Expeditionary Force. When peace came, he applied for a job with the Alberta Provincial Police.[10] "Do you understand the care and management of horses?" the APP asked on the job application, and "Can you ride?" Sullivan answered no, but somehow landed in the Grand Prairie district in the summer of 1919, in the isolated northern half of the province.[11] The local detachment in Beaver Lodge would have rejected him, but they were in need of a stranger to go undercover to investigate a missing homesteader named Jack Dougherty.[12]

There were signs that something was amiss at the Dougherty homestead. Jack's wife, Henrietta, and their son had been on their own for months, giving different excuses about Jack's absence.[13] Sullivan ventured across the "broad prairie lands" wearing overalls and a cowboy hat, posing as a cattle buyer from the nearby town of Sexsmith.[14] Henrietta was a striking woman a few years younger than Sullivan, with a "splendid physique," glistening black hair, and big brown eyes.[15] Sullivan pretended to be interested in her livestock, and they became friendly. She told him that her husband, Jack, had left in April to set up their new life in the United States.[16] She showed him the letters he had written, telling her to sell all the animals, rent the farm, and join him in St. Louis, Missouri, where they met as teenagers.[17] Sullivan sent a telegram to police in Missouri and caught a break. They informed the APP that Henrietta had served a few years in the state penitentiary for trying to poison her husband's family not long ago. Her husband had come north to Canada with their son, and Henrietta had joined them for a second chance at happiness upon her release from jail.[18]

Sullivan kept visiting Henrietta, and she kept talking. "I sometimes think that Jack is dead," she said one day, and then, on another visit: "I really believe Jack is dead, and might be found in the cellar."[19] Sullivan returned with another officer and found Jack Dougherty in the basement buried under the winter vegetables, the top of his head blown off from a rifle shot. Constable Sullivan had solved the murder, but according to his personnel file, the success went right to his head. He considered himself the Sherlock Holmes of the district.[20] He was a hard-drinking, foul-mouthed lothario, who pestered women at the bars and slagged his co-workers.

According to written complaints from the locals, Sullivan's tirades covered, but were not limited to, the following topics:

1. A true Irishman hated the very sight of England; England was the dirt and scum of Europe.
2. The English were trying to subdue the Irish, "the grandest and most enlightened people in the world."
3. He would like to cut the throat of every Englishman.
4. The British flag was a dirty old rag, and he would curse England with his last breath.[21]
5. He hated Prohibition, which had been enforced (very weakly, evidently) in Alberta since 1916.
6. A bootlegger was no criminal.
7. There was nothing so wonderful as becoming gloriously drunk and passing out.

8. One of his co-workers was "an ignorant old lump" who was "no good" at his job.

9. Another was a failure who would soon be fired.²²

His boss had been considering a promotion but changed his mind—Sullivan was too "fond of talking" for undercover work.²³ The APP would have fired him, but they needed him to give evidence at the Dougherty trial.²⁴ Beating them to the punch, Sullivan resigned and left town without permission. The APP found him in Edmonton and brought him back for the trial, where Henrietta was found guilty of manslaughter and sentenced to twenty years in prison.²⁵ Sullivan was celebrated by the local newspapers for his "clever piece of detective work."²⁶

Basking in the public praise, Sullivan lobbied to get his old job back. He knew that he was erratic and insubordinate, and that the "fire water" made it worse. But he drank to dull the memories of the war, he said.²⁷ He promised to quit alcohol if the police force gave him another chance. Police work consumed him like the rush of first love: it made him restless; he ignored danger and hardship; his brain thought only of the criminals he needed to find. "I have turned over a new leaf and will mind my own business in future," he wrote to his old boss. "I regret the unpleasantness I caused, And I apologize for any offence I may have been guilty of."²⁸ The APP took a pass. Patrick Sullivan was too much trouble.²⁹

Not long after, Sullivan was arrested in Edmonton on a liquor charge. He jumped town on bail and travelled east, applying for police jobs along the way.³⁰ He also wrote letters

to powerful people, hoping to ruffle feathers. He wrote to politicians about the incompetence of the Alberta Provincial Police
and advised the newly created Royal Canadian Mounted Police of
the "wretched depredations" in the West. "We are not worrying
about anything that Sullivan is writing about, as the man should
be in some lunatic asylum," a top APP official assured the RCMP.[31]
The APP became accustomed to receiving inquiries about
Sullivan's claims and had a short summary of his inglorious
career ready for mailing. "This man Sullivan is a notorious agitator," an APP detective wrote in 1920. "He is well educated and
clever enough to be dangerous in causing trouble and dissatisfac-
tion in any community in which he may be at large."[32]

In the midst of his letter-writing campaign, Sullivan wrote a
story about Alberta's unsolved murders for *Jack Canuck*, a muck-
raking Toronto tabloid, in 1920. He called his series "The Trail of
Blood."[33] The APP wrote to the editor of *Jack Canuck*, offering
her a peek at Sullivan's file, which would show that "this man is
not worthy of credence and his story and theories . . . are utter
bosh and nonsense."[34] Sullivan loved the attention but hated
being dismissed as "crazy." "Top of the morning to you, Shamus,"
he wrote to one of the high-ranking Alberta police officials
when he found out they had written to *Jack Canuck*. "Did 'The
trail of Blood' get stuck in your gills? Did it get your 'goat' Jim?
How did the old fossilized, dormant-brained sots, who call
themselves police officials, swallow it? Have I roused them from
their torpor?" He continued, "My pen is powerful, and my sar-
casm is withering. . . . I was a thorn in the side of the monster
of corruption—Alberta government. You thought the matter

would end there, did you? Aha, Shamus, 'old chap' you people know little of the characteristics of the Irishman if you think he surrenders without a fight." He concluded, "Happy Xmas."[35]

As he made his way across the country, the APP tracked his progress, writing to police forces in advance: "Personally I have nothing against the man," one official warned the Montreal police, "but there is something wrong with his upper storey."[36] In the spring of 1921, Sullivan landed a job with the Sudbury police, but it didn't take long for the APP to inform them that Sullivan was an "Irish agitator of the worst type," who drank so much he "does not know what he is doing half of the time."[37]

He showed up in Toronto in May 1921, when the big story in the papers was about a man sentenced to six years in Kingston for stealing bonds from his boss, a millionaire named Ambrose Small. Sullivan liked to say that he heard the "cry" of the poor, defenceless Small sisters and felt compelled to help, but journalist Fred McClement wrote that Sullivan offered his investigative services to Theresa Small first.[38] The loudmouthed Irishman was not Theresa's sort of fellow, and she rebuffed him.[39] But not the Small sisters, who were grateful that somebody was willing to listen. Sullivan created a flash-in-the-pan tabloid called *On Guard* to spread the word about the Ambrose Small mystery. "It will be a shock to the people of Toronto when they read, in my next issue, the names of influential persons who have attempted to interfere with the publication of the 'A.J. Small Mystery,' he wrote. "Subtle means have been resorted to, but the conspirators have failed to baffle or bulldoze me. Their bullyragging attitudes only added fuel to the flames. . . . I am satisfied that the cogs and levers of the machinery protecting the criminals in the Small mystery will snap under the pressure of my terrible exposure."

Sullivan relayed the story of the "frail" Small sisters, who left home in 1919, believing Ambrose would support them forever. They hated their stepmother, Josephine—Theresa's sister. Their father, Dan, was a nice man, but too old and feeble to help, Sullivan wrote.[40] He explained that Gertrude and Florence had applied to the trustees of their brother's estate for a monthly allowance, but were rebuffed.[41] Theresa Small, who sat on the committee of the estate, had fared much better. By 1922, the Capital Trust Corporation had handed over more than $800,000 to her, along with a yearly allowance of $30,000.[42] The payments were rubber stamped by J.A.C. Cameron, the master-in-chambers at Osgoode Hall.[43] (The master-in-chambers role was a judicial position. Cameron had no jurisdiction in trials or appeals, but he made rulings on smaller matters to keep business moving at Osgoode Hall.[44]) Cameron had approved the payments based on handwritten documents that Theresa showed him. The first was an agreement indicating that she and Ambrose had agreed to split the $1 million cheque, and the second was Ambrose Small's 1903 will that left everything to her.

"I am firmly convinced that the Small sisters will get the bulk of their brother's estate as soon as the true facts . . . are known,"[45] Sullivan wrote in On Guard. "This scandal is frightful, but I promise my readers that it will fade into insignificance in comparison with the exposures I will make in my next issue."[46] Sullivan ended the issue with some poetry:

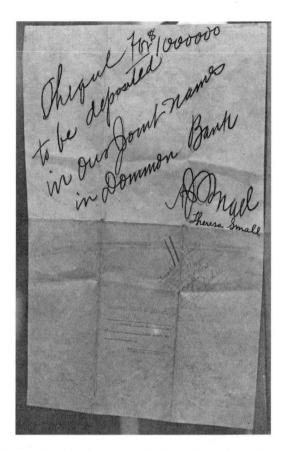

Theresa Small produced this document in the aftermath of Ambrose's disappearance. She said they agreed to split the $1 million cheque 50/50, but had no witnesses to this document.

To the ladies of the "upper crust" of society: -
What care I for your glances cold,
Your dresses aglimmer with pearl and gold,
And your puny love that is bought and sold

--

> The Misses Small say to somebody: --
> "Now there you go! You still of course, keep up
>   your haughty bearing,
> And we're too poor to hinder you, but by the coats
>   we're wearing,
> We'll prove to you that we're the girls that nothing
>   ever daunted,
> For you have wished our brother be unchronicled,
>   unchanted."[47]

In the fall of 1922, Gertrude and Florence Small filed a challenge against the payments Theresa had received. There was no proof that their brother was dead, and even if he was, his will had not been tested in court.[48] At Osgoode Hall, Chief Justice Meredith agreed that the payments were improper since Small's other family members had not been notified. He told Theresa she had to pay the money back into the estate.[49] But he had some sympathy. While it was typical for the courts to wait seven years to declare a missing person dead, he told Theresa that she could make a legal case that Ambrose was dead, given the worldwide publicity of the case. "If you prove the will, what you have will not be taken from you," he said.[50]

In the winter of 1923, Theresa Small, who had once speculated about memory loss and mistresses, had no further explanations to offer regarding her husband's undetermined state of existence. She petitioned the court to declare Ambrose dead, swearing that he "died, as I verily believe, on or about the second day of December 1919, at the city of Toronto, in the county of York."[51] Gertrude and Florence Small challenged the attempt to consign their brother to the graveyard. In March 1923, the feuding family members met in court, along with a newspaper boy, a barber, a detective, and an engineer who told stories about whether Ambrose was alive or dead. This time, it was Judge Emerson Coatsworth, seventy, who would be forced to sort through the anecdotes and make a ruling. Known as "Emmie" to his close friends, Coatsworth had spent his entire life in public service. He had been mayor of Toronto in 1906, and a member of federal Parliament before the turn of the century.[52] He believed that bitter personal disputes didn't belong in the courts. It was

Mrs. Theresa Small at one of the many court battles of the 1920s.

Theresa Small leaves court with her laywer W.N. Tilley during the estate battles of the 1920s.

always better for families to work things out on their own, and although he had encouraged the Smalls to settle, nobody had relented.

Theresa Small had William Tilley, one of the top lawyers in the country. He had tried cases at the Hague and Privy Council and had the gravitas you'd expect from such experience, but he was known for his gentle manner with his clients.[53] The lawyers always shook their head at good old Tilley, a man who read the funny pages before court but came in razor sharp every time, unsparing in cross-examinations.

The Small sisters had Arthur Slaght. A few years younger than Tilley, Slaght was pure ambition, much like Ambrose Small had been (or still was, as Slaght argued). Slaght had moved north during the mining boom to set up a law firm, and he'd done well. He was a prominent Liberal and a good friend of Mitch Hepburn, the man who would be a populist premier of Ontario within the decade. The two men were bon vivants who liked to spend the winter partying in Havana, Bermuda, and Florida, living "on the edge of scandal."[54] Back in the city since the Great War, Slaght was a well-dressed dandy known for his love of a good time and "his merciless cross-examinations" that left audiences spellbound.[55]

The Toronto Police had not discovered Ambrose Small's body, but Detective Austin Mitchell supported Theresa Small's claim in court by filing an affidavit that he believed Ambrose was dead. It was a curious move, and Slaght pushed Mitchell to explain himself.[56] Had Mitchell been telling people that he knew the location of Ambrose Small's corpse "within 78 acres?" Mitchell said that he had made a comment like that to some "Ouija board person" or "clairvoyant," and maybe a few of his friends.[57]

"Well, tell us where that 70 acres is, then, because that will help Mr. Tilley tremendously to establish that he is dead," Slaght said.

"I don't know how helpful that is," Tilley interjected.

"Well asserting that . . . you believe he is dead, tell the Court where that 70 acres is, and there should not be any nonsense about it,"[58] Slaght said.

"There is no nonsense about it," Mitchell replied.

"It won't do any harm to dig Mr. Small up, if you are right?"

"No, not whatever," Mitchell said.

"It might help us solve this mystery, that in your mind there is a 78 acre piece of ground where if we had enough of us to dig and look properly we may find Mr. Small's body," Slaght said.

Judge Coatsworth said he didn't want to force Mitchell to say anything that would jeopardize his investigation.

"Then I would ask this, that Mr. Mitchell should divulge that area to Your Honour."

"No, I do not want to know it," Coatsworth said. "Of course I have the same desire for information that everybody else has, but I do not wish Mr. Mitchell to communicate to me any fact that he cannot communicate in open court now."

"If you allow me," Mitchell said, "I do not know whether I am thick in the head or whether you are or who is, but I am trying to make it as plain as I possibly can that of—"

"Mr. Slaght is not," Coatsworth said.

"I do not want to be untruthful," Mitchell said. "I want to be in every way a perfect gentleman from the heels to the head."

"Do you think that on December 2, 1926, you will have concluded your digging or investigation of this area?" Slaght asked.

"That depends," Mitchell replied.

"Well now, you are not going to take me beyond the seven-year period, are you?"

"I might take you on to [the] grave," Mitchell said.[59]

A half dozen people gave evidence about Ambrose Small's existence, citing memories both crisp and hazy. Tilley hoped to appeal to Judge Coatsworth's practical side: He told the court that Theresa's allowance had been cut off. The estate was in a mess, and they needed a decision, so they could probate the will. The police had searched for years. It was time to give up the ghost.[60] Slaght countered that the court couldn't rule out the possibility that Ambrose had left town with some money in his pocket—perhaps somewhere along the way he suffered a nervous breakdown. Judge Coatsworth agreed with Slaght and the Small sisters in his ruling. "It may be that he was in a highly nervous condition and the mental strain of attaining the financial position he achieved was too great, and in the very climax of success something snapped and he drifted away, with mind and memory wrecked, and may turn up again later, as others have done before," Coatsworth wrote.[61]

It was a somewhat fanciful ruling from a sober court, but losing one's self was a romantic, melancholy notion after the war.[62] Men of science were perplexed by lost souls.[63] Sometimes it was the drinker on a wander to another city with no memory of how he came to be there. Or maybe a man who had been hit in the head and began to act differently.[64] The most drastic cases showed a complete break from the past, as though it was the brain's last defence against shattering heartbreak.[65] Maybe something inside Ambrose Small had broken like one of those returned soldiers staring too long into the shop windows on King Street. There were still thousands of men missing in action in France. The lack of closure was painful, but there was also something hopeful in it because it allowed room for the story to continue. If a soldier in England could wake up in hospital and remember he was from Manitoba, why couldn't Ambrose Small have the same chance, wherever he was?

But Theresa Small wanted closure. Police had searched for years, helped by a world of amateurs keen to claim the prize money, offering up amnesia victims, a legless man, and water-logged corpses. Theresa's legal team appealed Coatsworth's ruling, and it took only a few months before she got her way. By the summer of 1923, Ambrose Small was officially dead.[66] There was no funeral, no cemetery plot, no engraved stone. There was nowhere for his family to grieve except the courts.

FIFTEEN

SMALL VS. SMALL

TORONTO, SPRING 1924

As soon as Theresa Small filed the paperwork to prove her husband's will—a document that left everything to her—Gertrude and Florence Small filed their challenge. Millions of dollars and a life of comfort were on the line. Justice William Logie would hear the case. Logie was a serious man who had served as the commander of the military district of Toronto, overseeing recruitment and training camps during the war.[1] Arthur Slaght had returned for the Small sisters, joined by Gideon Grant, who was not as colourful but just as fierce. William Tilley was back by Theresa's side.* He knew the Small

---

* In a few years, William Tilley would represent Canadian general
    Arthur Currie, when Currie successfully sued a Port Hope newspaper
    for libel after the paper claimed that Currie's actions had needlessly
    killed Canadian soldiers on the last day of the war in his desire to keep
    pushing ahead to Mons. The entire country watched the case—and
    though Currie won it, the financial reward was small.

The Ambrose Small estate was based on this 1903 handwritten will, which left everything to Theresa Small.

sisters and their legal team would build their case on marital scandal. He wanted to spare Theresa the cross-examination, so he called her sister to talk about the day when Ambrose asked them to witness his 1903 will.[2] It was written on a scrap of paper no bigger than a recipe card, and it left everything to Theresa.[3]

Gideon Grant objected to Theresa ducking out of an appearance, and Justice Logie agreed: if she wanted to prove this 1903 will, she'd have to open herself to questioning. Theresa faced the court with a woodland animal draped across her shoulders.[4] Tilley lobbed softballs that allowed Theresa to showcase her role in the theatrical empire, implying that she was a deserving

partner to the riches.⁵ Both Theresa and Tilley knew an attack
was coming, so they tried to get ahead of it. Theresa explained
that Ambrose had been "in the hands of a designing woman"
named Clara, who wrote her husband "rotten" love letters.⁶
Theresa had found some of the letters, but she said the unpleasantness was behind the couple in 1919. As proof, she mentioned
a note that Ambrose had written to her one night when she was
out at a show and he came upon her stash of Clara's love notes,
which Theresa had kept in a black box on her dresser. Ambrose
took Clara's letters out of the box and replaced them with an
apologetic note dated April 2, 1919:

Theresa Dear Theresa

Don't bother your dear little head about this rotten stuff
anymore. It's all over and no earthly use digging it up
and more. You left the Black Box wide open the night
you went to the Academy of Music Musical. I saw it and
destroyed the whole business to get it out of the way
and not bother either of us again. God bless you. AMBY.⁷

Standing before the packed courtroom the next day, Gideon
Grant began his cross-examination of Theresa Small by pulling
a stack of Clara's love letters from an envelope. "I understand the
press is not to publish these letters," he said. For the first time,
Justice Logie noticed all of the young women sitting in his court,
riveted by the scene as though it was a matinee melodrama. He

tried to shoo them away. Surely they didn't want to hear the "malodorous details" of the love letters. Grant began to read a letter from Clara to "darling" Ambrose, written in 1919. Theresa had acknowledged that her husband had a mistress, but she was trying to make the point that the marital troubles were behind them in 1919. In late 1919, Clara was living in Minneapolis, married to Douglas Jennings. "I am the most unhappy girl in the world," she wrote Ambrose. "I want you. Can't you suggest something after the first of December? You will be free, practically. Let's beat it away from our troubles."[8] As Grant read the letters, he hammered Theresa with questions.

"I do not suppose you knew anything about Ambrose wiring to her?"

"No."

"Or [her] cooking his dinner for him not long before?"

"No."

"I suppose you did know that she lived in an apartment here in Toronto, I will not say where?"

"I have heard since that she and Mr. Flynn had an apartment there."

"And you don't know who paid the rent?"

"I have heard since."

"And you knew that she would send bills to him to pay?"

"No."[9]

Grant began reading another letter, but Theresa stopped him. "The press are taking these letters down," she said. "Can you not give them to me? It is very humiliating."[10]

"We cannot change the facts, Mrs. Small," Grant responded.

Gideon Grant didn't think Theresa and Ambrose were a happy couple in 1919, when the theatre magnate disappeared. He guessed that Theresa—or somebody close to her—fudged the date on the conciliatory letter her legal team had filed with the court. The second 9 in 1919 looked suspect, he argued, like it had been birthed from the 7 of 1917. Theresa was adamant that wasn't the case. She remembered that she had been out to see a show at the Academy of Music when Ambrose left this letter on her dresser in 1919. Grant asked her what that conversation with Ambrose was like, when she returned home and found this

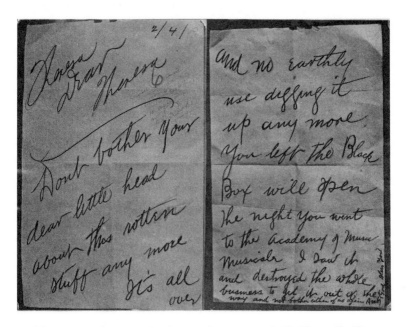

This note was a key piece of evidence in the 1924 estate battle. Theresa Small's legal team used it to show that the Smalls' marriage was in good shape by 1919. The opposing lawyers thought the note had been doctored and changed to 1919 from 1917.

new letter? She didn't remember. "I should think that was something which would stick in your mind eternally," Grant said.[11]

The existence of a mistress was humiliating enough for Theresa, but Grant wasn't done. It wasn't only Ambrose who had an affair during the spring of 1917, was it? Hadn't Theresa's husband accused her of having a romance with a soldier in the 208th Battalion? Theresa explained that this was a "diabolical plot" by Ambrose and his friends, a blackmail salvo in his bid to keep Clara in Toronto in 1917. To avoid embarrassing the man, the court called him Mr. X. Theresa said that Ambrose wrote a letter to Mr. X, accusing him of having an affair with Theresa. Ambrose told Theresa he wouldn't send it if she allowed Clara to stay in Toronto. Theresa refused—"I wouldn't be scared," she said, describing an escalating game of bluffs.[12] When the men left for England, Ambrose entrusted the letter to his cousin, fully expecting that Theresa would go behind his back to retrieve it, but she didn't. Ambrose was mortified, she claimed, and cabled to Mr. X to apologize for dragging him into this mess.[13]

Tilley had heard enough. This gossip was irrelevant and he asked that it be excluded from the record. The judge was sympathetic, but responded, "now that I am in it, I am afraid I will have to do the best I can."[14]

"It is to my regret that I put this evidence in at all, my lord, but I have to," Grant said.[15] Grant doubted Theresa's story. He believed that Theresa received the same letter from Ambrose, accusing her of adultery. Grant asked Theresa if the letter arrived while she was visiting her sister-in-law in Yonkers after the battalion sailed.[16]

"No," she replied.

"Did you get any letter, while at Yonkers, from your husband, stating that he had sent this letter with a copy of the schedule I have indicated, and saying to you that you had better find a place in a convent or a retreat?" Grant asked.

"Never in my life," Theresa said.

"Did you ever make a confession to your husband that there had been some improprieties between you and the man referred to?"

"Never in my life," she said.[17]

There was a two-week break before the next court date. Reading the newspaper accounts of the trial at his home in Toronto, Thomas Herbert Lennox, a Conservative MPP and the commanding officer of the 208th Battalion, was clearly uncomfortable. The good name of the battalion and its patron saint, Theresa Small, were being soiled (not to mention his own good name). "I desire to say that I am not Mr. X," he wrote to both the *Star* and the *Globe*. "The gentleman referred to was one of my most highly respected officers. . . . I have no hesitation in saying that, in my opinion, there is not a word of truth in the suggestion of any impropriety on his part."[18]

Justice Logie tried to convince the Small sisters and Theresa to settle during the two-week break, but they refused to give in.[19] When the parties gathered again in late April 1924, Theresa answered more questions about the family's finances. The story was a little different than last time. She said she and Ambrose agreed that she would receive $200,000 of his Victory Bonds (which included $100,000 for charity) for her dower, and then she would get half of the $1 million cheque.[20] Grant was incredulous that Ambrose Small would make a deal where Theresa would receive $700,000 straight away and he would get only $500,000 and take his chances on the money to come.

"No, I don't mean that," Theresa said. "If the property was figured up it would be just about what the intention was—half and half."

Theresa Small outside of court during the estate battle of April 1924, when her home life was "aired" in court.

As she continued to be grilled about her husband's final days, Theresa offered an impressive medley of "I don't knows," "I cannot tell yous," and "Not exactlys." When Grant suggested that Ambrose and Clara made a love nest of the family's Rosedale home in October 1919 while Theresa was visiting her sister in the United States for six weeks, Theresa said she'd "never been away six weeks" in her life.[21]

Grant painted a picture of the final weekend before the theatres were turned over to Trans-Canada. Ambrose returned to Toronto from Montreal and the couple had a blowout fight about the theatre, the marriage, the money. Theresa challenged every word of Grant's story. She and Ambrose weren't on bad terms. She and Ambrose didn't argue. They had a discussion and came to an agreement. Grant might believe their marriage had been imploding, but according to Theresa Small, everything was fine.[22]

The most unexpected development came the next day. The Small sisters and Theresa reached a settlement. Had the public shaming worn Theresa down? Did she worry that the judgment wouldn't go in her favour? Was she just tired?

Inside Justice Logie's chambers, they hammered out the deal. Florence and Gertrude would not challenge the 1903 will that gave Theresa control of the estate. In return, Theresa would set aside a $100,000 annuity for each sister so they could live off the interest, expected to be about $5,000 a year. The principal would return to the estate after each sister died.[23]

Justice Logie ended the ordeal with praise for Theresa, who left court without a "stain upon her character," he said. She walked into the spring day, arm linked with Tilley's, carefully managing the steps of City Hall. "It is just about the same as I had been willing to do at first," she said to the reporters waiting outside. "If the other parties had been willing to agree and to quit persecuting me."[24]

When the papers hit the streets, some of the reporters called it the final chapter of the Ambrose Small story. There might have been peace if Patrick Sullivan had moved on to the next injustice, but he was just getting started. Gideon Grant had been impressed by Sullivan's digging, and he thought the federal justice department might be interested in Sullivan's assistance since the case had gone cold.[25] "The detective department in Toronto has completely fallen down, and I would say have never made a thorough investigation of this case," Grant wrote to federal justice minister Ernest Lapointe in 1925. "I do not wish to impute any wrongful motives to anyone, but only one detective was detailed on this matter, and he evidently gave information to people whom he did not suspect which headed off every avenue of information which he might have followed up."[26]

Sensing the sort of reception this kind of letter might receive, Grant assured Lapointe that he wasn't a quack. They had met at the Ontario Club and had some mutual friends like Prime Minister William Lyon Mackenzie King. Grant told Lapointe that the reward money should be restored and the mail of certain people monitored—including a number of theatre men now living in the United States, Jack Doughty and his family, and Theresa Small and her sister Josephine. "I can assure you I would not think of making a request like this," he wrote, "if I were not persuaded that the parties named are very likely to be getting correspondence which will help solve the mystery."[27]

Sullivan also wrote to Lapointe. He knew the federal government had no jurisdiction in the case, but he said he didn't trust the Toronto or Ontario officials who had mixed "stinking politics" with the murder of Ambrose Small. "The Roman Church and the Methodist Church are crotch deep in the corruption surrounding the crime," he wrote. "Lovely country!"[28]

Word about Grant's request bounced around Ottawa. RCMP commissioner Cortlandt Starnes wanted to know if anyone in his Toronto detachment had any theories on Small or knew anything about this Patrick Sullivan fellow. RCMP officers tailed Sullivan, watching as he downed the light beer the Ontario government had legalized in 1923. "This man is a four-flusher and is no good," they wrote in their report, using an old-timey word for a bluffer in poker.[29]

Alfred Cuddy, the former commissioner of the Alberta Provincial Police, now worked at Queen's Park as the assistant commissioner for the Ontario Provincial Police, where he found himself ensconced in another Patrick Sullivan conspiracy campaign. "Pat is giving a great deal of attention to one side of the case and evidently making love to one of the Small sisters and I think she should know that Pat has a wife in Ireland," he wrote to his old colleagues in Alberta, asking for a copy of a letter that Sullivan's wife had once sent to the force detailing her abandonment.[30] The APP were surprised by Cuddy's update. They hadn't heard from Sullivan in a long time, which was strange, so they figured he left the country. It turned out he had found a new use for his time, and a new source of income, with the Small sisters. "He got $1000 at one time, several hundred at later date and he is now asking for $10,000," Cuddy informed his pals in the West.[31]

SIXTEEN

DOUGHTY'S FREEDOM

KINGSTON, 1926

The prisoners of Kingston Penitentiary were typically notified a few weeks before release. That gave a man enough time to grow his hair back, and if his civilian clothes had disappeared, it gave the other inmates enough time to rustle up a "freedom suit" for their friend.[1] Not Paris-nice, but Paris, Ontario-nice for sure.

Jack Doughty had worked every angle to shave time from his six-year sentence, and while he'd lopped off a few months for good behaviour, his official requests to the clemency branch of the federal justice department had been denied.[2] He convinced the prison chaplain to make the case for an early release on his behalf. (A prisoner could only write one letter per month, so this was a good workaround.) Doughty saw himself not as an innocent man or a "citizen unjustly dealt with," the prison chaplain wrote, "but rather as a guilty man already well punished for his crime and anxious to close this shadowy chapter in his life and get out and set his feet in the way of well-ordered lawful living."[3] As the sentencing judge, Herbert Denton could change the term of imprisonment, and the chaplain asked him to consider Doughty's pretrial stay in the Don Jail. How about freedom in August 1925 instead of February 1926?

"My own view is that the time has not yet nearly arrived when Doughty should be allowed his liberty," Judge Denton wrote in an internal memo.[4]

In February 1926, nearly five years after he'd arrived at the Kingston Pen, Doughty walked free, pocketing the ten-dollar bill they gave every inmate for a fresh start. As the prison gates shut behind him, the sun struggled to peek through the cloudy sky.[5] He wore a dark green fedora, a dark grey coat, and a suit of green-grey tweed. He was battling a cold, and took a deep breath of frigid air, waved at the reporters nearby, and climbed into the prison transport truck for the ride to the train station. Next to him was a convicted murderer heading home to finish his sentence in Finland.

The warden came to the station to wish him luck, like he did with all his famous prisoners, and the photographers got their photo. Afterward, Doughty waved them off. His boys were getting older, and he didn't want to cause them any grief, didn't want to make any big fuss, just wanted to quietly slip home by himself. He grabbed an egg sandwich and a coffee and walked into the station.[6] "The past is a closed book, as far as I can make it so," Doughty told a reporter on the train as the ducks bobbed in the ashy blue of Lake Ontario.

Jack Doughty before he boards the train at Kingston in February 1926, after his release from
Kingston Penitentiary.

But wouldn't he like to make a few thousand on a book?

"That would be the last resort," he replied. "I am not sure that I would not starve first. I hope that after today I am through with publicity."[7]

As the train slowed through the cities and towns, Doughty admitted that he felt like a time traveller. The last time he was a free man, the women were wearing long dresses. Now they were flappers with bobbed haircuts. "I have been buried alive these past five years and I didn't see any of these changes come in gradually," he said. "It is a peculiar sensation to leave the world with women of one type and come back to it and find women of another type altogether."[8] Doughty asked if the new light government beer was drinkable, but the reporter wanted to know about life inside Kingston. "You have seen it from one angle. I have seen it from my angle," Doughty said, biting his lip. "Don't ask me any further."[9]

He wanted the public to let him be. If people were humane, he said, they'd just forget about him.[10] As he settled into his old life in the Beaches, spring turned to summer and the reporters were busy covering other scandals, like the constitutional crisis that erupted when governor general Lord Byng refused Prime Minister William Lyon Mackenzie King's request to dissolve parliament. That autumn, when the trees outside Queen's Park began to turn and the squirrels looked plump enough for the long winter ahead, Ontario premier Howard Ferguson received dozens of postcards.* For two weeks, they came—images of new

---

* Howard Ferguson had been premier since 1923. He was a Conservative, and he was the premier who gradually ended Prohibition, legalizing light lager not long after his election.

infrastructure, like the bridge over the Humber River, and a steamer chugging along moon-dappled Lake Muskoka. On the back of each, in strange and practised handwriting, were variations of the same message:

"A J Small Case is Corruption X 1,000,000"

"Say guy! What're ye gonna do about the Small case"

"Poor Small was not an orange-man."[11]

The postcards were not signed, but their postmarks came from Toronto—and a few from the Back Bay neighbourhood of Boston, Massachusetts, where Patrick Sullivan's sister happened to live.[12]

In the midst of the bombardment, Premier Ferguson received a handwritten invitation from Patrick Sullivan to debate the Ambrose Small case. No premier would ever consider debating a criminal matter with a known agitator. It was best to ignore people like that. The problem, of course, was that Sullivan hated being ignored. It only made him angrier.

His government would introduce controlled liquor sales, giving birth to the modern LCBO in 1927. Historians said he "personified Ontario" with his nineteenth-century values and twentieth-century ambitions, steering the province through the 1920s with his collaborative style.

SEVENTEEN

THERESA SMALL MAKES SOME FRIENDS

TORONTO, 1920S

With her close circle of friends and family, Theresa Small loved reminiscing about the old days, when she had rounded up hospital beds for the Spanish flu epidemic and brought sacks of Christmas gifts to the struggling families in the Ward neighbourhood of Toronto. Life after Ambrose's disappearance had worn her down, and she no longer ran in those circles. It was "as if she could not bear to take up the thread and go on," a friend said.[1] "Watching her trying to be inconspicuous in a gathering reminded me of bear-baiting. I never thought humans so cruel, so intolerant as when they began talking about her."[2] Theresa's days among high society were largely over, but one vestige of the past returned to her like a boomerang: the Grand Opera House.

Trans-Canada's plan to supply Canada with the very best of British theatre had been "an artistic and commercial disaster."[3] It was tough to fill theatres from the Atlantic to the Pacific with high-quality British drama, and they'd been reduced to offering fare like *Boob McNutt*,[4] a play based on a Rube Goldberg comic strip about a dopey man who botched every task, much like they had botched this. In the midst of the struggles, the Shubert brothers suggested they make the Grand Opera House a vaudeville theatre. The building would need a complete overhaul ("There is no use going into it half shod," Lee Shubert wrote[5]), but Trans-Canada could not afford it.

The Montreal-based theatre company was bleeding money by 1923. With the advent of radio and the proliferation of silent film, the public wasn't willing to "patronize good drama" like they used to.[6] The original agreement for the A.J. Small circuit had been $1 million cash and $750,000 of stock paid out in yearly installments. As the company struggled, Theresa offered the owners a cash investment, but in the summer of 1923, Trans-Canada decided it was better to wind down operations.[7] A company called Famous Players Canada[8] picked up most of the holdings.

Since Trans-Canada wouldn't be paying out their stock options, they returned the Grand Opera House to Theresa Small.[9] Theresa leased the theatre back to one of the ex–Trans-Canada men to manage, and from there, it sputtered into irrelevance.[10] The old timers spoke wistfully of the golden years, but memories weren't enough. The Grand, a sad, old barn of a place, was something you walked by, not something you walked to.[11] "There is a pathos all its own about an old theatre that stands empty and unused, its stage silent and deserted, and its bare walls seeming to make mute appeal against the fate that

The Grand Opera House in 1921.

has overtaken the building," a reporter noted. "Within these walls must hover at times the ghosts of the dead past, the shadowy figures of players who have uttered immortal lines upon its stage and gone their way—a part of the evanescent life they portrayed."[12]

Theresa Small wasn't going to waste her money on the Grand. She had found another worthy investment. She didn't join a convent, but she came as close as any secular woman could when she helped buy a mansion across the street from her own house, for the Sisters of Service. The Sisters of Service were a new religious institute dedicated to missionary work in the prairies, and they wore fashionable grey hats by Holt Renfrew and drop-waisted dresses by Edgeleys, designed for the religious woman who travelled by horse.[13] The venture had been the brainchild of Catherine Donnelly, a woman who had taught in one-room schools across Canada, including in the prairies. While the Anglicans had invested in schools, hospitals, and churches for the immigrant population there, the Catholics had not, and that worried her.[14] The prairies had been home to Indigenous people for thousands of years, before the settlers arrived.[15] In the late nineteenth century, government officials had been told to "withhold food" until the starving First Nations moved into reserve lands, away from the new Canadian Pacific Railway.[16] Indigenous people had been told the government would protect them, but "the 'protections' afforded by treaties became the means by which the state subjugated the treaty Indian population," historian James Daschuk writes in *Clearing the Plains*.[17]

Ever since the West was opened to "settlement" by the railway, immigrants had streamed in, many from Eastern Europe. These people struggled in the harsh landscape, and Donnelly wanted Catholics to establish a mission based on social work and teaching, so she set out to become a sister and convince others of her plan. When the Sisters of St. Joseph turned her down,[18] she created a new religious institute with the help of a few priests.

The motherhouse of the Sisters of Service in Rosedale—a gift from Theresa Small, located across the street from her mansion.

The Sisters of Service launched in 1922 as an apostolic institute under the Archdiocese of Toronto,* and Archbishop McNeil asked Theresa Small for a cash infusion.[19] (The archdiocese had long been aware of Theresa's financial situation. Back in 1920, they were informed that Theresa Small was updating her will. Make "doubly sure," one of their well-connected parishioners wrote in a letter to the archbishop, that Catholic charities were empowered to hold "property for charitable uses."[20]) Theresa was keen to help the new religious institute. She donated $3,500 so the sisters could build their first mission in a farming town north of Winnipeg.[21] Theresa gave another $5,000 for a hospital in Alberta.[22] She made her most generous gift in 1927, donating $25,000 in memory of her parents so the sisters could buy the mansion across the street on Glen Road. They transformed the beautiful old manor into a novitiate, where they trained new recruits.[23] "No one knows more than your humble servant what this generous act means to our little missionary endeavor," Father George Daly, the Redemptorist priest in charge of the operation, told Theresa.[24] Theresa gave them a record player, a badminton set, furniture, a stove, paintings, carved angels, a radio, chairs, costumes, vases— anything she thought they might have a use for was hauled across the street.[25]

---

* The Sisters of Service are not nuns but sisters. Nuns take solemn vows and live a cloistered life in a monastery, and orders are established by Vatican decree. The sisters take simpler vows, and dedicate their lives to a particular mission—like service and teaching in the prairies.

Life at the Rosedale novitiate followed a satisfying rhythm: midnight mass, hymn singing, prayers, and picnics in the summer. ("Though the weatherman threatened to send a storm several times, they were happily averted by recourse to the souls in Purgatory and we were let off with a few sun showers," one sister cheekily wrote in their community annals.[26]) In the same notebook, they wrote that Santa was good to them at Christmas, that Father Daly blessed their new car, and made note of all postulants receiving the "Holy Habit." Theresa had a room in the novitiate, and full access to the garage out back, which made a handy apartment for her chauffeur. The "great and thoughtful benefactress" was honoured every Christmas and celebrated with special prayers and masses throughout the year. There were no reporters, no lawyers, and no uncomfortable stares.

EIGHTEEN

ONE MORE CHARLATAN

n 1928, a "Viennese criminologist" by the name of Maximilian Langsner declared that he would solve the Ambrose Small mystery using the powers of his mind. He was neither Viennese, nor was he a criminologist, but nobody knew those crucial details when he promised to deliver the skeleton of Ambrose Small to the attorney general's office.[1]

Believing in the unseen wasn't *that* taboo in the 1920s. Respected figures like Arthur Conan Doyle and Oliver Lodge believed that they could communicate with their sons who had been killed in the Great War. The spiritualist movement had its roots in Victorian times, but it became a healing balm after the war. Even Prime Minister Mackenzie King partook. He was fascinated by tea leaves, fortune tellers, and making contact with the "spirit world," but had more time for his "psychic research" when he was in opposition.[2]

Because the police never explained what became of Ambrose, plenty of mystical explanations filled the vacuum. There was the woman who sent a map of the cosmos to Small's lawyer, and the single mother who offered her trance-based services to the Small sisters, certain that Ambrose wasn't too far away, like a misplaced set of keys.[3] There was a fine line between celestial assistance and cash grab, and at first, Maximilian Langsner said nothing about money. He claimed that he had already solved eighty-four murders and that Ambrose would be number eighty-five. He was a sensational fellow, but you couldn't dismiss him completely. In the summer of 1928, Langsner had helped police in Alberta solve a triple homicide.

Three people had been killed on a farm, and the lone survivor of the attack—young Vernon Booher—was locked up at the rural detachment. The police suspected Vernon, but they couldn't locate a murder weapon, and Vernon was not cooperating.[4] Langsner, who was then on a speaking tour of the West, visited Vernon in jail. He told the reporters that he had burrowed deep into his subject's brain with his own mind and had seen the murder weapon behind the barn. (He was right—police found it there.[5]) Langsner also claimed that he'd seen the motive floating around Vernon's brain as well. The young man was upset because his parents had not approved of a romantic match. The local press said it was all so overwhelming that Vernon confessed to the triple homicide soon after Langsner's visits. Before the legal system ruled the confession inadmissible and lifted the curtain on his hypnotic tricks,[6] Langsner was the toast of the prairies. At circus-like events, he subdued fighting cocks with his mind. He made sure the audience knew these were local birds he'd never met, and not planted poultry. That summer, at the apex of his fame, he told the world he'd find the killer of Ambrose Small.

The Toronto papers were happy for another twist and gleefully reported on the mysterious investigator who showed up that October, wearing a mask like the Lone Ranger and carrying a suitcase of costumes (because holding the powerful to account came with great personal risk). Langsner told Toronto reporters he had recently unravelled a diplomatic mystery overseas and had solved a historic murder at the Egyptian pyramids by testing his poisoning theory on a local cat.* Langsner's accent was hard to place, but he said he had "recently emerged from seven years spent in the jungles of the occult mentality and psychopathy of the Orient."[7] The stories were written so breathlessly it was hard to tell if journalists *really* believed them, or if they were giving Langsner enough rope to hang himself. He claimed to be a close friend of Arthur Conan Doyle, and told a long, detailed yarn about how he'd met the author in a fender bender. When questioned, Doyle said he had never heard of Langsner ("An utter stranger," he said); neither had the Viennese medical community.[8]

Eventually, the hypnotist made his ask: he needed money to solve the Ambrose Small mystery. (He also needed cash to pay his hotel bill. He'd come to Toronto because one of the city newspapers had promised to pay the freight, but they'd become fickle when he'd given an interview to a rival.[9]) Earlier that summer, when Langsner's assistance was first offered, the Toronto Police didn't think it would be a good use of taxpayer money.[10]

---

* RIP.

The OPP had been less polite: "I will not give thirty cents for the result he achieves," said OPP acting commissioner Alfred Cuddy. When Langsner came to town that autumn, Cuddy figured he should hear him out. At a meeting at Queen's Park, Langsner said that he knew where Ambrose Small was buried, but he needed money for excavation. Cuddy was firm: skeleton first, payment second.[11]

Ontario's acting top cop agreed to help the hypnotist in one small way. Langsner didn't want to face the press, and Cuddy knew there was a trapdoor somewhere in his office that led to the basement. He thought it would be hilarious to one-up the reporters perched outside his door by helping Langsner escape, so the "little criminologist" disappeared into the hole, followed by deputy attorney general Edward Bayly.[12]

While the reporters waited for the meeting to end, the two men were scurrying through the vaults and cellars of Queen's Park.[13] Langsner escaped out the western entrance, skipping over the flowerbeds and shrubbery, while the deputy attorney general glided down the main staircase of Queen's Park like a lounge singer, in view of the journalists waiting outside Cuddy's door, where Cuddy was now standing, visibly pleased with the effect of the trick.[*] ("Great Trapdoor Mystery Enacted by Deputy Attorney-General, Acting Provincial Police Chief and 'The Doctor,'" the *Globe* noted the next day.[14])

Downtown, Langsner brushed by the pack of reporters who were waiting for him at his hotel. Calls to his suite were met

---

[*]   Excellent use of taxpayer resources.

with gruff replies. The next day, he checked out, explaining that he was "forced" to abandon the Small case for a lecture tour that would fund his investigations. He promised to return incognito to solve the case, but for now, he said, "My opponents are all too strong financially."[15] A mysterious group called the 200 Society was very disappointed with this turn of events. The society claimed to represent two hundred Catholic women who were upset over the treatment of Gertrude and Florence Small. The women threatened to leave the Catholic Church, along with all their male relations, and sent a letter outlining their demographic blackmail to the archdiocese, trying to drum up funds for Langsner. "The Small sisters for some time past, had definite knowledge of those responsible for the disappearance of their brother . . . but they have lacked funds to supply the culprits with their dessert. . . . LACK OF FUNDS—and their brother a millionaire. Why should this be?" the anonymous president wrote, sounding an awful lot like Patrick Sullivan. "It is a blot on any Government to stand idly by and allow a Dominion-wide crime like this to lie dormant," the letter concluded.[16]

The *Star* wasn't ready to give up on Langsner either. They sent his handwriting in for analysis by the "psycho-graphologist" employed by the federal government.[17] Handwriting analysis was a burgeoning field of criminology, and the bureaucrat saw the strange spacing between letters, the "queer stencil appearance," and inferred that Langsner was a man "off the beaten track," a master of thrills who had hypnotized himself. "When the doctor is through with the Small case and feels he has done enough to entertain the Toronto public he should think seriously of a trip down south to recuperate his strangely attractive personality," he suggested.[18]

By the end of 1928, thick envelopes began to arrive at City Hall from Asia, Europe, and sun-drenched islands in the Pacific Ocean. The police had reached out to their global contacts when Langsner arrived in town, and the world had responded, sending their case files on the con man who never stayed long enough for the international mail to come in.[19] Langsner was wanted for fraud and slander in Austria, and he'd been run out

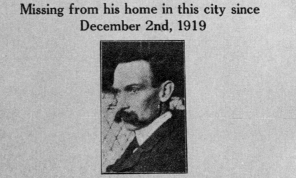

Missing from his home in this city since December 2nd, 1919

Ambrose J. Small

Description: Age 53, 5 ft. 6 or 7 ins.; 135 to 140 lbs.   Blue eyes, reddish complexion.   Brown hair and moustache, streaked with grey.   Hair receding on temples.   Is very quick in his movements.

Mr. Small, who was well known in theatrical circles in the United States and Canada, was owner of Grand Opera House, Toronto, and was last seen in his office at this theatre on afternoon of December 2nd, 1919.

When last seen he was wearing a dark tweed suit and dark overcoat with velvet collar and a soft felt hat.

The above photo, although taken some time previous to his disappearance, is a good likeness, except that for a considerable time he had been wearing his moustache clipped short.

Wire all information to the undersigned.

POLICE HEADQUARTERS
TORONTO, CANADA
October 1st, 1928.

D. C. DRAPER,
Chief Constable.

Toronto Police sent missing posters around the world, including this one in 1928, nine years after the millionaire was last seen.

of India, refused entry in Japan, jailed in Manila, and "pronounced a charlatan" by Hawaiian officials when he hypnotized the wife of an official before a dental operation.[20] "Langsner is morally and educationally unfit to use hypnotism because he uses it for his own gain," one letter read.[21] One correspondent guessed at Langsner's plan vis-à-vis the promised skeleton: He was going to dig up some bones and have a dentist and a masseuse claim that the teeth and spinal column matched those of Ambrose Small.[22]

Langsner was back in the news in 1930 when he arrived in Poland to investigate Satanist cults.[23] It was two years after his Toronto appearance, but one reporter was still smarting from the Queen's Park escape act, when the hypnotist and provincial officials had "prowled around the cellar of the parliament buildings one day for a reason that has not yet been cleared up."[24] Popping his head into the deputy police commissioner Alfred Cuddy's office, *Star* reporter Gordon Sinclair quipped, "We are interested to know if you have heard anything from your old pal and colleague." ("It would have been nice to report today that Mr. Cuddy was busy at work solving murders or catching robbers or something heroic, but he wasn't," Sinclair wrote.)

Cuddy set his pipe on his desk and frowned. "You're a great little kidder, aren't you?" he said, turning his eyes back to his newspaper. "Well you can't kid me."[25]

Langsner never dragged Ambrose Small's corpse up the stairs of Queen's Park. He was a footnote in encyclopedias of twentieth-century murders, perhaps most fittingly in the *Complete Idiot's Guide to Forensics*.

NINETEEN

SKYSCRAPER CITY

I n the eight years since Ambrose Small had vanished, Toronto had grown up.

Toronto's new Union Station—a "granite and marble temple to the age of steel and steam"—opened in 1927, followed in 1929 by the Royal York Hotel across the street.[1] The automobile opened a new frontier of suburban development. People poured into the city from across the world, building bridges and digging sewers and gas lines to new neighbourhoods. Real estate investors bought gently used buildings and tore them down to create something grander. It was a "cocky" decade for a country that had proven itself an international player during the Great War and was now seeking more independence from Britain.[2]

Toronto felt like the centre of all that progress and ambition. Land values were rising faster than the skyline. Newspapers like the *Globe* and the *Star* had their eyes on buildings they could demolish to build soaring towers. Eaton's built a flagship store on

College Street, and the Gayety Theatre on Richmond Street was torn down for an art deco office building that would be named the Victory Building, in honour of the war.[3] "Great Buildings are Projected and Property Values Increase—The Dreams of Business Men are Coming True," the *Globe* said about the "Wonderful Boom."[4] In the summer of 1927, a group of investors pitched Theresa Small on a hotel and office complex called the Toronto Towers, which looked just as magnificent as the Royal York Hotel. It would be a downtown hub, like the Grand had once been. The basement would house a cafeteria, coffee shop, barbershop, and shoe shiners; and underground corridors would connect pedestrians to a banking tower planned across the street. Above ground, it would be non-stop luxury, with a ballroom, banquet hall, deluxe penthouse suites, and an "exceedingly expensive" bank of elevators that didn't require operator assistance. The lobby would feature a marble staircase and lounge, writing rooms, and a beauty parlour. There were plans to include a chapel in memory of Ambrose Small.[5] Location to be determined—like that of the man himself.

The investors behind the towers said they'd have shovels in the ground in the new year, so the Grand would need to be demolished. "They may put up skyscrapers that knock the dark spots off the moon," one reporter reminisced, but never would there be a spot that made people feel "more vividly the sensation of a great city," than the Grand Opera House.[6] Before the wreckers came, stagehands and actors were invited back to choose a souvenir—like the framed dime that had been an ancient tip from famously cheap actor Joe Murphy.[7] The prop room had an oversized nest and eggs the "Great Herman" left behind, and the gondola Sir Henry Irving used in *Macbeth*.[8] Amid the memorabilia harvest, a reporter found Theresa standing alone inside the theatre. It was December 2, the eighth anniversary of her husband's disappearance. "I hadn't thought of it," she said, when reminded of the date.[9]

Was there any news?

"Oh, I suppose they are always searching," she replied. "It would be a pretty hard thing to find a body after eight years."[10]

In the eulogies to the theatre in the local papers, the Grand's former manager O.B. Sheppard recalled the days when he chatted up Toronto's most respectable citizens before each show. His days on earth were just as numbered as the Grand's: he died a few months before the razing began.

Toronto 1930

In the summer of 1928—a historic year for construction that saw a handful of million-dollar skyscrapers change the skyline— the Hall of Strange Delights was smashed to rubble. Workers guarded the dusty ruins at night. The only intruder was the whistling wind, which dislodged a few bricks from a wall that still stood. "If this building was not near a garage and people and police around all the time, I would not stay here five minutes," one of the watchmen said.[11] The theatre came down, but the Toronto Towers did not rise. In the years to come, the parcel of land that once held the Grand Opera House would serve Toronto's new obsession. It would become a parking lot.[12]

TWENTY

BEHOLD THE MAN OF GOD

TORONTO, 1929

A t five cents a pop, tabloid newspapers—gutter sheets as they were often called—sold well in Toronto between the wars. In 1926, Patrick Sullivan—private investigator, troublemaker, ex-policeman—became the owner of one such publication.[1] "The Thunderer Tells the Truth," the masthead read, and by 1929, the main editorial purpose of the "fearless independent weekly" seemed to be the destruction of Theresa Small. The tabloid dealt in conspiracies, and there was none bigger than the Ambrose Small case—"one of the most horrifying stories ever heard since the dawn of Christianity," according to Sullivan, who promised, "The Thunderer will prove before this battle is over, that you, government of Ontario, are not even as honourable as the maggots that crawl and creep in the scruff and dandruff that cover the cuticle of Mother Earth."[2]

The *Thunderer* was so popular that Sullivan had advertisements for legitimate businesses like "W.S. Fife picture framing" and "Ed's Radio and Electric Service," and a half page of classi-fieds for local homes, orchards, and missing persons.* The colourful tone of tabloids like *Jack Canuck* and the *Thunderer* made them stand out from daily newspapers like the *Globe* and the *Star*. No two such papers were alike. Some, like *Jack Canuck*, investigated issues like public health reform, while others, like *Hush*, went after the upper class, armed with gossip from Rosedale and the Granite Club: "Each new venture bore the indelible mark of its editor/publisher, each of whom was assailed widely for publishing 'scurrilous' and 'corrupting' material," historian Susan Houston notes.[3] They poked fun at the elites, and were popular, because "Schadenfreude can be addictive."[4]

Sullivan was a natural. He occasionally raised legitimate concerns about the Small case, but it was impossible for authorities to take him seriously when he attacked the Catholic Church in an all-caps screed: "AND NOW THE VENGEANCE OF GOD IS UPON YOU, YOU COWARDLY BEASTS, YOU FILTHY BRUTES!"[5] Sullivan railed against the public menace of "puss doctors," Queen's Park sugar daddies, aluminum utensils, organized religion, gambling, and the corruption of the "vile" King government,[6] but his choicest turns of phrase were reserved for the Small mystery. "It is safe to say that the spiders of imbecil-ity have long since weaved their webs in every corner of the brains of Toronto's Detective Department," he wrote.[7]

---

*   Historian Susan E. Houston notes that many of the tabloid papers that flourished between the wars were "ephemeral" creatures. Sustained runs of these papers are not easily found, and very few business records survive.

The tabloid was on the radar of the authorities, but nobody wanted to shut it down, because they knew Sullivan would relish the martyrdom.[8] But as the ten-year anniversary of Small's disappearance loomed and Sullivan began to make "terrible disclosures" the paper became harder to ignore.

In November 1929, Sullivan wrote an article claiming that Theresa Small's maid came to his home to warn him that he had

Patrick Sullivan appears on the cover of the February 8, 1930 issue of his tabloid. Sullivan was in the midst of several legal battles over material that was deemed libelous and obscene by the courts.

been probing too deeply and Theresa's Italian friends were plotting to kill him. Or, as Sullivan reported it, the maid told him: "You are going to be in the soup."[9] (When police visited Rosedale to investigate, the maid was asleep, but she later denied everything he had alleged. "I would not care if anyone had made a plot on his life," she said.[10]) Sullivan persisted. In the *Thunderer* he wrote an article claiming that the publisher of a local Italian newspaper was involved in the plot. Sullivan accused his would-be assassin of gangsterism and immigration schemes, and was eventually charged with criminal libel (a "frame up," he spat in the pages of his paper.)[11]

In early January 1930, with his libel trial a few weeks away, the *Thunderer* published another exposé, claiming that Theresa Small's alleged wartime lover Mr. X was the battalion chaplain and United Church minister Bruce Hunter. ("Behold, the man of God," the *Thunderer* headline screamed.[12])

Hunter was a popular minister and decorated war veteran who was awarded the Military Cross during the final months of the war, when he was attached to the 85th Battalion: "He not only dressed the wounded but repeatedly and under fire assisted in carrying wounded men back to safety," the official citation read.[13] He had been a Methodist minister at that time, but the church no longer existed. In the middle of the 1920s, the Methodist Church had been folded into the newly formed United Church of Canada. Hunter now lived in London, Ontario, where he was minister of London's Metropolitan Church, a congregation that included the city's "foremost citizens."[14] (It was just around the corner from that city's Grand Opera House.)

In the midst of Sullivan's latest "disclosures," the attorney general's office told the police to watch him "from the time he gets up in the morning until he goes to bed at night."[15] At the first day of his libel trial in January, one of Toronto's morality cops handcuffed Sullivan as he left the courthouse.[16] The police officer explained to the reporters nearby that there had been a complaint about an article in the *Thunderer* "involving an alleged statement made against the characters of Rev. Bruce Hunter and Mrs. Ambrose J. Small." Sullivan was charged with publishing obscene literature—"intending to corrupt morals."[17] The police raided the printing press that Sullivan used and tore through his Brunswick Avenue home. Bail was set at $25,000:* "You would think he had committed murder," the Small sisters said.

Bail was reduced and Sullivan's friends cobbled together $10,000 to free him from the Don. Not long after, a fresh issue of the *Thunderer* hit the streets: "Oh! The Scandal!" the January 11 edition read.[18] Inside there was a summary of a 1922 affidavit, purportedly from Clara Smith. According to the document, Clara had seen "Old Theresa" dining at the Queen's Hotel with Hunter in the spring of 1917. Clara called Ambrose and they returned to Rosedale, where they climbed a ladder and spied on the alleged lovers through a window into the first-floor music room.[19] Ambrose then sent accusatory letters to Bruce and Theresa. According to the affidavit, Bruce received his letter on his way to war, and Theresa was in New York

*   About $374,000 in 2019 dollars, according to the Bank of Canada's inflation calculator.

visiting her sister. "We thought she would jump in the Hudson, but instead she landed back here on the next train," Clara said. Theresa, she claimed, was so furious that she threatened to strangle Ambrose in his sleep, and tried to kill herself. "He was afraid she would do it. He really thought her insane," Clara declared.[20] There was no other evidence to link Bruce and Theresa—only this affidavit from a less than objective "witness." It had never been tested in court, and Clara, who was nowhere to be found, had her own motivations as the mistress of Ambrose. The authorities figured it was a fake, but when they found the lawyer listed in Sullivan's story, he confirmed that he'd recorded Clara's account in the proper legal manner.[21]

An older preacher noticed Hunter's face on the front of the tabloid as he walked up Yonge Street. The reverend didn't believe a word of the filth, and wrote to Hunter to tell him so. "I phoned to the Honorable W.H. Price, the Attorney General, whom I know fairly well, giving him only a brief statement of what the article contained but telling what kind of man you were and what position you hold in the Church in the City of London," he reassured his friend.[22] "I suggested to Mr. Price, that if no law existed today on the Statute Books to prevent a scavenger-monger making his living out of digging into the cess pools and casting up its filth to the disgust of the better citizenship, there should be."[23]

As the gossip in the *Thunderer* spread, the church leadership was supportive. They knew Hunter had been dealing with this nonsense since the war, when Ambrose Small had dragged Hunter into his drama in a bid to tarnish Theresa's name and divorce her.[24] Hunter had told them that there was no truth to it.[25] The church elders were completely on his side. So were the people in the pews. Carry on and hold your head high, they wrote to him by the dozens.[26] Even though he walked through the valley of the shadow of death, he should fear no evil. "I admired your pluck amazingly for carrying on through the day," read one of the letters he received. "Life plays some rather wry jokes on us at times."[27] One legion branch in London had seven hundred men ready to support Hunter in a lawsuit, but lawyers had advised against any publicity.[28] "I am sure you all can appreciate the embarrassing position in which I find myself," Hunter told the London Rotary Club, who had given him "three cheers" of support at a recent meeting. "During my service as chaplain of the battalion, I always conducted myself as a Christian should."[29]

The Thunderer viewed similar articles from what it called London's "Sheep Faced Methodist Press" with disgust. "Hunter is all we say and worse! Get it! Come out you bible whacking hypocrites! Come out and fight PAT SULLIVAN!"[30]

Hunter ignored the *Thunderer* dispatches, but his church steward sent telegrams to the attorney general: "THUNDERER AGAIN ATTACKING REVEREND BRUCE HUNTER . . . HAVE POLICE STOP SALE."[31] The attorney general didn't want to create any sympathy for Sullivan so close to his libel trial. The courts would be the best place to sort this out, the attorney general's office said, trying to soothe the anger in London. And sure enough, Sullivan was found guilty in both the libel case and the obscenity matter: "I have some doubt to his sanity, which was not raised as an issue at the trial—and I respectfully suggest that he be submitted to a mental examination," the judge ruled in the obscenity case.[32]

With Sullivan locked up, Hunter wrote letters to his supporters and thanked staff at the attorney general's office. Hunter went back to his busy life, his honour restored. "While this attack was no doubt distressing, it neither slowed Dr. Hunter down nor discredited him," one of the books in the church library states. His reputation "was enhanced rather than diminished."[33]

TWENTY-ONE

THE OLD ORDER IS GONE

TORONTO, 1935

I n January 1935, Prime Minister Richard Bedford Bennett stood inside the recording booth at an Ottawa radio station and made a coast-to-coast address outlining his economic plan to save Canada from the Great Depression. Bennett's Conservatives had been in power since 1930, and the country had fallen deeper into helplessness with every year that passed. Millions of Canadians were out of work, the drought in the prairies had brought years of crop failure, and the spread of communism was a real fear in Ottawa. Relief camps had been created by the federal government to keep single young men distracted with hard labour in exchange for room, board, and a pitiful wage. The camps had essentially become prisons, "hotbeds of discontent."[1]

"The time has come when I must speak to you with the utmost frankness about our national affairs," the prime minister began. "In the last five years, great changes have taken

place in the world. The old order is gone. It will not return."
Bennett had a deep voice that sounded good on the radio. He
had been inspired to give this speech—the first in a series
that he had paid for with his own money—by U.S. president
Franklin Delano Roosevelt, who had started his series of
"fireside chats" about the American economy in 1933. The two
world leaders had created appointment listening in their respec-
tive countries, and in Canada, neighbours gathered for "Bennett
parties,"[2] to listen as the prime minister pitched his plan of
progressive taxation, the eight-hour work day, unemployment
insurance, and a minimum wage.[3]

Bennett's family had owned a shipyard in New Brunswick
when he was a boy, but the business had failed and he had made
his living as a teacher, lawyer, businessman, and politician.[4] He was
wealthy but liked to point out that he had made his own way. (He
did not look like a man of the people, he looked like a man per-
petually dressed for the opera in his double-breasted waistcoat.[5])

For the last five years, Bennett had hoped that high tariffs and
trade with Great Britain would pull Canada out of the Depression,
but on the radio, he sounded like a different politician, talking
about "corporations without souls" who were counting on his
government to protect their "immemorial right of exploitation."[6]
An election was looming, and the Liberals scoffed at the timing
and the vocabulary lifted from Leon Trotsky. It was the "last desperate plunge of the gambler," the "conjurer pulling a rabbit out
of a hat," and the "11th hour repentance" of a desperate man,
they said.[7]

In Toronto, the man on the street thought that the reforms were long overdue. A minimum wage was a nice idea, but the manufacturers would never go for it—Bennett would need to be a dictator to bring about this much change, one man said.[8] But another respondent—a lawyer—countered, "Mr. Bennett is exactly the opposite to a Hitler or a Mussolini. I don't think he had any Fascist ideas. I thought it was the most democratic speech I've heard."[9] In his diary, Liberal leader William Lyon Mackenzie King called it "a political gambler's ambition to be a second Napoleon, the Mussolini, the Hitler of Canada . . . but Bennett will lose because he is in the wrong."[10]

Fascism was on people's minds. A week or so after Bennett's first radio address, the citizens of Saarland, one of the mining districts the Allies had taken from Germany after the war, prepared to vote on whether they would return to the Fatherland. After the last war, the coal-rich region had been governed by the League of Nations. In January 1935, journalist Coralie van Paassen, on assignment for the *Star*, saw swastikas woven into tablecloths, framed photos of Adolf Hitler, and storm trooper dolls in the toy shops of Saarbrucken. "The plebiscite is a foregone conclusion: Herr Hitler has the Saar in his pocket," she wrote.[11] (She was right. Saarland voted 90 per cent in favour of a return to Germany.[12])

The Nazis were rumoured to have plans for concentration camps, and anyone fighting against the country—the socialists, anti-Nazis, Catholic priests—were all thought to be "marked men." More than a hundred Jewish people had already sold their

businesses in Saarbrucken and were waiting to leave.[13] "If the
Saar goes to Hitler, Austria is next, and after that Alsace-
Lorraine," van Paassen wrote. "If Hitler is beaten, it will be the
Waterloo of Nazism in Europe!"[14]

In Canada in the 1930s, the accepted mythology was that hard
work solved all problems. There was deep shame in going broke,
but little help to avoid the fate. In Toronto, families crowded
into single-room flats. Homeless men slept rough in the Don
Valley flats. Theresa Small's real estate and stock market investments were hurting, but she still had household staff and cash
in the bank, which she used to help her brothers and sisters.
The Depression years had been hard on the Kormanns.
Theresa's younger sister Mary had drained her savings to take
care of her husband, who was now dead. Her older brother
Frank was retired but poor, and another brother, Frantz, had
died in 1934, leaving his widow with nothing but worthless real
estate. Her older brother Henry was also struggling, and his
only income was the $160 a month Theresa gave him.[15]

Theresa was a fairly nervous person, and was particularly
scared of automobiles. She had been in the back seat when the
family chauffeur had killed a pedestrian in 1906, and in 1928, a
cab driver fell asleep at the wheel and crashed into her car as
Theresa and two Sisters of Service were en route to the hospital
for charitable work. The cab driver was a new father who had
been working non-stop to support his family, and Theresa sent

a baby carriage to his house and made sure he had a lawyer. "The law will have to do something to stop excessive hours," she told a friend.[16]

"Hasn't she a nerve to show herself in public," she'd sometimes hear on summer days when the chauffeur stopped at a traffic light, and her windows were rolled down for the breeze. Late at night, the phone would still ring and strangers would shout, "Go down to the cellar and you'll find your husband's body!"[17]

Mentions of Theresa's name in the society pages were a rarity by the 1930s.[18] In 1933, the *Star* reported that Theresa was confined to her home, critically ill, but there was no word on the nature of her condition. The *Thunderer* didn't exist anymore, but there was a tabloid called *Thunder*, also associated with Patrick Sullivan. The paper "wished" Theresa Small a speedy recovery in the summer of 1934: "Death will overtake each and every one of us, for Nature transforms all things into its opposite."[19]

That same year, long-serving Catholic Archbishop Neil McNeil died and his replacement, James McGuigan, arrived to find the Toronto archdiocese on the verge of bankruptcy. McGuigan came from Regina, where his austere measures had saved that diocese during the first years of the Depression.[20] In Toronto, he restricted loans and expenses and put a stop to bacon and eggs at the seminary breakfast.[21] He asked parishioners for help. Widows sent $20, and Frank O'Connor, a prominent Catholic senator, gave $500,000. As McGuigan tried to stave off financial ruin, he visited the ailing Theresa Small.[22] In October 1935, she was weak with pneumonia and unable to get out of bed. Outside her window, crisp autumn leaves fell from the trees, and the postulants across the street sent their prayers skyward.

On the heels of Prime Minister Bennett's "New Deal" radio speeches, Liberal leader William Lyon Mackenzie King knew the Prime Minister wanted him to oppose the reforms so he could paint the Liberals as the party that chose politics over progress. King refused to play that game, and the Conservatives found an unsettling lack of opposition to their ideas.[23] They pushed a few of them through the House of Commons, but the measures "proved to be only a hollow echo of the flow of fulsome rhetoric with which they were announced," as one Liberal MP said.[24] When the federal election was called later that year, the Liberals had a crackerjack of a slogan: "King or Chaos." The vote on October 14, 1935, proved to be the "most one-sided since Confederation."[25] The Liberals took 173 of the 245 seats, in a victory that "flabbergasted prognosticators."[26]

Theresa Small died on election day. The Sisters of Service knew she had been failing rapidly and they had been praying for her "happy death." Word came during their scheduled time for spiritual reading and reflection. They rushed to the chapel with their rosaries and prayed "for the repose of her soul." They held nightly vigil over her body, "beautiful" in death.[27] Cerebral thrombosis and hypostatic pneumonia were the official cause, but some said it was the years of agony Theresa had endured.

The Sisters clipped all of the tributes from the newspapers. There was one story that stood out, written by an "anonymous friend" in the *Toronto Telegram*. Theresa, the friend said, once talked about Ambrose's disappearance while they sat inside her home, a roaring fire glowing off the jade tiles. Theresa imagined her husband's office at the Grand, an argument, an accident, a man carrying a heavy bundle out of the theatre, oars slicing through the black water of Lake Ontario, a splash, a body sinking to the bottom of the lake. "I could almost hear the sucking of the oars, smell the soft breeze that comes from the open lake in winter—and I felt the terror in my heart for anyone who had to do such a thing," the friend wrote. "This of course, was only a theory . . . but it was such a reasonable theory that it has stuck with me—that I can hear the tone of voice, the very inflection of the word 'lake' and see the dimly lighted room." There were too many people still living to name names, but whatever happened to Ambrose, "Mrs. Small did not know," the friend asserted.[28]

The papers said that more than a thousand people came to the funeral at Our Lady of Lourdes church on Sherbourne Street, just south of Rosedale. There were enough sisters and priests to bring the city's ecclesiastic productivity to a halt.[29] J.A.C. Cameron, the Osgoode Hall official who had wrongfully approved payments to Theresa, was also there. He had recently been disbarred for using client funds for his own purposes, but not many people knew that—it hadn't made the papers.[30]

Theresa was buried at St. Michael's cemetery next to her parents. Initially built on the northern outskirts of the city,

the historic cemetery was now in the middle of a bustling neighbourhood. Its Yonge Street frontage had been sold to a developer
in the 1920s, and a line of shops shielded it from view.[31] That was
convenient for Theresa Small. She did not want a stone, or any
official listing for her grave. She did not want to be bothered.
People were curious, so they came to Rosedale to stare at her
red-brick mansion instead. Many of them saw the religious
sisters across the street, preparing their gardens for winter.[32]
"Everyone that passes stares at us and on the least pretense, will
stop and ask us something—if Mrs. Small's house is occupied, or
some such thing, anything to obtain information concerning
Mrs. Small," the sisters wrote.[33]

Father George Daly, the Redemptorist priest who was still in
charge of the Sisters of Service, had been visiting the western
missions when the great benefactress died. It had been an odyssey
for him to get home—from Vancouver to Spokane to Minneapolis
to Chicago to Toronto, a mixture of trains and airplanes, the lat-
ter flown by "very clean-looking," steady, and polite young men.[34]
Back in Toronto by the end of October, Daly stopped by the Glen
Road novitiate, and he and the sisters stayed up late in the home
Theresa Small had purchased for them avowing to "never forget
her and often pray for her soul."[35]

———

By 1935, the Orange Order didn't have the same grip it once
had. The Great War had united the city in some respects.
During the war, The Knights of Columbus—a Catholic

fraternal organization—wanted to create places of respite where soldiers could eat, relax, pray, and read, no matter their religion: "Catholic Army Huts, All Are Welcome," they declared.[36] It was a national campaign and non-Catholics—like Sir Arthur Currie, the commander of the Canadian Corps on the western front, and then Toronto mayor Tommy Church—sent money.[37] In Toronto, close to $200,000 was raised, but one Orange Order newspaper "never eased up on its accusations that Pope Benedict was aligned with the Central Powers, that Catholics shunned the Allies, and that the Catholic people were priest-ridden," historian Mark McGowan notes.[38]

Toronto was changing demographically, and Canadian-born children didn't always share the previous generation's passion for the Orange and Green divide. While the archdiocese still felt the need to keep a list of well-placed Catholics that they could call in a pinch, Martin J. Quinn, the head of the Catholic taxpayers group, thought it was best to ignore the Orange Order and their fading clout. In 1933, he advised Archbishop McNeil— then in the final years of his life—"I have become convinced that if every last one of the alleged shock troops could be gathered together in a hundred acre field with a barbed wire fence so high that they could not escape, that any ten first class Scotchmen with spears, or four ordinary Irishmen with chair legs would chase them until 75 per cent of them would fall unconscious with the blind staggers, the other 25 per cent having been trampled to death in the initial stampede."[39]

In spite of the progress, a hint of the old bias was evident in the papers when Theresa died. The populist *Telegram*, "intensely pro-Orange, anti-French and fanatically anti-clerical,"[40] described Theresa's strange and spooky final years in her den of Catholicism in Rosedale. Patrick Sullivan told the *Telegram* that a former maid told him that "Mrs. Small used to go to the cellar and there pray over a certain spot with candles lighted."[41] The *Telegram* interviewed Hilda Weiss, now living in California, who said that Theresa Small roamed the mansion at night, rosary in hand.[42] "Often times she went to the cellar alone, but I could never see what she did," Weiss said.[43] "There was something strange, mystic about the household." The descent-into-the-basement narrative recalled bestselling Victorian-era books by religious men and women who had turned against the Catholic faith, like *Awful Disclosures of Maria Monk* and Charles Chiniquy's *50 Years in the Church of Rome*. Both authors described a religion in which scandalous things happened in dark corridors.[44] The *Star*, which was known as "the only daily that gave the minorities in the city any kind of fair break," painted Theresa in a better light.[45] Their reporter found a former cook of the Smalls who thought her boss "behaved with a great deal of courage in the face of her loss and all the talk."[46]

"After Mr. Small's disappearance, Mrs. Small seemed to acquire a number of enemies, people who talked a lot but were in no position to know anything about the case," Catherine Dunn said. A few days later, the *Star* quoted her again. "I am positive Ambrose Small's body cannot be concealed in the cellar of his home," she said.[47]

The *Star* and the *Telegram* waged war with incremental bits of hearsay and gossip. Patrick Sullivan, a few years removed from

his stay in jail, couldn't resist entering the fray. He told journalists that Theresa Small was rumoured to have made a shocking
deathbed confession to a nurse. The nurse reluctantly reached
out to the *Star* to say that Theresa had a "beautiful and peaceful
death." There was no eleventh-hour confession, no finger
pointed in the direction of the cellar, no headless husband buried under a pile of root vegetables.[48]

TWENTY-TWO

THE WILL

"In the name of The Father, The Son, The Holy Ghost, Amen," Theresa's will began. "Blessed and praised forevermore be the Holy and Undivided Trinity."[1] On first glance, Arthur Holmes—Theresa's nephew, and one of two executors of her estate—saw that there was about $20,000 in the bank, $3,000 in assorted jewellery, a $200 Pierce Arrow car (which Theresa had earmarked for him), and $5,000 worth of religious paintings. On paper, there was roughly $2 million of assets, but most of it was tied up in real estate and stocks. It wasn't money you wanted to touch during the Depression unless you absolutely had to.[2]

The executors were also facing the long-term effects of Theresa's stubborn streak. She had refused to pay the succession tax on Ambrose's estate. She was in arrears back to 1924, and now there would be a similar bill on her estate. (All told, $922,304.22 was owed to the province in "succession duties" on both estates.[3]) Theresa may have been a millionaire on paper, but there was very little liquidity.

Before anybody understood that reality, the Sisters of Service looked to be the early winners. They were due to receive $5,000 a year, all of Theresa's religious paintings, and a couple of future payouts, including the residue of the estate.* Father George Daly, the director of the Sisters of Service, tried to be helpful and asked Archbishop McGuigan to have a word with Catholic businessman Frank O'Connor, who was a good friend of the premier. Maybe the government would be willing to negotiate on the succession tax. "It means in the ultimate end so much to the Church at home and abroad," he wrote to the archbishop.[4] (In the end, they did reach a settlement—the estate paid around $300,000 for both Ambrose and Theresa inclusive.[5])

Theresa hadn't singled out the archdiocese for any gifts, but many Catholic organizations were lined up for a one-time payment of $5,000: St. Augustine's Seminary, the Jesuits, the Redemptorist Fathers, the St. Francis Xavier China Mission Seminary, the Monastery of the Precious Blood, the Catholic Truth Society, the Carmelite Sisters of the Divine Heart, the Sisters of Misericorde, and the Loretto Ladies School and Colleges. Theresa had also set aside more than $15,000 for a few religious organizations and priests "to be used for masses for my soul"; had earmarked $5,000 for masses for her parents; and allotted $2,000 for prayers for the souls of priests who had given

---

*   When the Small sisters died, Theresa wanted $100,000 of the $200,000 court-ordered investment from the 1924 settlement to transfer to the Sisters of Service for missionary work.

her the "Blessed Sacrament" in her lifetime.[6] "Mrs. Small Wills Millions to Nuns" and "R.C. Sisters and Church Get Fortune," the headlines screamed in capital letters as the content of the will began to leak. There were some notable absences: The Sisters of St. Joseph, where Theresa had studied as a young woman, were not included. Neither were the Basilian fathers, who had married her and Ambrose back in 1902.

There were onetime gifts for nieces, a "little blind girl," and Theresa's "faithful maid," and yearly allowances of $5,000 for her niece and nephew (and Ambrose's siblings) Percy and Madeleine, and for some of her brothers and sisters, depending on their needs. The executors and lawyers worried that the siblings who received nothing might say that Theresa wasn't in her right mind when she'd written the will in 1931, or charge that the will was "procured under influence" perhaps by the Sisters of Service and the Redemptorist Fathers—both organizations that Father George Daly was connected with.[7] (Executor Arthur Holmes "did not seem to think that the allegation (of a lack of mental competency) was entirely groundless," one lawyer noted.[8]) They knew if a challenge was filed, it would look bad in the press: the Kormann family versus the Catholic Church.

The forgotten were already circling. Some of the family members had retained a lawyer and were talking about a settlement. There was a friend of Theresa's who demanded money for a painting Theresa had damaged, and a former chauffeur who said that Theresa had docked him money from his pay for a rat-infested apartment in the garage over on the Sisters of Service property. "In justice to me I don't think I should have paid five dollars a week for a place I couldn't use, to suit the whim of an old lady," he wrote. "I think I should be given some consideration for that money."[9]

But all of those issues were minor. The real trouble lurked in a handwritten court ledger at City Hall, thick with decades of betrayal and hurt feelings. On every page of the surrogate court book of caveats were the names of people who challenged a will in court. It wasn't Theresa's siblings who added their names to the periwinkle pages, but Patrick Sullivan and Florence Small. They believed the estate of Theresa Small was the ill-gotten gains of fraud, perjury, and forgery, because Theresa Small was the person who was responsible for the death of Ambrose Small, and they had the confession to prove it.

TWENTY-THREE

CONFESSION

TORONTO, 1936

The way Patrick Sullivan described it, a series of strange events occurred in November 1929. He was living with Gertrude and Florence Small and undertaking swash-buckling acts of journalism in his *Thunderer* tabloid, preparing to accuse Theresa Small of having an affair with the chaplain of the 208th Battalion. Theresa, he said, heard about his plans, came by the Brunswick Avenue home, and, in a bid to stop Sullivan from attacking her in his paper, offered up a confession of her role in Ambrose's death.

In preparation for the eventual hearing for the estate challenge, preliminary interviews were held in one of the city's newer skyscrapers on Richmond Street in the spring of 1936. The lawyers for the Theresa Small estate were incredulous about Sullivan's story. Why would Theresa Small confide in a man who called her an "old bitch"?

"She was man mad, and I was pretty good looking then and she might probably have fallen from a physical standpoint," Sullivan said in the room on the eleventh floor.[1]

"Do you think she trusted you?" asked Thomas Phelan, one of the lawyers for the estate. "You had been viciously critical of her up to that time."

"Not *viciously*," Sullivan said.

That afternoon in November 1929, Sullivan said, the Small sisters were out at a show, and he was entertaining two friends when Theresa knocked on the door. She was dressed in a heavy coat, wearing a hat that looked like a German military helmet with the spike on the top. Her hair was flattened to the sides of her face.

"I have been informed," she allegedly said, "that you are going to publish an affidavit attacking my character, my virtue."

"It does not matter what I publish, I could not injure your character or your virtue," Sullivan said. "You are a monster, a monstrosity."[2]

Sullivan said that Theresa poured her heart out to him right there. She had travelled to Rome to confide in the Pope, who had forgiven her sins and given her an admit-one ticket for Heaven in exchange for a will that left a good chunk of her millions to the Catholic Church. But Theresa wanted to make things right with the Small sisters, because "perhaps this imaginary fellow up in the sky would not look very favourably upon her" if she didn't, Sullivan claimed.[3]

To ease her spiritual burden, she had written a letter to her sisters-in-law, explaining what had happened on December 2,

1919. The Small sisters weren't home, but Sullivan said he convinced Theresa to give him a peek at the typed confession:

Dear Florence and Gertrude

I feel unwell, downhearted and lonely. I spend the most of my time in prayer and preparing my soul for a happy life with God after death.

I received absolution from our Holy Father for the great sin I committed on the 2nd December 1919, but still I feel I should not leave this world to face my Eternal Father without telling you what happened to your brother.

Poor Ambrose was killed on the 2nd December 1919 and I know that a part of his body, the trunk, was buried in the Rosedale Ravine dump, and the other parts of the body were burned in the Grand Opera furnace. You will be surprised, my dear Florence and Gertrude, to learn that I am, more than any other person, responsible for your brother's death. God forgive me.

I will not cause any more pain to a living soul, and that is why I will not reveal the names of those who are involved in this gruesome crime: but I will tell you one thing: it cost me plenty to close their mouths.

I am leaving the bulk of your brother's estate to those who are doing Christ's work on earth; they will always pray for the repose of our souls.

I have told many untruths about you and Ambrose in court, and I said unkind things in many unsigned letters which I have sent to you. I hope you will forgive me, and your forgiveness will be pleasing to God.

I request in the name of Christ not to give the contents of this letter to any other person; leave the matter rest.

This confession, which relieves my mind of a great burden, is typed by a very dear friend of mine, who will deliver it to you after my death.

Forgive me, my dear Florence and Gertrude, and pray for the repose of my soul when I pass away.

God bless you.
Your loving sister
T. Small.[4]

Sullivan said Theresa took the letter back for safekeeping, promising it would be delivered after her death. Sure enough, a good-looking woman from Hamilton (who was likely a criminal, Sullivan said, because "most of the people who are hanging around the late Mrs. Small were of the criminal type") delivered the confession to Sullivan as scheduled. And now, here he was, using it to challenge the estate.

At the preliminary hearings, the lawyers also interviewed Sullivan's friends who claimed they were visiting when Theresa showed up with her confession. Bert Brown was a pal who helped out with odd jobs around the Brunswick Avenue house, and Albert Small was a country cousin of the Small sisters. Both men backed up the story, word for word. So did Florence Small.

"Is it a fact," Thomas Phelan asked Florence, who was nearly sixty, "that you waited until after the woman was dead and unable to answer for herself before you revealed your knowledge of this confession to anybody?"

"We didn't speak to anybody. We didn't talk about it—what would we talk about it for?" Florence replied.

"Is it a fact you waited until after the woman was dead and unable to answer for herself?" Phelan asked again.

"Yes," Florence replied.[5]

That was a fact.

After their preliminary interviews, the estate lawyers believed the "confession" was a forgery. It was odd that it was typewritten except for the signature—almost like someone was too lazy to fake the handwriting for an entire document. The signature was also bizarre: "T. Small" instead of her full name. The estate lawyers asked the Catholic beneficiaries to go through their correspondence: Did Theresa ever sign anything as "T. Small"?

"While I must admit that I do not believe the story which has been told by the various witnesses under oath," one lawyer wrote, "I must say that [Sullivan and his friends] do give their evidence in apparently a straightforward manner and I think no stone should be left unturned towards the gathering together of evidence to discredit their stories."[6]

Father Daly wrote to his western missions to inform them of the impending court date. "As this court case is so important to us I would ask you to make a Novena to St. Joseph . . . saying together in common, 'The Glory be to the Father,' three times, and three times the invocation, 'St. Joseph, pray for us,'" he wrote, also requesting a mass for Theresa's soul.[7] He wrote to his top sister in Saskatchewan on the eve of the trial in November. "Pray that God may confound the scoundrel who is making this trouble, a man by the name of P. Sullivan, a pervert and a vicious character."[8]

The challenge was heard in November 1936 before Justice Nicol Jeffrey. Theresa's alleged confession was the main point of contention. Sullivan, of course, said the document was real, and that it was Ambrose Small's handwritten will of 1903 that left everything to Theresa that was the true fake. Handwriting experts for the estate pointed to the heavy shade on the S in "T. Small," a sign of practised deliberateness. Analysts for Sullivan and friends said that Ambrose was a quick writer but the 1903 will was written slowly and the spacing between the lines was tighter than his normal scrawl.[9] It was also perplexing that a businessman who dealt with contracts had used such a small scrap of paper for such an important document.

Sullivan repeated the story about Theresa swinging by his home with the confession, but cracks emerged during this telling. One of the "friends" who had backed up his story at the preliminary hearing admitted on cross-examination that he was heavily in debt and had been told he might receive $30,000 if the will was "broken."[10]

Florence Small was full of venom. When she was a teenager, she said, Theresa Small hounded her rich brother into an unhappy marriage.[11] "He told me that Mrs. Small had threatened to choke him and that he put a dresser up to his door at night," she said. She claimed further that her brother had recorded all of the threats his wife made in a book. It should have been found in the safe at the Grand Opera House, but it wasn't there.[12] Detective Austin Mitchell "got lots of money out of my brother's estate and did nothing," she said. "He ought to be put in custody as well as John Doughty."[13]

The Toronto Police were sensitive about the case. They sent Detective Sergeant James McIlrath to take notes during the challenge, and to watch for signs of perjury from Sullivan. "Expectations were high that there might be some wonderful disclosures when he took the stand, but disappointments were common," McIlrath wrote. Sullivan and his cronies were "well-schooled and well paid for their services," in his opinion. "My observation of the case is that the plaintiffs are badly disappointed because they were not allowed to use gossip and were held to the strict rule of evidence by His Lordship," he wrote.[14]

Justice Jeffrey grew impatient with each passing day. The case was part coroner's inquest, part criminal trial, part group-therapy session. Sullivan went on interminable tangents and his mystery blonde confession deliverer from Hamilton was now being described as a brunette from Buffalo. She never showed, which Justice Jeffrey attributed to her lack of existence.[15] An aging cast of characters weighed in on random aspects of the case, including Jack Doughty's state of mind in 1919. An old typesetter named Thomas Shields told the court how he drank in the old "coal hole" of the Grand and once heard Doughty threaten to throw Ambrose in the furnace during a "heated" arugment the night before Small went missing.[16] Then there was Elizabeth Chapman who said she had met Theresa Small during the war when her first husband, a Catholic, signed up for the 208th Battalion. Chapman claimed Theresa had tried to convert her to Catholicism, and confided in her that she didn't get along with Ambrose and wanted to "get rid of him."[17] "I told her not to talk like that. I thought she had been drinking and I told her not to be foolish."

After a few days, Justice Jeffrey had heard enough. This was supposed to be an estate matter, but it had veered completely off the rails. Motivations were muddled by time, bias, and money. There was still no body, and the evidence fell short of implicating anyone in the murder of Ambrose Small, he said. He dismissed the case. "There is no doubt in my mind there has been for many years much bitterness between the misses Small and the late Theresa Small," he wrote in his decision. "I think I am not overstating the situation when I say there was an undying hatred between them."[18] He continued, "I cannot find language quite strong enough to condemn the conduct of Sullivan. Not only had he, down to the date of the confession, accused this unfortunate woman of being unfaithful to her husband, but accused her of adultery and murder. Not only that, but he held up to ridicule the church to which she belonged, something which she held sacred."[19]

Theresa would never place herself at the mercy of such a man, Justice Jeffrey argued. And why did Sullivan, who had pursued her for years, let her walk away on the day of her alleged confession? He had shown no restraint with the other stories he printed in the *Thunderer* that year. He'd gone to jail for two separate stories relating to Theresa Small even though he knew there was a document that would "utterly destroy" her?[20] This seemed highly improbable. Justice Jeffrey believed the testimony of the handwriting experts who saw too much hesitancy and care in the signature of "T. Small." The alleged confession was a "web of scandal and blackmail" all the way through, he declared, a "tissue of lies" from an infamous villain. If Ambrose Small was killed, he insisted, "there is not a scintilla of evidence that the late Mrs. Small was in any way connected with the killing or assaulting of her husband, unless the confession, which it is alleged she signed, compromises her." And Jeffrey didn't believe the confession was real. "I thought it proper to protect at the earliest opportunity the reputation of a dead woman who in her lifetime interested herself in charity and in doing good," he said.[21]

The Sisters of Service were jubilant. Patrick Sullivan, "pervert and vicious character," had been vanquished once and for all. "This ends a long and painful litigation, and I do hope it is the end of the mischievous doings of an unscrupulous villain,"[22] Father Daly wrote to the sisters, granting them a "free day" to celebrate, with ice cream for dessert as a special treat.[23]

TWENTY-FOUR

THE LAST SMALL

Patrick Sullivan had been bested, but the Theresa Small estate was plagued by legal issues and a cash-flow crisis. "If we don't pay taxes, we shall lose the Concourse Building fairly soon and other real estate in time," one lawyer connected to the estate wrote in 1936. "There is no possible way of maneuvering the situation except by getting extra funds. Failing this, the entire residue of the estate—largely real estate—not at the moment productive—will simply disappear."[1] There were occasional settlements to creditors (the "little blind girl" was given one of Theresa's homes and a $574 payment in 1940[2]) but most of the money seemed to evaporate in the Great Depression or was sucked up by lawyers and estate tax.

Father George Daly kept a constant vigil, writing to the executors when he recognized that one of Theresa Small's properties had sold. He was just curious, he would write, about how that windfall would be distributed, seeing as the Sisters of Service still had a claim.[3] He had spent years trying to sell Theresa's religious art, convinced that one wall-sized piece was by Flemish painter Peter Paul Rubens. Daly wrote to art experts and collectors talking up the painting's provenance and connection to Ambrose Small. "His widow told me that they could have bought a theatre with the money her husband paid for it," he wrote to a potential Chicago buyer.[4] He had employed an art dealer to try to sell some of the collection—and while a few paintings had earned modest amounts, the Rubens was proving a tough piece to move, as there were doubts about the painting's authenticity.[5] "I should say that your picture has no actual comparison with Rubens' own hand," the director of the National Gallery of Canada told Daly matter-of-factly in 1939.[6] Daly didn't let such details get him down. He even wrote an article about the "rather romantic history" of the "Rubens" painting and submitted it to Time magazine in 1942, hoping to stir a flurry of interest. The editor gently rejected the submission.[7] The headlines about the Catholic Church earning a big payday from Theresa Small's death had been exaggerated. "Poor Mrs. Small did not know into what trouble she was leading us through," Daly wrote in the early 1950s.[8]

The Sisters of Service were supposed to receive $100,000 when the Small sisters died and their annuities reverted back to the estate; and when the final Small sister, Florence, died in 1953, Daly prayed that God would see fit to give his order "something" for their trouble. But the entire estate was worth $141,000 at that point, with outstanding claims and debts of around $174,000. The kitty was split, cents to the dollar, between Percy, Madeleine, a few of Theresa's family members, and the trust company. The lawyer for the Sisters of Service figured his client was owed $390,000—"not a cent of which they touch."⁹ The court took the view that because the religious organization did not answer a summons in 1939, they were "precluded" from trying to assert their rights now.¹⁰ They could have fought for a piece by trying to set aside the ruling, but the wrangling had gone on long enough. Father Daly was now a white-haired man in his eighties. "We can now write 'finis' to a case which has kept us guessing for many years," he wrote.¹¹

The biggest payouts went to Ambrose's siblings Percy and Madeleine.¹² As part of the 1924 settlement that gave Theresa control of Ambrose Small's estate, they were both supposed to receive $100,000 trust funds similar to those created for Florence and Gertrude, but Theresa had never formalized the arrangement for her niece and nephew. She had been generous to them in life, and had set aside $5,000 yearly payments in her will, but she had left them in legal limbo when it came to the trust fund. Lawyers had been fighting on their behalf for years, so when the last of the money was distributed, Percy, Madeleine, and a trust company were the biggest creditors.¹³

Madeleine Small was the youngest child of Dan Small and Josephine Kormann. She was twenty-five years old when Ambrose disappeared, and she stayed by Theresa's side as a companion in those years of swirling suspicions, before embarking on a life far away from the scandal in Paris, Scarsdale, San Francisco, and Cape Cod. She married, divorced, and had two children, but she never returned to her maiden name. "Madeleine McMaster" was a good shield from the infamy, and, "If anyone asks, tell them your mother's maiden name is Holmes," she used to tell her children.*

The press had hounded her family, and the notoriety of being a Small upset her already anxious disposition. Part of Madeleine was worried that someone might come after her family, or her children. If some nefarious gang had kidnapped her brother, she didn't want to take any chances.[14] She wanted to live as quietly as possible, with no ties to the past.

She lived in New York, wore sensible shoes, and practised her driving in a parking lot to keep up her skills. Like her Aunt Theresa, she believed in education, and both of her children became university professors. Madeleine never became a U.S. citizen, so she didn't have Social Security, but she had "her money from Canada," which she invested in stocks.[15] She had a good, long life, and the money paid for her nursing home in Cape Cod. When she died on her 104th birthday, the accounts were nearly empty, and her obituary was headlined: "East Sandwich resident homemaker loved animals." It continued, "Born and educated in Canada, she graduated from Toronto University. During her junior year in college, she studied in Paris." Madeleine McMaster, née Holmes, the obit noted, was an avid reader who spoke several languages, loved animals, and pursued world travel. There was no reference to her parents, or her siblings, Ambrose, Gertrude, Florence, and Percy.[16]

---

*   After Theresa Small died, Madeleine was referred to as "Madeleine Ryan" in the legal documents. Her grandson said that was her mother-in-law's maiden name, and Madeleine used it sometimes.

A daughter and grandson were mentioned in the obituary. I called and left two voicemails about a mystery from another century. An hour later, Chuck Hutchings phoned me back. Had his grandmother Madeleine been alive when I called, he said, "she would have hidden in the closet."

CAPE COD, 2017

Cape Cod, where the last dregs of the Small estate dwindled away, feels like a trip back in time. Children sit on the boardwalk to catch crabs in the salt marshes. In the evening, wet sandy towels are draped on the porches around town with exhausted satisfaction. Madeleine McMaster spent the twilight of her very long life here. Her daughter, Nancy Hutchings, had a shingled grey cottage in a small seaside town just past the Cape Cod canal. Madeleine spent her summers with Nancy and her grandson, Chuck, and in her later years, she moved to the seaside town full time. In her nineties, she would stare at the water and lament that she never learned how to swim.[17] She had sailed on the same deep blue water a lifetime ago, with Ambrose and Theresa, but she never talked about those days.

Her grandson Chuck Hutchings still lives in the same grey house. It is dark inside, with wood panelling and nautical knick-knacks. The bedrooms pop in Easter egg shades of purple, blue, and pink. A framed photo of a middle-aged Josephine Small—Madeleine's mother—sits on a table near the back door. She looks grand and elegant in the same way her sister Theresa did—radiating a serene sort of confidence. Madeleine's daughter, Nancy, has genes from both the Kormanns and the Smalls—but she is taller like her dad's side of the family. Nancy is in her late eighties, a retired professor of social work, the product of a long line of Kormann women who believed in education. She earned her Ph.D. in her early sixties. She wears a soft sweater, pearl earrings, and her fingernails are painted dusty rose. She calls her son Charles, but most people call him Chuck.

Josephine Small was Theresa's oldest sister. She married the widower Daniel Small when his first wife died, becoming Ambrose Small's stepmother, even though she was only three years older than him.

Chuck, who is exactly forty years younger than his mother, is more casual in a T-shirt and jeans. He didn't know about Ambrose Small until his grandmother Madeleine died. One day, he asked his mother about the family history, and she told him that his grandmother's *real* last name was Small. Chuck was told there had been a "family member who had been rich and had been kidnapped and never found," and because of that his grandmother changed her name and moved to New York.[18]

Chuck cooks burgers for lunch and sets a bag of salt-and-vinegar chips on the table. Nancy raises her eyebrows and laughs. "No bowl?" We set the family photo album aside for

Nancy Hutchings, the daughter of Madeleine (Small) McMaster, with her son Chuck Hutchings in the Cape Cod home where Madeleine spent her later years. The Hutchings are the closest living descendants to Ambrose Small. Nancy was Ambrose Small's niece. (He disappeared before she was born.)

lunch. It's the first time I've seen a photo of Madeleine Small, and I am struck by how similar she looks to her sisters Florence and Gertrude.

We talk about Theresa's possible involvement in Ambrose's disappearance as we eat the chips, and discuss the theories— that maybe it was an argument over money gone wrong.

"That could be another reason why she ran away," Chuck says of Madeleine.

"Hmmm," Nancy says, sitting in a chair with a blanket around her legs. "Because she didn't like Theresa? No."

"Give me one second to form my hypothesis," Chuck says, moving to the couch, which is a better spot to think. He stares

Madeleine Small, Ambrose Small's half-sister, and Theresa Small's niece, was born in 1894 and spent her adult life distancing herself from the scandal. She died on her 104th birthday in Cape Cod.

at the ceiling, deep in thought. What if, on one of their trips together, Theresa told Madeleine what happened—"what she felt she needed to know," he says. What if that is why Madeleine moves to New York, and changes her name? What if that's why Madeleine never wanted to talk about it?

Nancy shakes her head. Her bird clock on the wall starts to chirp, and she laughs at the tinny warble.

Before I head to the airport, I drive along the curving highway bordered by old willows and stop by St. Peter's Cemetery. Madeleine Small is in the last row, her stone laid in the ground, her name facing the blue sky: Madeleine McMaster, 1894–1998.

Nobody ever found her. If she knew what happened to Ambrose, she never told anyone.

"I'm sorry to bother you," I whisper.

And then I leave her alone.

TWENTY-FIVE

DINNER WITH THE DOUGHTYS

W hen Jack Doughty was released from prison, he politely told the reporters to scram. A year into his freedom, he and his nephew George Lovatt started an automotive business on Danforth Avenue, selling motor oil and other accessories for the car craze. His sister Eliza loaned them $1,000 to start Universal Battery Service, with the under-standing that they'd pay her back.[1] He worked there, took care of the few properties he still owned down on River Street, and puttered away in the garden on Kingswood Road. He lived the rest of his days with his sister Eliza at the end of the streetcar line.[2] (Her husband had died in 1933—surrounded by his wife's family until the end of his life.) Jack grew old in relative peace.[3] His oldest son, John, became a justice of the peace. George Doughty—the twin who lived—had two sons of his own.

When I first called Bruce Doughty, son of George, grandson of Jack, his daughter answered the phone. I had the right family, Nancy Doughty cheerfully told me. She knew all about the story of her great grandfather, and in fact, she had nearly solved the mystery a few years ago. Back in 2014, when she was finishing her master's degree, an old wooden box arrived at the family home on her birthday. Inside, there was a skeleton key, bundles of handwritten notes, and a letter from an Oregon lawyer. The box had been sitting out west for several generations, and the descendants of the lawyer had been instructed to pass the box on to Jack Doughty's descendants, she told me. Nancy read the letters and deciphered a few messages in code. She was so swept up in the excitement that she figured she had possibly determined the location of Ambrose Small, and might need to call the police. But before she could make the call, her parents intervened. The family had recently learned of their connection to the Ambrose Small mystery, and the box of letters was an elaborate joke played by her brother.

When I visited the Doughtys east of Toronto, Bruce and his wife, Carol, prepared a spread of crackers, grapes, cheese, and prosciutto, and brought out their impeccably organized documents relating to Jack Doughty, a man they never knew until recently. When he was released from Kingston, Jack had said that past was a closed book, but his descendants have a different take. Nancy brought out the old wooden box, shaking her head over her brother's trick. Bruce brought out a delicate gold tie pin made of a wishbone and a pearl: it had been Jack's.

Bruce is taller and leaner than his grandfather, but there was something in his eyes that reminded me of the old photos I'd seen of Doughty. Standing in the dining room as I scanned documents with my phone, he told me he didn't think there was any connection between the Victory Bonds and Ambrose

Small's disappearance. "I think you've got two stories running in parallel," he said.

Bruce's father never talked about any of it: how Jack took off to Oregon and was hauled back to Toronto by police and then imprisoned after a sensational trial. "My father probably thought there no value in me knowing that my grandfather spent time in jail," Bruce says.[4] His father, George Doughty, died in 2003. A year later, Bruce got a call from Margaret Santon, a second cousin he had lost touch with. She invited Bruce and his family to her home in a small town a two-hour drive east of Toronto. It wasn't long into the visit when Margaret, the granddaughter of Eliza Lovatt, asked them a question: What did they think about the story of Jack Doughty?

They had no idea what she was talking about.

Toronto takes up a lot of room, but once the traffic on Highway 401 thins out, there are places where life is quieter—where parents drive their children to hockey games, worried about the black ice and the snow squalls, but they drive anyway, past the variety store with the Subway restaurant inside, past the billboard in the farmer's field that is up all year, advertising the fair that comes to town for one weekend.

Margaret Santon—the keeper of the Doughty family story—lives in one of these towns, tucked into the hilly landscape of Northumberland County, east of Toronto. Her grandmother, Eliza, was Jack Doughty's most loyal supporter. The siblings lived together until Jack suffered a stroke in August 1949.

"With him in death went whatever he may have known concerning a baffling case that has earned a legendary place in police records," the *Star* wrote at the time.[5]

Margaret and her husband welcome me inside their home, which is filled with light, books, and an excitable pug boxer named Ruby. It is a windy but sunny autumn day, and there is chili simmering on the stove and a wood fire burning. Margaret tells me that when she was a little girl, she spent many of her Saturdays at her grandmother's house. It was a four-year-old's dream—a lakeside paradise of freshly baked cookies, a piano, and a sweet older man named Uncle Jack. Once a month, if Margaret was lucky, she and Uncle Jack rode the streetcar downtown to collect the River Street rents.[6] The tenants who rolled their eyes when they saw Jack coming had no idea what a softie he was. He always bought her something special at Eaton's Toyland—like a piece of furniture for her dollhouse. She remembers those Saturdays vividly. How she held his hand, how it always felt safe and warm. Jack died when he was seventy-one and Margaret was four. Her family took Eliza to Europe that summer to distract her from her sadness and the newspaper stories.

After Jack was gone, Eliza moved in with Margaret's family at their home on the Scarborough Bluffs. Margaret sometimes slept in the same bed as her grandmother. As she fell asleep, Eliza whispered stories about her childhood in Toronto. She talked about a horse burned alive in a fire, a child she played with on the rooftops of River Street, and how her father once won a bear the family then kept in a cage in the backyard. She never told the story of Ambrose Small. "Not a whisper," Margaret says. The little girl in the bed would have to wait until she was fully grown to learn about that.

As we sit in front of the woodstove, Margaret, now in her seventies, white hair styled in a short cut, talks about the old resentments: how Eliza hated Ambrose, how Eliza tried to bring the Victory Bonds back to Theresa Small, how some of the family believed that Theresa had fixed things against Jack. I tell her some of what I've found in the archives and ask her if it's

Margaret Santon with her grandmother Eliza Lovatt.

possible her great-uncle Jack might have been involved in the disappearance. As her dog snores in the sun she tells a story that her mother once told her. Before Jack's first wife, Berthe, died in 1911, a Catholic priest came over and told Jack that his wife would go straight to hell for marrying a Protestant. Jack threw that priest down the stairs. (At least, that's what her mother had said.) That was the only violent act she had heard of.

The other story—the one where Ambrose escapes to a quiet life, always seemed more likely to Margaret, given Ambrose's wealth and power. She has always been taken with the fate Michael Ondaatje imagined for Ambrose Small in his novel *In the Skin of a Lion*. Ondaatje's novel is set in the Toronto of the 1920s. People from all over the world arrive in the city for a new start, and many of them have the most dangerous jobs building the infrastructure that will transform the old Victorian town into a metropolis. Ambrose Small is one of the characters woven into the story: "He was a hawk who hovered over the whole province, swooping down for the kill, buying up every field of wealth, and eating the profit in mid-air," Ondaatje writes.[7] After he vanishes, a character named Patrick moves to the city and becomes a searcher, hoping to claim the reward. Patrick tries to gain the confidence of the people closest to the theatre magnate, like his mistress, here named Clara Dickens. Clara insists she doesn't know anything, but Patrick follows Clara to eastern Ontario, where he finds the couple hiding in the small town of Marmora. He confronts Ambrose and it turns violent.[8] By the end of the book, Ambrose, still hidden in Marmora, spills his secrets to Clara—all of the lives he kept separate, "bitten flesh and manicures and greyhounds and sex and safe combinations and knowledge of suicides."⁹ Then he dies.

Before I leave Margaret's home, I ask how far it is to Marmora.

"That's just a story," her husband says, sitting at the computer desk, a map of Ontario on the screen.

"No, it's not," she says, because maybe Ambrose Small disappeared into a quieter life somewhere, and maybe her uncle was the scapegoat because the police had no other leads. As I put on my shoes, she mentions that a magician saw Ambrose Small in Mexico in 1920.

Harry Blackstone, a vaudevillian of the floating light bulb and dancing handkerchief variety, swore that he saw Ambrose at a casino in Juárez. He waved at the millionaire across the roulette table. "When the play was finished, I went around to talk to Small, but when I moved toward him he was gone in a twinkling," Blackstone recalled a few years later.¹⁰ He didn't mention it to anyone, because he figured Ambrose didn't want to be found. By the time Blackstone brought it up in 1923, it was either a swift bit of public relations for his act, or a legitimate loose thread that nobody pulled.

In the summer of 2018, I met up with some of the Doughty descendants for a barbeque at Bruce and Carol's home. It was a rainy summer day and Bruce was wearing his grilling apron. He told us all to help ourselves to the fizzy tangerine soda and wine while he grilled the burgers and made jokes about all the smoke. We sat in the dining room talking about summer plans and the century-old mystery. We talked about Eliza's loyalty and wondered what the siblings discussed behind closed doors. "I just want to know: what was happening in the world that this story took on a life of its own?" Bruce said.

In the 1920s, the newspapers were filled with serious stories about post-war reconstruction and Canada's quest for independence from Britain, but the public thirsted for scandal. "It was the age of F. Scott Fitzgerald hedonism, of the outlandish feats of glamourized celebrities, of the sports heroics of idolized athletes, of the deeds and misdeeds of the famous, the notorious and the obscure," one historian observed, noting that it was a carefree decade in hindsight, sandwiched between the Great War and the Great Depression.[11] There was the Black Sox baseball fix; there was Al Capone's violent campaign to control the illegal booze market in Chicago; and there was Ambrose Small, who was not so much a victim as a villain, the perfect low-stakes foil for the times. The story grew wilder every year with sightings, legal fights, and accusations. It never ended.

Night was falling at the Doughty-family gathering, and everybody was contemplating the journey home. Before we dispersed, everyone gave their best guess about the fate of Ambrose Small.

He took the opportunity to disappear.

Took some money and got out of town.

He was tired of his life and jumped on a boat.

He went to Europe. Hid out in Germany.

Died in Marmora.

I don't know.

It was an escape plan that went wrong.

I was the last to speak.

I did not think Ambrose escaped to a quieter life, jumped on a boat, or hid out in Europe. He was a man who relished a scheme. He liked winning, and I did not think he would leave the $1 million cheque in his account. Only death could separate him from such a sum. The conversation veered in another direction, and Carol Doughty looked at the clock. She reminded me that we had to leave soon if I wanted to make my train downtown. There was no time for anything else. "You can't go," Bruce deadpanned. "What about the dishes?"

TWENTY-SIX

SPOT THE RED HERRINGS

---

once dreamed that I was inside the Glen Road mansion, sitting in a room with wooden wainscoting and pink accents with Ambrose and Theresa. Nobody talked to me, because even in my dreams, they refuse to help. In my mind, Ambrose Small exists in alternative realities: He is murdered, he has escaped, he is found in an asylum, humming the best songs from the 1909 theatrical season. It is quicksand, and I am sinking. I keep a file on my computer, just to make some space in my brain:

Ambrose Small was buried in the cellar of his mansion.

Ambrose Small escaped to be with his lover.

Ambrose Small was buried in the Rosedale dump.

Ambrose Small was drugged, driven to Montreal, and locked in a basement.

Ambrose Small was tied to a cement block in the bottom of Lake Ontario.

Ambrose Small was wandering the countryside near Kingston.

Ambrose Small was floating in Lake St. Clair.

Ambrose Small was decapitated and tossed in a shallow grave.

Ambrose Small lived on a mink farm.

Ambrose Small was buried in High Park.

Ambrose Small was kidnapped by a New York gang who wanted a big payday.

Ambrose Small was burned in the furnace at the Grand Opera House in Toronto.

Ambrose Small moved to Germany, where he was sheltered by his wife's relations.

Ambrose Small was burned in the furnace at the Grand Opera House in London.

Ambrose Small lived in Manitoba under the alias of Smitty. He looked different because his nose had frozen during a bad winter.

Ambrose Small was burned in a pig furnace.

Ambrose Small lived in seclusion in Toronto.

Ambrose Small was buried under a gas station in St. Thomas.

Ambrose Small was murdered by a hitman.

Ambrose Small received a chiropractic treatment in Winnipeg before he escaped to Austria.

Ambrose Small was buried under the willow trees by the Thames River in London.

Ambrose Small liked to skulk around a bank in Perth, Ontario.

Ambrose Small lived in Halifax, in the form of a mysterious man with large teeth, small wrists and "several tiny sphere-shaped sacks" suspended from thin strands of skin in his armpits.

Ambrose Small was buried in a stretch of rural land near Danforth Avenue.

Ambrose Small lived in Whitby at the Royal Hotel.

Ambrose Small was killed after he spent some time in a house of ill repute in London, Ontario, and his body was carted in a wheelbarrow and dumped in a gravel pit.

Ambrose Small hid at St. Michael's College in Toronto, where he lived peacefully for several years.

Ambrose Small was drugged and taken to Montreal, where he was placed in the cellar like a bulky piece of luggage.

Ambrose Small was murdered and his body decomposed in the cellar of a house on Charles Street in Toronto.

Ambrose Small escaped to a quiet life with Jack Doughty's help.

Ambrose Small's ghost haunted the farm.

Ambrose Small was spotted in the backseat of a car driving up Yonge Street in early December 1919.

Ambrose Small was bedridden in Windsor.

Ambrose Small was gambling in Mexico in 1920.

Ambrose Small was killed in his office on December 2.

Ambrose Small haunts the Grand Theatre in London, where he likes to steal the scissors in the wardrobe department.

TWENTY-SEVEN

THE HAMMOND REPORT

TORONTO, 1936

By 1936, the Ambrose Small case was an embarrassment. The millionaire was still missing, the investigation had stalled, and the combined scandal of it all was a constant source of newspaper copy. When Patrick Sullivan and the Small sisters challenged Theresa's will with Theresa's alleged "confession," they filed several affidavits at Osgoode Hall in support of their claim. The challenge was dismissed by Justice Jeffrey that November, but the allegations filed in the spring of 1936 created such a stir that Attorney General Arthur Roebuck ordered an immediate investigation into the Small case.[1]

That May, the Ontario Provincial Police sent Inspector Edward Hammond to help the Toronto Police re-examine their files, pore over court transcripts, and interview anybody who was still alive. Hammond was a senior investigator with the OPP. He had dark hair and a dimpled chin and had been an inspector with the prestigious Criminal Investigation Bureau for most of his career. Although his name hadn't come up in the press, Hammond had been called in to help with the case in early 1920, according to journalist Fred McClement. In McClement's 1974 book *The Strange Case of Ambrose Small*, he detailed the strained relationship between the two detectives: Austin Mitchell was inclined toward psychics and astral advisors, while Hammond thought the Toronto Police needed to go harder at Theresa Small. His bosses reminded him that it was Toronto's file. Hammond faded away and the Ambrose Small case became synonymous with Austin Mitchell—for better or worse.[2]

At the request of the attorney general, Hammond took a deep dive. It was a sensitive file, and Hammond was a good choice in this respect. He didn't mind asking uncomfortable questions or criticizing colleagues, and he had done his fair share of both in his career.[3] Hammond teamed up with Toronto Police Detective-Sergeant James McIlrath to get a "true grasp" of what had happened to Ambrose Small. Many people were dead, and some of those who survived still repeated old rumours. The two police officers sifted through memories, official records, and what remained of Mitchell's notes, and then Hammond wrote a scathing twenty-page report. The answer to the mystery had not been "abroad in distant lands," he said. It had been here all along, and sincere people had tried to help. "The chief complaint seems to be, that it mattered not who volunteered information to Detective Mitchell, he invariably 'put them off' and told them to keep their nose out of things that did not concern them," Hammond wrote in the report marked "secret and confidential."[4]

Hammond felt that Ambrose "was the victim of a cunningly and well-conceived plan in which Mrs. Theresa Small his wife was the prime mover, and furthermore, I believe that she was actually present when her husband was murdered, for there is no question that she knew all along what had happened to him, also that John Doughty her husband's secretary was one of the murderers too."[5] The report was dropped on Mitchell's desk in the summer of 1936. He went through it line by line and produced twenty-four pages of rebuttals.

"Some competent person," Hammond wrote, should have confronted Theresa with this theory before she died.[6]

Nobody ever did.

"There surely was a reason," Hammond wrote.[7]

HAMMOND'S THEORY

THE ALLIANCE

By 1919, Ambrose and Theresa Small had a complicated relationship at best. Theresa knew all about Clara, and Ambrose accused his wife of having an affair of her own.[8] Theresa went out of her way to make it seem like their troubles were resolved in 1919, but Hammond didn't buy that. He believed that conciliatory note from Ambrose that her legal team filed in court back in the estate battle had been doctored from 1917 to read 1919, "the 7 being changed to a 9."[9]

Hammond had an undated letter from Clara Smith in 1918 that stated that Clara, Thomas Flynn, and Ambrose Small were conspiring to "get" Theresa "one way or another." The same trio had allegedly spied on Theresa in 1917—with Clara making an affidavit to the effect that she saw Theresa and Rev. Bruce Hunter "having sexual intercourse" before the 208th Battalion shipped out for the war, something they both denied.[10] Not long after, Ambrose wrote a pair of accusatory letters, filled with "lurid details" to Theresa and her alleged paramour outlining what he had supposedly seen. (Hunter told police he had received the letter, which contained a threat that Ambrose would "get even with him." Both Theresa and Hunter had denied the affair, and Theresa explained it as a rather theatrical salvo by her husband to keep his mistress in the city. There had never been any hard evidence of the alleged affair, but Hammond spoke to D'Arcy Hinds, the court registrar who had helped assemble the 208th Battalion. Hinds told Hammond that a very anxious Hunter came to him and "practically admitted his associations with Mrs. Small as the letter accused him of," Hammond writes.[11]) Ambrose hoped the accusatory letters would be his ticket out of his marriage and financial obligations, Hammond wrote. The theatre magnate believed "that Mrs. Small would feel so ashamed and fear publicity, that she would be willing to stay away from Toronto and possibly commit suicide rather than face the shame and disgrace of exposure,"[12] Hammond noted.

If that was his plan, it didn't work. Theresa Small returned to Toronto "quite prepared to meet Small on even grounds,"

Hammond wrote. The OPP investigator believed that Theresa began to do a little plotting on her own, which may have "culminated with the final disappearance of Small out of her life."[13] As the sale for the theatres loomed, she likely "sought the aid of Doughty, whom she knew had no use for Small."[14] There might have been another reason for the alliance: Hammond had found an old statement from theatre manager James Cowan that claimed that Jack and Theresa had a sexual relationship.[15]

Jack Doughty had been a loyal employee, but he soured as Ambrose's wealth grew, Hammond said. In the year before Ambrose became a millionaire, Doughty had been peddling a plan to "bring Small to his knees."[16] When the sale of the theatre chain finally wrapped up in late 1919, there was no acknowledgement of Jack's toil and sacrifice as he helped to build Small's empire.[17] While the biggest deal of Small's life was underway, he noted, Doughty made some "very queer moves" to line his pockets.[18] Doughty knew all the accounts and the details of the deal, and he had turned over Ambrose's mail to Theresa the weekend before the sale closed—when Ambrose was in Montreal. There was a love letter from Clara in there too. "Surely this was an act of treachery on his part against his employer, and on the other hand it clearly shows that Mrs. Small was in the 'know' of what was being done."[19]

Hammond believed that Theresa expected to find the $1 million cheque in the bank account she shared with Ambrose, but that her husband had tricked her by depositing it in his own account, out of her reach.[20] The long-simmering tension reached a breaking point with these final betrayals. According to the bank records, Doughty was in Ambrose's vault for three minutes on December 2: "Just long enough to clean out the box of its contents."[21] Later that evening, Jimmy Cowan heard strange noises on the back stairway of the Grand Opera House. Cowan had initially believed Doughty was moving some of his belongings out of the office, but Hammond figured there had been a violent altercation in the office, which explains why Theresa was so "distracted" that night, running around town in a panic.[22] If Theresa didn't take part in the "doing away" of Ambrose, "she was indeed an accessory after the fact," Hammond argued. "For at no time did she divulge her knowledge of Small's murder to the Police. She instead shielded Doughty all along."[23]

Doughty was supposed to start his new job with Trans-Canada Theatres Ltd. in late November. His bosses had been sending telegrams wondering where he was, and he cabled back that he was tying up loose ends. Mitchell "took it for granted," Hammond noted, that Doughty left for Montreal the night of December 2, 1919.[24] Once in Montreal, "We find Doughty so worried he could not sleep or work . . . that he quits his job as suddenly as he takes it," Hammond observed.[25] A Peterborough theatre manager ran into the usually friendly Doughty at the Montreal train station in mid-December. He was huddled in a corner, a look of worry on his face. It was late, and the sight was strange enough for the theatre manager to recall it.

"I have troubles and I have a good notion to take the train for Toronto," Doughty allegedly said.

What kind of troubles?

"I have troubles that no person knows about," he supposedly replied.[26]

When Doughty returned to Toronto to fetch some paper-work for Trans-Canada at the end of December, he telegrammed his bosses to say he was too sick to return to Montreal on the train. But on December 29, he met Theresa Small in Rosedale. Theresa had long described the meeting as an interview between a grieving wife and a trusted employee, but Hammond believed the pair were plotting.[27] Doughty left Toronto that same day, leaving the Victory Bonds with his family. His sisters said they tried to take the bonds back to Theresa months later, but she refused them. Theresa knew the police were searching for the bonds, so why didn't she pass along this information to Mitchell?[28] "Mrs. Small took all the precautions in the world to keep the police off Doughty's track," Hammond noted. "During all the long years that elapsed between that time and her own death, not once did she tell the Police, the Truth of what she actually knew about her husband's murder by John Doughty. She was paying for the investigation, and it was to her benefit, and the benefit of John Doughty."[29]

———

Austin Mitchell agreed with Hammond's theory about Doughty as the faithful worker turned sour.[30] His conduct was indeed "suspicious from beginning to the end," and Mitchell said he was "firmly convinced" that Doughty was the principal "in the kidnapping or murder of A.J. Small."[31] He also agreed that, with the sale of the theatre chain finalized, it was the logical time for the "commission of murder."[32] Doughty had experience with bonds and knew they could be traced back to him if he cashed them. "In all probability he intended to negotiate these bonds in small quantities as the opportunity presented itself," Mitchell guessed.[33]

But Mitchell was stunned with Hammond's take on Theresa. It was true that Ambrose and Theresa's marriage was "somewhat complicated," but had they really been plotting against each other? That was conjecture, he argued.[34] He had heard his fair share of stories about the Smalls' intimate lives, but he had never heard about a fling between Theresa and Jack Doughty.[35] "It does not seem logical and is contrary to human nature that she should be intimate with Doughty and still pay a $15,000 reward for his arrest," he wrote.[36] Mitchell didn't have much to say about Doughty turning Ambrose's mail over to Theresa before the deal closed. He pointed out that Ambrose valued his wife's advice, so this act wasn't *that* unreasonable.[37] It was true that Theresa had never told Mitchell she'd met with Doughty at the end of December 1919. But she didn't know that police were looking to talk to Doughty at that point, so you could hardly blame her.[38]

Mitchell pointed out that none of the lawyers who had investigated the case for the Crown had ever suggested that Theresa was an "accessory after the fact."[39] Recalling the final court battle over Ambrose's will in 1924, Mitchell reminded Hammond that Justice Logie had said that Theresa was leaving the court without a "stain upon her character." He took those words as gospel truth.

As for Theresa's frantic actions on the night of December 2, 1919, "Is it not just as logical to suppose that she did not know what had happened to A.J. Small?"[40] Mitchell continued, "Are the actions of Theresa that night enough to say she was the murderess along with Doughty? Was there evidence of such a bond between them that would justify her in placing her life in the hands of Doughty?" He answered his own question, "From my investigation I have never been able to find this evidence."[41] But he noted, "Not only did Mrs. Small believe that Doughty killed her husband or knew all about who did, it is the consensus of opinion of the officers connected with the case that Doughty knew all about the disappearance of Small."[42]

THE SHAKY TIMELINE

Theresa Small had told police that she was expecting Ambrose for dinner on December 2, 1919, at 6:30 p.m. When he didn't show up, she spent the next few hours searching for her husband. Ambrose Small was a known carouser, so what was the "acute abnormality" of it all?[43] Hammond pointed out that Theresa's timeline had shifted over the years. Her initial account to Mitchell was sparse and involved only a few stops at her sisters' homes. She told Mitchell that she had made a phone call to the Grand Opera House to look for Ambrose, but the court heard a different story in 1924 when Theresa said she visited the theatre in person, then walked to the orphans home, and then over to Pembroke Street searching for Thomas Flynn. She never told police about any of those stops. Flynn's neighbours, the Kellys, said that Theresa came by Pembroke Street at 8 p.m. "in a most excited state," looking for Flynn and asking to use their phone.[44] "Mrs. Small told Mrs. Kelly that her husband had been taken away in a car, and she was afraid he had met with an accident," Hammond noted. "Not a word of this was ever told to Police. Why?" he asked. "If she had any such fears then why did she not tell the Police?"

Hammond wrote that Dan Small—the wife of Josephine Kormann and the father of Ambrose—said that Theresa arrived at his home at 9:30 p.m., looking terrible. She was still there at 10:45 p.m. when the phone rang, and she ran to it, "listened for a minute, and then without saying goodbye rushed out of the door and apparently went to her home," Hammond wrote.[45] Mitchell had not pushed Theresa Small on her inconsistencies and had done "nothing to show her lying statements up," Hammond pointed out.[46] Theresa Small's movements on that night were of "the utmost importance," he said, and Mitchell had let them slip away.[47] "His notebooks are gone too," Hammond wrote. "Here again, however, it is hard to believe that this woman could get away with all this, without giving an account to the Police and the Courts."[48]

———

THERESA SMALL'S WHEREABOUTS:

EVENING OF DECEMBER 2, 1919

	As told to Austin Mitchell December 17, 1919	As told in court in 1924
5:00 p.m.		51 Glen Road
6:00 p.m.	51 Glen Road	streetcar to 10 Bloor Street East
	10 Bloor Street East	
	51 Glen Road	walks to 51 Glen Road
7:00 p.m.		51 Glen Road / calls Grand Opera
8:00 p.m.		
		Calls Jack Doughty,* calls Grand Opera box office
9:00 p.m.	10 Bloor Street East	streetcar to theatre
		walks to Orphans' Home
	97 Kendal Avenue	walks to 101 Pembroke Street
	calls to maid and Grand Opera House	walks to 10 Bloor Street East
10:00 p.m.		streetcar to 97 Kendal Avenue
		streetcar to 51 Glen Road
11:00 p.m.		

* In 1924 trial, Theresa says she called Jack Doughty at 8:30 p.m., but she couldn't be sure of the exact time. She did not provide timestamps for her subsequent actions until she arrived home at 11 p.m, so those actions are merely in the same sequence she described. Timestamps are unknown.

Mitchell was defensive. He had confirmed *parts* of the timeline. Staff at the orphans home had said that Theresa had been there on the afternoon of December 2, and Theresa's sisters had backed up her version of events.[49] It was true that Theresa Small had omitted from her account the visit to Thomas Flynn's home at 8 p.m. But when Mitchell asked her about it later, she said she had forgotten.[50] As far as that bit about the Kellys and the car, Theresa had never said anything like that to him.[51] Mitchell acknowledged that there were different time-lines, but he pointed out that "the police did not know that the statements were false."[52]

Mitchell brought Theresa to speak with the chief constable, Lieutenant-Colonel Henry Grasett, in February 1920, but he didn't stay for the chat. He was never told to bring Theresa in for further questioning. "Had I received these instructions and not complied with same," he wrote, "the matter would certainly have been brought to my attention by my superiors."[53] He continued, "Unfortunately, my note books are gone, for the reason that in moving to Police Headquarters from the City Hall to 149 College St., some 3 years ago, a large quantity of old documents and records were shipped to No. 5 Division and we have made a search and so far have not been able to locate my missing books."[54]

THE KEYS

For years, Patrick Sullivan had published lists of Ambrose Small's belongings in the *Thunderer*. Ambrose had vanished, but many of his personal items—including a bank book that showed the $1 million deposit of December 2, a set of keys, his watch and jewellery—had turned up in Rosedale.[55] That was curious. "There has been a lot of confusion as to how Mrs. Small came into possession of many of the personal articles," Hammond wrote.[56] At various court appearances, her answers varied, just like her timeline had. Once, she said she found the keys on the afternoon of December 2; another time, she said she found them on the night of December 2. She also said that she found them in "Mr. Small's bedroom" on December 3.[57]

Given the acrimony between the Smalls, surely Ambrose would not leave his keys at home, or hand them over to his wife, Hammond thought.[58] He believed instead that Theresa came to possess her husband's pocket flotsam after something went down at the Grand Opera House. "It is proven beyond doubt," he wrote, that Theresa was at the theatre "when Small was taken away in an automobile."[59] "She knew then that Doughty, herself and Small had a quarrel over money matters, and she knew quite well that Doughty had struck Small and killed him there and then," he wrote.[60] According to Hammond, Theresa had told this story to Star reporter Roy Greenaway in 1930, and to Dr. Joachim Guinane, a Toronto surgeon who, before he died, told the story to J.A.C. Cameron, the former master-in-chambers at Osgoode Hall.[61, 62]

Cameron, an Orangeman who lived in Rosedale, had made some conspicuously pro-Theresa rulings on the Ambrose Small estate, approving an allowance and lump sum payment in the neighbourhood of $800,000. In 1922, Theresa produced an agreement she claimed Ambrose had written that entitled her to half the million-dollar cheque, which Cameron accepted. Hammond believed that note was a forgery, likely done by Theresa's friend Felix Devine, a government lawyer who worked at the provincial department of succession duties and was a "very clever penman" who "could copy any writing."[63] Cameron's ruling was later reversed because it was improper given the unsettled nature of the case. Hammond had a look through the receipts for the trust company that handled the Ambrose Small estate during the absentee period and saw an "account fee" of $15,000 for Cameron. Another court filing showed that Cameron had been paid $4,500. What was this money for? Patrick Sullivan had once accused Cameron of accepting payments above his salary in his On Guard tabloid. Some judicial officers who had special appointment as "official referees" at Osgoode Hall had come under fire for this during the war, and Cameron had been one of them, Sullivan said.[64] The government reminded these men that they were salaried government employees and were not supposed to accept extra cash. (Cameron's legal career ended when he was disbarred in 1934 for misappropriating client funds.)

Hammond didn't know if the payments had any significance, but thought it "as well to point this out, especially so, as many people think that anyone who had any dealings with the case were 'fixed' by Mrs. Small," he wrote.[65] On the topic of payoffs, there was some confusion about the amount of Victory Bonds Doughty had taken. The widely accepted figure had been $105,000, but one of Mitchell's early investigation notes mentioned that $150,000 of Victory Bonds were missing.[66] Hammond had also seen the $150,000 figure in an affidavit that Patrick Sullivan filed. In the affidavit, Sullivan alleged that Clara Brett Martin (one of Doughty's old lawyers who was now dead) had told him that Theresa Small instructed Doughty to take the $150,000 in Victory Bonds "and leave Canada and change his name before the Police opened Mr. Small's Bank safe, and the whole affair would soon be forgotten." If the total of the missing bonds was actually $150,000, where was the extra $45,000?[67]

———

Theresa never made any explanations to Mitchell about the keys, but he figured her different answers were honest mistakes owing to "the lapse of time."[68] "If the keys and other articles referred to did come into the possession of Mrs. Small on the date of his disappearance, we have nothing to prove this," he wrote.[69] He didn't think Theresa was at the Grand Opera House on the night of December 2, because according to his timeline Theresa Small was in her own home by 9:30 p.m.[70] The alleged quarrel between Doughty, Ambrose, and Theresa that was making the rounds in certain circles "was never reported to the City Police by Mrs. Small or anyone of the three persons mentioned," he said.[71]

Mitchell never found "any evidence" that people were "fixed" by Theresa Small.[72] He certainly was not. There was confusion about the Victory Bonds in the early days, but the Dominion

Bank of Canada told police "definitively" that $105,000 worth of bonds were missing. They were all recovered.[73]

THOMAS FLYNN

Thomas Flynn was a confusing character to police. He was an associate of Ambrose, but his first priority had always been himself. After Ambrose vanished, Flynn tried to sue the estate for a portion of the $1 million cheque, claiming he had been consulting on the deal since 1917.[74] (It was an absurd claim, and Small's lawyer wrote to Theresa to let her know that. The case was quickly thrown out.[75])

Flynn was a colourful, "horsey" fellow about ten years older than Ambrose. According to Clara Smith's 1922 affidavit, he had been an ally to Ambrose during the marital scandals of 1917, promising, along with Clara, to be a witness to Theresa's alleged affair. When Flynn was confronted about that in court, he painted himself as a double agent. "Anything I did in the line of plotting," he said, "was to protect Mrs. Small." He further yelled, "I protected her life. Do you call that protection?"[76]

Hammond believed that Flynn was Small's "pimp" and knew something bad had happened to his friend. "It does seem strange that Flynn should have remained so quiet," he wrote, "unless of course, he was afraid of his own contemptible game becoming known also. There is little else to be said for him, with the exception perhaps that he was also 'fixed' to say nothing by Mrs. Small."[77]

———

Mitchell didn't have a lot to add about Thomas Flynn. He agreed he was a shady sort, but noted "there is no evidence to show that Flynn was fixed by Mrs. Small." Flynn had been antagonistic to Theresa Small, he said, at "all times."[78]

THE CORPSE

If he was killed, as Hammond believed, what became of the mortal remains of Ambrose Small? Hammond figured that his corpse was taken away from the theatre. Dismemberment in the office would have been too messy; the smell of human flesh in the furnace would have permeated the entire building.[79] Hammond recalled the story of Alfred Elson, the school care-taker who saw a group of men drive to the Rosedale dump on the night of December 2. As Elson was flooding the lawn for an ice rink, he saw four men in the valley below drag a large pack-age from their car. Elson mentioned this to Mitchell, who made a "very belated" search at the dump but didn't dig in the right place. "I told Det. Mitchell that I was far from satisfied with the search and I also felt that the public would not be satisfied," Elson recalled in 1936, "and Mitchell just laughed at me and took no notice of me."[80]

———

Mitchell believed that Jack Doughty was responsible for "whatever happened to Small" and that his brother William "assisted
him."[81] He acknowledged there were many theories about
Ambrose's body. It might have been dumped in the lake, buried
in the "rear of Doughty's house," the Rosedale Ravine, the cellar
of the Rosedale house, possibly the backyard, or it might have
been burned in the furnace of the theatre.[82]

THE DETECTIVE

As he interviewed the people connected to the case who
were still alive, Hammond heard troubling things about Austin
Mitchell. Percy Small said that Mitchell told him that Ambrose
was murdered at the theatre.[83] A Toronto psychic reported that
Mitchell knew where Ambrose was buried and that he had said
"that he would protect Mrs. Small, and the public be damned."[84]
Then there was a man who overheard a conversation about
Ambrose and reported it to Mitchell, who snapped at him "to
mind his own damn business."[85]

There was barber Burton Keyser, who said that Mitchell
had been "sick and tired" of the case in the early 1920s and
had told him that if he came up with a human bone he would
"do the rest" and make sure Keyser got the reward money.
Keyser had heard a few theories about Small's murder, and
when he told Mitchell about them, he replied, "Burt, forget all
about it, have nothing more to do with it, it all happened in
the Grand Opera House."[86] And there was the time, in court,

when Mitchell swore on oath that he knew Ambrose Small was dead and buried in a seventy-acre plot, but wouldn't elaborate on the location.[87]

If Mitchell was going around town telling people that he knew what happened, why did he waste everyone's time on excavations in High Park, in the ravine, at the dump? "It looks like a case of 'any red herring will do' to spoil the scent and fool the public," Hammond said.[88]

Going through the legal bills, Hammond saw that one of Theresa's lawyers had billed her for a "consultation" where she was asked every "conceivable question" about the two-week lag time between her husband's disappearance and police involvement in the case. According to the paperwork, the lawyers went over her answers in the presence of Det. Austin Mitchell, and, according to the bill, "made such corrections in your answers as are in your interest." There were other meetings with trust company officials where Mitchell was present, Hammond said.[89] When Hammond looked through the paperwork, he saw that Theresa had paid Toronto Police around $35,000 for the investigation—"the greatest bluff that was ever put over," he wrote. "And yet when the sisters of Ambrose J. Small ask any questions regarding their brother, they are immediately shut out as it were, and no satisfaction has ever been accorded to them."[90]

———

Mitchell took issue with Hammond's "caustic" tone and responded with a series of denials about his actions (or lack thereof): "At no time did I ever tell Percy Small that I knew A.J. Small was murdered in the Grand Opera House"[91] and "I most emphatically deny ever making the statements attributed to me by [Toronto psychic] Madame Rayme."[92] He denied the account of the barber, and said he was not in the habit of telling people to mind their own business. That whole "70 acre" plot in the east end had come from a psychic, and there was nothing to it. Mitchell said he made an "honest endeavor" to find Small's body, "and not, as suggested by the writer, to draw a red herring across the trail or fool the public."[93] Mitchell said that Theresa Small and the estate had paid closer to $24,000 for costs associated with the investigation. $15,000 for the Oregon City reward, $4,000 in legal fees, $700 in advertising, $2,700 for police investigations, and $795 for miscellaneous expenses, including drilling, excavation, telegrams, and a small model of the office.[94] Mitchell said that he did not help Theresa draft her statements. The incident that Hammond referred to occurred when he was building the case against Jack Doughty and needed a statement from Theresa "pertaining to the said charges." If she had her lawyers with her, that was her privilege. He thought Hammond was trying to make him look nefarious, assisting Theresa Small as she prepared her evidence. "I wish to most emphatically state that such is not the fact," he wrote.[95] "I do protest in the strongest manner possible the insinuation that at any time I favoured Mrs. Small or any other persons in this case."[96]

In the summer of 1936, the Hammond report made its way through the attorney general's office, the Toronto Police, and the OPP. It was a slim but sensational document that dug into all the places nobody dared venture before.

Mitchell, now an inspector with the force, reminded his superiors that he had constantly reviewed the case with his superiors, the lawyers for the Crown, the attorney general's office, and OPP superintendent Joseph Rogers. "I at no time received advice from any of them to the effect that additional charges could be laid against any person in this case," he wrote.[97]

At Toronto Police headquarters, Deputy Chief George Guthrie—the man who had assigned Mitchell to the case back

Deputy Chief George Guthrie and Inspector Austin Mitchell, third and fourth from left, at a funeral for a colleague in 1931. Guthrie assigned Mitchell to the Small case and later signed off on Mitchell's response to the Hammond report.

in 1919—signed off on Mitchell's response. That fall, Justice Jeffrey heard Sullivan's wild tale of Theresa's supposed confession. Jeffrey ruled the confession a phoney and dismissed the challenge to the widow's estate that November, praising Theresa as a charitable woman who had spent her life doing good works for others. Nothing was said about Hammond's conclusions in the court case or in the press.

Mitchell was inching closer to retirement, Doughty was puttering around the garden, and Theresa was buried in the old Catholic cemetery. The Hammond report was buried too. To borrow a phrase from its author, there surely was a reason.

TWENTY-EIGHT

ANNIHILATION OF THE I

Every time a building met the wrecking ball, the joke came easily to wiseacres who were quite pleased with themselves: Any sign of Ambrose down there? Newspapers delighted in the rehashing of the story that came on the big anniversaries, but for those close to it, the mystery was a life-long affliction. "Most of them have been interviewed and cross examined into a state of neurosis and just want to be left alone," a *Maclean's* reporter wrote in 1951, after approaching a man connected to the case at a Toronto pub. The man played dumb at first. He drank in silence for a few minutes. Then he spoke. "If you mention my name," he said, "I'll murder you."[1]

GERTRUDE SMALL, 1883 TO 1939

Gertrude had been four years old when her mother died, and her older sister, Florence, became a mother-like figure. For most of their lives, the two were inseparable—renouncing Theresa

Small and Catholicism, the religion of their birth and early years. According to Sullivan's writing in the *Thunderer*, the sisters felt betrayed by the Catholic Church, an institution they felt had sided with Theresa. Sullivan had been born Catholic, but criticized the religion every chance he had, and the sisters followed his lead—if not in vitriol, then with their financial and emotional support, bailing him out of jail, standing by him at his court cases, living with him for years. (At his trial for publishing obscene literature, he objected that the judge was a Catholic: "Your honor knows the Roman hierarchy is behind this prosecution. I therefore consider it my duty, although it is a painful one, to object to your honour's occupation of the bench."[2] The judge stayed on, found Sullivan guilty, and doubted his sanity in his ruling. In 1936, when Sullivan challenged Theresa's will, he initially wouldn't tell the lawyers the location of the alleged confession because he believed that a secret "militia" controlled by Pope Pius XI (the "chief of the big opium joint") might bomb the house.[3] The sisters were Catholic in the official ways, but they made sure that the property tax on the home they purchased in 1927—where they lived with Sullivan—supported the public school board.* Florence was the sister who was always more willing to go along with Sullivan's plans. She supported Sullivan in court with his challenge against Theresa's will in 1936. Dismissing that case, Justice Nicol Jeffrey said that regrettably, he didn't

---

* The house still stands. Pope Pius XI was never seen lurking around Brunswick Ave., and it was never bombed by the Vatican.

believe a word she had said since she was under "the malign influence of Sullivan."[4]

Gertrude didn't give evidence in that case. After a lifetime by her sister's side, Gertrude broke away in May 1939 when she and a friend named Miss Jamieson moved to the lakeside community of Midland, Ontario. Gertrude, age fifty-six, had recently undergone an operation[5] and was hoping to recover in a smaller town outside Toronto. Midland was the home of the Martyrs' Shrine, a famous Catholic church dedicated to early missionaries who lived and died among the Indigenous population. Many people came to Midland to pray for healing at the shrine.

Gertrude stayed at the Georgian Hotel, which was where she met electrician Warren Bell when he came to her room to fix her radio.[6] He was thirty-nine years old, almost twenty years her junior, and something sparked between them. They went on picnics, boating adventures, and fishing expeditions. "She told me again and again that she never knew what a good time was before," a friend said. "She was just a lonely woman starting out to enjoy life."[7]

Florence and Patrick Sullivan were still living together at 535 Brunswick Avenue, and they thought Gertrude had gone mad. She no longer told them when she came to Toronto for weekend visits, and there were rumours that she was attending a Catholic church in Midland, despite Sullivan's repeated warnings about the religion.[8] Florence was suspicious of the suddenness of Gertrude's romantic relationship, and of the couple's age difference, and she tried to talk some sense into her sister when she returned to Toronto to pack up her furniture, dogs, and cats for a permanent move to Midland. But Gertrude would not be swayed: she and Warren were going to marry.

The modest wedding was held on October 26, 1939, in Stayner, Ontario. The only witnesses were another couple from Midland. Both couples left Stayner at dusk for the drive home along the coast of Lake Huron, but the newlyweds never made it home. The next morning, two duck hunters were walking along Wasaga Beach, a lakeside community that was not far from Stayner. It was the off-season, quiet and lonely, and one of the men thought he saw a human face in the water. He shook it off but then saw a man's coat floating in the lake. When he fished it out, there was a marriage licence in the pocket for Warren Bell and Gertrude Small.[9]

The men walked down the beach and found a car partially submerged at the mouth of the Nottawasaga River. A young boy found Gertrude a half mile from the car, her grey travelling suit soaked through, a pair of gloves protecting her icy hands. Her purse was nearby, with pawn tickets for jewellery inside. Bell's body was found a day later, his nose badly injured. The night it happened, the "sea was low," a local said. "Just about as low as it ever gets." The people in town thought Bell had mistaken the sandbar between the river and the lake for a road. He must have been going a pretty good clip, they reckoned, when he struck something like a log, and he and Gertrude catapulted through the roof of the car.[10]

Was it a suicide pact? A murder? A freak accident? The first autopsy didn't find water in Gertrude's lungs, and attributed her death to shock, but an official inquest found that she had drowned, and that both of the newlyweds had alcohol in their system.[11] There was no sign of foul play found by the "medico-legal" experts, but Florence was adamant that her sister had been doped and murdered by the same shadowy, anonymous people who had gone after Ambrose. Warren Bell had bought a few bottles of commercial-grade ether back in September. "My brother's death was hushed and kept down and I am not going to do the same thing about my sister's death," Florence declared.[12]

"Gertie wouldn't take my advice about coming back to Toronto to live," Sullivan said, when the media came calling. "I told her, 'Gertie, you are doomed. You are in the enemy's camp

Gertrude and Warren Bell's car.

and you'll meet the same fate as your brother Ambrose. You are out of your realm altogether.' But she wouldn't listen to me."[13]

Florence Small buried her sister under her maiden name in a Protestant cemetery, even though her sister had returned to the Catholic faith.[14] Their brother Percy was a pallbearer. So was Sullivan.

I went looking for Gertrude's grave at Mount Pleasant Cemetery in Toronto. I walked up and down the section of the cemetery where her plot was supposed to be, sweeping aside leaves to read the names of the stones laid in the ground. I could not find her.

After thirty minutes, I called the front office.

They checked their records. There was no stone.

Florence Small did not pay for a gravestone for her sister.

AUSTIN MITCHELL, 1874 TO 1950

Austin Mitchell, who had chased Doughty to Oregon City and palled around with him on the train ride home, died five months after Jack Doughty in January 1950. He was seventy-six years old.[15] His funeral program quoted Alfred Tennyson—"Sunset and evening star / And one clear call for me! / And may there be no moaning of the bar / When I put out to sea."[16] When he retired in 1945, he had spent half a century in policing. The boy from Beeton, Ontario ("a small village renowned for black flies and mosquitoes," Sullivan once said[17]), had seen the transition from horses to cars, had risen from constable to inspector, but he never found Ambrose Small. That would be his legacy. Mitchell was "a skilled and competent officer," a police official said when the reporters called looking for a comment.

FLORENCE SMALL, 1878 TO 1953

After Gertrude died in 1939, Florence Small and Patrick Sullivan moved to the Beaufort Apartments on Davenport Road. Florence changed her will to leave everything to Sullivan after her sister's death, and later added a clause to acknowledge the deep rift in her family: "I give the sum of One Dollar to my half-brother Percy Small and also the sum of One Dollar to my half-sister Madeleine Ryan."[18] She wanted her body cremated, with no religious service. She explicitly stated that no Catholic relatives were to enter her home after her death.

She died on March 19, 1953, seventy-seven years old. She was the only child of Dan and Ellen Small whose death did not provoke an official inquiry.[19]

CLARA SMITH, 1894 TO ?

When Clara's name came up in the case, she was known as Clara Smith, but the last name was a fleeting accessory, picked up in an early marriage that didn't last. Born Clare Shepard, she was said to have grown up on a farm near Grimsby, a small lakeside community between Toronto and Niagara Falls.[20]

Ambrose and Clara's love letters suggest that they had a romantic relationship dating back to 1914, when Clara was around twenty years old, and that she had lived in Toronto for part of their affair.

City tax assessments for 90 Park Road—the apartment where Ambrose "kept" Clara—show a "Clara Smith" as owner in 1916. During the war, Clara's letters to Ambrose were written from different locations, including Toronto, Hamilton, New York, and Niagara-on-the-Lake. In 1917, she divorced her first husband, Jimmy Smith, with Ambrose's help; but in 1918, she married Douglas Jennings and moved to Minneapolis, which did not stop her affair with Ambrose.[21] She told Ambrose that it was a mistake marrying Jennings and that she wanted to run away with her much wealthier paramour.[22]

She was living in Minnesota when Ambrose vanished, and she came to Toronto to talk to the police in 1920 and 1922. It is unclear whether her husband ever made the connection that his wife was Ambrose Small's mistress. Her married name never appeared in the newspapers, and her trips to Toronto seemed to coincide with her husband's sales trips.

Clara petitioned for a divorce from Jennings in 1921, citing "cruel and inhuman" treatment. (He made no appearance in court and gave no defence.) She left the home in 1921 and was granted an absolute divorce in 1922.[23] She then disappeared from the public record. Attempts to find traces of Clara outside the fiction of Michael Ondaatje, where she is called Clara Dickens, have so far fizzled out.

PATRICK SULLIVAN, 1885 TO 1958

Patrick Sullivan loved to write, and as he grew older and his enemies died off, he channelled his passion into writing his final story—a series of wills he was constantly updating. "I believe death is the end—complete annihilation of the I," he wrote in 1953. "My mind or 'soul' is adjusted to that belief."[24] After Florence died, he updated his will to include a lengthy screed against one of his favourite enemies: "The Roman Catholic Church is not a religion; it is an economic-financial corporation, as far removed from the teachings of Jesus as Queen Ann's musket is from the H-bomb."[25] While Catholics believed in eternal damnation, he said, he believed in evolution—that death fulfilled the cycle of life. It shouldn't be feared.

In March 1958, Sullivan died of a stroke in the room he was renting in Toronto's west end. His friend Bert Brown took care of the arrangements. Brown had always been willing to do Sullivan's bidding. When Sullivan had been sentenced to jail in 1930, it was Brown he wrote to, giving detailed instructions on how his thoughts should be submitted to the newspapers. When Sullivan claimed Theresa visited the Brunswick Avenue home to deliver a confession in 1929, Brown corroborated the account in court in 1936. (Justice Jeffrey dismissed Brown as a liar and noted that he was a member of the Ku Klux Klan, that he believed communism was good for Canada, and perhaps most tellingly, that he was a great admirer of Sullivan.[26])

Brown, loyal to the end, followed Sullivan's detailed instructions and had the notorious agitator's body cremated, as instructed. "Cremation is the most sanitary and sensible method of disposing of the dead that has yet been devised," Sullivan's *Thunder* tabloid advised in 1931. "The Commercialized Christian Church opposed Cremation because it would destroy their CEMETERY RACKET—a Racket that brings millions of dollars to the CELESTIAL DOPE PEDLARS."[27] The Catholics hadn't come around on cremation yet, and this was Sullivan's final chance to stick it to Rome. He left Toronto, more or less, the same way he'd arrived: with a sizzle.

TORONTO POLICE INVESTIGATION, 1919 to 1960

In December 1960, the Toronto Police destroyed their files on the Ambrose Small case and declared it closed. "Finally Admit Can't Find Ambrose Small," the newspapers reported.[28] Four decades of paperwork went into the discard pile, along with the key to the long-demolished theatre. The Toronto Police gave up the search, but the world didn't take the hint. Letters still arrived with sightings and tips. I may seem crazy, they'd say, or I promise I am not another old woman trying to be smart, but here's what I know.[29] The police responded with variations of a canned answer: Nearly everyone was dead, the reward was lapsed, and in spite of an exhaustive search, the case had never been solved. The man you saw in Halifax, Manitoba, Windsor, could not be Ambrose Small.

In 1976, a Timmins, Ontario, man wrote to say that his father had been involved in the murder of "Mr. Ambrose"—that it was a contract killing with a partner. He always thought his father was joking about this, but his dad had been connected to organized crime and had done time in jail. The killing took place in the theatre, he said—they shot Small and tossed his body in a dormant "heating unit" to hide it before they took him to the dump in a garbage truck. He explained that his father had later killed himself. "Knowing my father as I do, even though he was sick, his conscience was bothering him," he wrote. Now that he was dead, his father couldn't defend himself or face any consequences, but his son was hoping to get the reward money.[30]

There were a couple of mistakes in the letter, including the year of the disappearance, and the police told him that they had no evidence to support his theory, or the involvement of his father. The reward was long expired.[31] The Toronto Police had a small recipe-card summary of the writer courtesy of the RCMP: "Believed to have subversive background, outspoken, feels govt. owes him a living. Capable of causing embarrassment to VIP's."

TWENTY-NINE

ENIGMA

TORONTO, 2019

I spend so much time imagining the ending. I picture a grand escape where Ambrose takes a wistful look at the moustache that grew to "exciting lengths" in his youth and was clipped shorter during the war. The moustache always makes me laugh, because a century's worth of narrators have described its splendour in the absence of so many crucial facts. When I imagine Ambrose Small escaping his life in Toronto, he shaves the moustache because he is nothing without it, and that's what he needs to become. He grabs a wig from the wardrobe room, in one of those twisting hallways of the Grand that nobody ever wrote about in great detail, and then he takes a cab, a train, a ship to a secluded island in the Pacific Ocean, where Clara is waiting for him, happy to shake the Minneapolis chill from her bones. Ambrose makes mojitos with his bountiful mint crop, as the turquoise waters lap the shore.

I have found so many fragments of Ambrose Small, but there

is no DNA to solve the riddle, no autopsy to narrate the final hours, no confession to guide our path, except for the one the courts dismissed in 1936.

Ambrose Small has been trapped in the infinite possibility of life and death for a century. "At best he was an amnesia victim, at worst a gibbering idiot, and in between an astral body, an anguished wail issuing from beneath a cement floor,"[1] one journalist noted in 1951. The story never ends, the last chapter always has a caveat: "The ghosts of this bizarre case have never rested easily," Fred McClement wrote in the final sentence of his 1974 book.[2]

The uncertainty is captivating, but to suggest that Ambrose spent the rest of his days in solitude when the world was looking for him—and $1 million was waiting in his bank account—ignores the man I found in the Shubert Archive, who chased down every dollar he was owed. What was the point of going through the hassle of the sale, the wrangling to keep his office, only to walk away? Even if there were secret accounts, I don't think Ambrose would leave the million behind, or the Victory Bonds, or the $225,000 in cash he had in his five other bank accounts.[3] I believe that only death could separate him from his money.

Since most of Austin Mitchell's police files have been lost, Hammond's report—which includes some Toronto Police files—is the best window we have on the events of December 2, 1919. Hammond believed that Theresa and Jack were at the Grand Opera House that evening. He believed they were involved in whatever happened, and that at the very least, Theresa was implicated in the cover-up. Hammond can't tell us conclusively whether it was a bullet, a misplaced punch, an act of passion, or the detached work of a contract killer from the greater Timmins area, but he believed there was a fatal scuffle in the office, and Austin Mitchell didn't want to see the facts that were in front of him.

When I told the Doughty descendants about the general points of the Hammond report, Margaret Santon said that although she wouldn't rule out Jack's involvement, she can hardly see it: "Because how do you dispose of a body that thoroughly? I just don't think he had the resources."[4]

Bruce Doughty, who was only four when his grandfather died, said that people tell stories all the time, woven from fact and fiction. "That doesn't mean that's how it happened," he said. "In a court of law there has to be actual evidence."

Hammond's theory is circumstantial, but I wonder how it would fare in court. What would a jury have decided if the conspiracy to kidnap charge against Jack Doughty had been heard? I find the clarity and the certainty of the Hammond report compelling. His theory seems plausible, but I don't have the same access to the files or people. I don't know how it was received or why it was buried. The same year that Hammond wrote the report, Justice Nicol Jeffrey dealt with similar allegations as Sullivan tried to unsettle Theresa's will. A few witnesses said they heard Doughty make threats against Small the night before his disappearance, in the basement of the Grand Opera House—but they had been drinking, and nobody ever told the police, and the information was vague. "The evidence falls short of satisfying me that Doughty . . . or someone associated with him, killed or murdered Ambrose J. Small," Jeffrey wrote in his decision.[5] Jeffrey was speaking to the evidence that he heard in court, and not the more fulsome story of betrayal and revenge that Hammond pieced together. Had he read the Hammond report?

I think that Jack and Theresa likely knew what happened to Ambrose Small, and the real shame was that nobody ever pushed them to answer questions in a meaningful way. In her statements in court, Theresa Small was never overly harsh on Doughty, even though she had every right to be furious with the man who stole $105,000 from her husband, changed his name, reinvented himself in Oregon. She never told the police that Doughty came to see her before he left town, or that his sisters had tried to bring her the Victory Bonds the police were looking for. Doughty, who loved to talk, kept quiet about the case for his entire life. He never testified at his trial, never spoke about it to the reporters who pestered him, never pointed a finger in anyone's direction.

In the halls of power—where the husbands of Theresa's luncheon guests grew wealthier every year—there was a great reluctance to question Theresa Small's narrative. It was best to stay quiet. It raised too many questions about police incompetence, payoffs, compromise, and how the rich and powerful were treated.

In Adjala, the rolling farmland where Ambrose Small's grandparents settled in the 1830s, some of the Smalls blamed Theresa in the long years that followed. They fell for all that propaganda, says Joe Small, a descendant of the family, a retired farmer now in his eighties.[6] Joe's grandfather, also named Joe, was a cousin of Ambrose. He came to the big city to see a show occasionally, bounding up the staircase at the Grand for a few complimentary tickets. He always got them, but Ambrose never had much time for him beyond that. A few years ago, Joe was in Toronto for cancer treatment. He was feeling healthy, so he left the hospital for a walk. He found himself in Rosedale, staring at the three-storey mansion on Glen Road. Joe Small doesn't think Theresa Small was involved, but "Why all those Kormanns couldn't get good German husbands," he says good-naturedly, "I don't know."[7]

In the nineteenth century, St. Michael's Cemetery was good and far from downtown. The early planners didn't anticipate how quickly Toronto would grow. Now in the middle of the city, it has been plagued by vandalism, dog walkers, and garbage, and the gate was permanently locked in 2005 to prevent further damage.[8] The cemetery is open only on holidays.

On a humid Father's Day, a security guard is eating a sandwich in an air-conditioned car near the winter vault, where the caretakers stored the coffins to await the spring thaw. She tells me to be mindful of the time. It is 3:50 p.m. and she is locking the front gate in ten minutes. I walk around the peaceful space, reading the names of Catholics who have been dead for 150 years. I see the grave of twenty-three-year-old Matthew Sheedy, killed in a religious riot back in 1859. In the cemetery register, his cause of death is "killed by an Orangeman," and the story goes that his stone used to say the same thing.[9] It had to be replaced about twenty years ago, and now reads: "He gave his young life in defence of peace." Times have changed.

Theresa has no grave, but I find her patch of grass next to her parents' red obelisk. It takes me a while to find Ellen and Dan Small, buried at the very back of the cemetery, past a group of postulants. It was Ellen's death in 1887 that brought the Kormanns and Smalls together. Dan married Josephine Kormann, and then Ambrose married her sister, Theresa. Happiness, heartbreak, and hatred followed. The Smalls and the Kormanns chose sides, and they're still doing it in death. When Josephine Small died in 1950, she was not buried with her husband. She chose her sister Theresa, in the unmarked grave at the northeast end of the cemetery.[10]

Ambrose Small is not here. He doesn't have a gravestone.

I return to the entrance, but the security guard is gone. It's 4:01 p.m. and the old iron gate is locked, as promised.

I will not spend eternity with the warring Smalls and Kormanns.

I walk back through the cemetery and climb a fence into a condo parking lot. I leave them all behind.

ILLUSTRATION CREDITS

———————◇———————

NOTES

———————◇———————

ONE: AMBROSE SMALL IS MISSING

1   "Little Red Riding Hood," *Toronto World*, December 30, 1919, 10.

2   "Big Canadian Circuit Is Rumored," *New York Clipper*, October 22, 1919, https://archive.org/stream/Clipper67-1919-10/Clipper67-1919-10_djvu.txt.

3   *Dictionary of Canadian Biography*, s.v. "Shaughnessy, Thomas George, 1st Baron Shaughnessy," by Theodore D. Regehr, accessed January 5, 2019, http://www.biographi.ca/en/bio/shaughnessy_thomas_george_15E.html.

4   Ibid.

5   Paul Bilkey, *Persons, Papers and Things; Being the Casual Recollections of a Journalist, with Some Flounderings in Philosophy* (Toronto: Ryerson Press, 1940), 25.

6   H.W. Beauclerk to A.J. Small, August 8, 1919. E.W.M. Flock Papers 1919–1924, Envelope 2, Marilyn & Charles Baillie Special Collections Centre, Toronto Reference Library, Ontario, Canada.

7   Brooks McNamara, *The Shuberts of Broadway: A History Drawn from the Collection of the Shubert Archive* (New York: Oxford University Press, 1990), 112.

8   "Kitty Marks describes A.J. Small," in Sheila M.F. Johnston, *Let's go to the Grand! 100 years of entertainment at London's Grand Theatre* (Toronto: Natural Heritage Books, 2001), 43.

9   Michael J. Piva, "Urban Working-Class Incomes and Real Incomes in 1921: A Comparative Analysis," *Social History* 16, no. 21 (May 1983): 143–65.

10 Hector Willoughby Charlesworth, *More Candid Chronicles: Further Leaves from the Note Book of a Canadian Journalist* (Toronto: Macmillan Company, 1928), 289.

11 Correspondence between E.W.M. Flock and H.J. Wright, January 5, 1920. E.W.M. Flock Papers 1919–1924, Envelope 1, Toronto Reference Library, Ontario, Canada.

12 Correspondence between E.W.M. Flock and James Cowan, December 26, 1919. E.W.M. Flock Papers 1919–1924, Envelope 1, Toronto Reference Library, Ontario, Canada.

13   "Battle of Ballots Was Waged All Day," *Toronto Daily Star*, January 1, 1920, 1.

14   "Need United Action to Rebuild World," *Toronto Daily Star*, January 2, 1920, 3.

15   "Looks for Solution of Mystery of Death," *Toronto Daily Star*, January 2, 1920, 1.

16   "Startling Disappearance of Toronto Millionaire Causes Grave Apprehension," *Toronto World*, January 2, 1920, 1.

17   Theresa Kormann Small, "Venice," *St. Joseph Lilies* 1, no. 2 (September 1912): 14–16. (Accessed Archive.org.)

18   Ibid.

19   "In Venice Then; Where Is He Now," *Evening Telegram*, January 13, 1920, page number not scanned.

20   Pretrial interview with John Spencer, Small vs. Holmes, RG 22-5800, Case 863-1936, May 1936. Archives of Ontario, Toronto, Ontario (hereafter cited as AO).

21   Ibid.

TWO: **THE HALL OF STRANGE DELIGHTS**

1   Donald Campbell Charles Masters, *The Rise of Toronto: 1850–1890* (Toronto: The University of Toronto Press), 1947, 11.

2   Katie Daubs, "In 1867, Toronto Faced a Frightened Mare Before Christmas," *Toronto Star*, December 24, 2017, https://www.thestar.com/news/ insight/2017 /12/24/toronto-1867-the-frightened-mare-before-christmas.html.

3   Robert Harrison, *The Conventional Man: The Diaries of Ontario Chief Justice Robert A. Harrison 1856–1878*, ed. Peter Oliver (Toronto: University of Toronto Press, 2003), 53. (This is from Peter Oliver's rich introduction to the text, which explains Toronto society in the mid to late Victorian era.)

4   J.M.S. Careless, *Toronto to 1918: An Illustrated History* (Toronto: Lorimer, [1984] 2002), 107. (The theatre opened in 1848.)

5   Masters, *The Rise of Toronto*, 51.

6   Harrison, *The Conventional Man*, 55. (Again, this is from the introduction, describing Harrison's 1872 reaction to a show at the St. Lawrence Hall later in his journal.)

7   Ibid., 468.

8   Ibid., 521.

9   Thomas Scott, *Behind the Footlights*, 10. In Thomas Scott Collection, Grand Opera House (c.1876–1900), Toronto Reference Library, Ontario, Canada.

10   Ibid. "We had very poor audience and on several occasions when I was ready to light up the house, I found no gas."

11   Ibid, 12.

12   Robert Brockhouse, *The Royal Alexandra Theatre: A Celebration of 100 years* (Toronto: McArthur & Company, 2008), 31–32.

13   Ibid., 31.

14   Ibid., 32.

15   "Disastrous Fire: The Grand Opera House Destroyed: Three Persons Perish," *Globe*, December 1, 1879, 4. (Lurid details were common in Victorian newspapers, where readers commonly read about unfortunate souls trapped in burning buildings, their torsos aflame, their bodies burned to a crisp.)

16   Alexander Manning, "Grand Opera House: The Safety of the Restored Building Vouched For," *Globe*, February 7, 1880, 4.

17   Charles Pelham Mulvany, *Toronto, Past and Present: A Handbook of the City* (Toronto: W.E. Caiger, 1884), 119.

18   "Toronto's New Opera-House: Opened by Miss Neilson in 'As You Like It'—Speeches and Much Enthusiasm," *New York Times*, February 10, 1880, 5.

19   F.A. Dixon, "Ode on the occasion of the Opening of the Grand Opera House, Toronto." Address, opening night 1880, Grand Opera House, Toronto. In Thomas Scott Collection, Grand Opera House (c.1876–1900), Toronto Reference Library, Ontario, Canada.

20   Tax Assessment for the Ward of St. Andrew, City of Toronto, 1881, page 27. City of Toronto Archives, Ontario, Canada (hereafter cited as CTA). (Daniel Small shows up as a tenant at the Grand Opera House in the 1881 city directory, suggesting he arrived in 1880, when the information was gathered.)

21   Mulvany, *Toronto, Past and Present*, 119.

22   "Toronto Directory for 1881," Might & Co., 1881. Accessed online, Toronto Public Library, Toronto, Ontario, Canada.

23   Mulvany, *Toronto, Past and Present*, 119.

THREE: THE SMALLS OF ADJALA

1   "The 'Separate' System," *Globe*, December 10, 1856, 2. (The *Globe* draws attention to the advertisement in this article.)

2   Andrew F. Hunter, "A History of Simcoe County," Barrie, County Council, 1909, 50.

3   "The Ministerial Mode of Canvassing," *Globe*, January 8, 1858, 2. (The *Globe* reported this story based on sworn statements from two East Gwillimbury men, who heard it from two of their friends. The acceptance of this gossip as news tells us a lot about attitudes toward Catholics.)

4   Rev. Jon Coburn, *I Kept My Powder Dry* (Toronto: Ryerson Press, 1950), 16.

5   Ibid., 18.

6   Ibid., 21.

7   Joe Small, in discussion with the author, Toronto, September 12, 2017.

8   Careless, *Toronto to 1918*, 77. (Here, Careless is commenting on rural changes.)

9   County Marriage Registers, 1858–June 1869. Series MS248, Reels 15 and 16, AO. Accessed at Ancestry.com.

10   Census Returns for 1861, Ward of St. Andrew, Division No. 5, Bathurst Street West Side, Library and Archives Canada (hereafter cited as LAC). Accessed at https://www.bac-lac.gc.ca/eng/census/1861/Pages/1861.aspx; *Hutchinson's Toronto Directory 1862–1863* (Toronto: Lovell and Gibson, 1863), 34. Accessed at Torontopubliclibrary.ca. (There is not much that is known about Ambrose Small's mother, Ellen. The marriage records say that she was living in Bradford at the time of the 1865 marriage. She was born in Ontario to Patrick Brazill and Mary Kelley. By the 1861 census, Ellen's father had died, and her widowed mother had moved the children to Toronto, first to a location on Bathurst Street, and by 1862, they lived on Hayter Street near Terauley. Both of those locations were close to Catholic churches—the first near St. Mary's, and the second near St. Basil's—the church where Ambrose Small would one day tie the knot.) Note: spelling of Brazill is sometimes Brazil in records.

11   *Gazetteer and Directory of the County of Simcoe* (Toronto: McEvoy & Co, 1866), 84.

12   "Lovell's Canadian Dominion directory for 1871," J. Lovell (1871) and in conversation with Joe Small, September 12, 2017.

13   Careless, *Toronto to 1918*, 120–22. (By 1891, Careless notes, the city had a Canadian-born majority nearing 100,000, with 23,000 English born, 13,000 Irish born, 6,300 Scottish born, 5,000 Americans, and 1,500 "foreign born," including the Germans, Italians, and Slavic backgrounds, and a few of the Jewish faith. Toronto's diversity was beginning to take shape.)

14   Tax Assessment for the Ward of St. Andrew, City of Toronto, 1875, page 94, CTA. (Tax assessments reflect data gathered in the previous year, which is how I have dated the 1874 arrival.)

15   Ibid.

16   Ibid.

17   William Smyth, *Toronto, the Belfast of Canada: The Orange Order and the Shaping of Municipal Culture* (Toronto: University of Toronto Press, 2015), 14.

18   "The Road to Northern Ireland, 1167 to 1921," BBC History, February 1,

2007, https://www.bbc.co.uk/history/recent/troubles/overview_ni_article
_01.shtml. "New policies for controlling the thinly-colonised island were
attempted, including 'plantation,' which was first introduced under Edward VI.
English settlers were given lands confiscated from rebellious Irish families."

19   Ibid.

20   Smyth, *Toronto, the Belfast of Canada*, 4.

21   Ibid., 14.

22   Ibid., 21. "At one stage Canada could claim more Orange lodges than
Ulster, and at the time of Canadian Confederation one-third of all adult
male Canadian Protesants were, or had been, members of the organization.
A century after its introduction to Canada, the Order still proclaimed its
slogan "Keep Canada British and Protestant," Smyth writes.

23   Ibid., 84.

24   Cecil J. Houston and William J. Smyth, "Community Development and
Institutional Supports: Life on the Agricultural Frontier of Adjala and
Mono Townships," in *Catholics at the Gathering Place*, eds. M. McGowan
and B. Clarke (Toronto: Dundurn, 1993), 15.

25   Smyth, *Toronto, the Belfast of Canada*, 21.

26   Ibid., 4. Smyth is quoting Canadian historian Maurice Careless in *Toronto to
1918*, 41.

27   John S. Moir, "Toronto's Protestants and Their Perceptions of Their Roman
Catholic Neighbours," in *Catholics at the Gathering Place*, eds. M. McGowan
and B. Clarke (Toronto: Dundurn, 1993), 314.

28   Ibid., 316.

29   Smyth, *Toronto: The Belfast of Canada*, 34.

30   Moir, "Toronto's Protestants," 317.

31   Ibid., 317.

32   Martin A. Galvin, "The Jubilee Riots in Toronto, 1875," *Report* (CCHA) 26
(1959): 93–107, http://www.umanitoba.ca/colleges/st_pauls/ccha/Back%20
Issues/CCHA1959/Galvin.htm.

33   Ibid.

34   Ibid.

35   Moir, "Toronto's Protestants," 318.

36   Stay tuned—a few decades later, when Ambrose was travelling the world
by steamship, he occasionally gave his religion as "Protestant" for the ship
manifests, shedding his Catholicism like a winter jacket in an overheated
shopping mall.

37   Tax Assessment for the Ward of St. Andrew, City of Toronto 1881, page 27, CTA.

38   "De La Salle College, Tenth Annual Commencement and Distribution of Prizes," *Irish Canadian* (Toronto), July 14, 1881. From De La Salle Archives, Laval.

39   Thomas Scott, *Behind the Footlights*, undated. Reminiscences of Thomas Scott, gas engineer of Grand Opera House, as told to his son Thomas Scott, Jr. In Thomas Scott Collection, Grand Opera House (c.1876–1900), Toronto Reference Library, Ontario, Canada.

40   Ibid.

41   *The Toronto City Directory of 1884* (Toronto: R.L. Polk & Co. at Toronto Reference Library. (PDF online on library website.)

42   *The Toronto City Directory of 1885* (Toronto: R.L. Polk & Co. at Toronto Reference Library. (PDF online on library website.)

43   Charlesworth, *More Candid Chronicles*, 278.

44   "Made Millions at the Grand," *Toronto Telegram*, January 10, 1920.

45   Israel T. Dana, "The Treatment of Chronic Bright's Disease," *Columbus Medical Journal: A Magazine of Medicine and Surgery* 4 (1885), 304-315.

46   Ibid., 312.

47   Ibid.

48   Ibid., 314.

49   Ibid., 310.

50   There is no photo of Ellen Small. As a working woman who died in the Victorian age, she was erased from history, except for her grave, and a few lines on a census. The detail about her ring comes out in coverage of Ambrose's wedding, cited later.

51   "In a Wicker Basket," *Ottawa Journal*, June 1, 1896, 5.

52   "Well Remembered as Theatre Official: O.B. Sheppard Had Also Been . . . ," *Globe*, May 1, 1928, 23.

53   Charlesworth, *More Candid Chronicles*, 278.

54   Ibid.

55   Ibid.

56   "Promiscuous Dancing and Roller Skating Rinks," *Globe*, December 11, 1885, 4; "A Roller Skating Victim: Brain Exhaustion Kills a Contestant in the Recent Tournament," *Globe*, March 18, 1885, 8.

57   Charlesworth, *More Candid Chronicles*, 278.

58   *The Toronto City Directory of 1890* (Toronto: R.L. Polk & Co. at Toronto Reference Library. (PDF online on library website.)

59   Scott, *Behind the Footlights*, 6.

60   "A Compliment to Mr. Small," *Globe*, October 1, 1895, 2.

61   "Presentation to a Popular Treasurer," *Globe*, September 18, 1895, 10.

62   *The Toronto City Directory of 1895* (Toronto: Might Directory Co. at Toronto Reference Library). (PDF online on library website.)

63   Charlesworth, *More Candid Chronicles*, 280.

64   Ibid., 279

65   Ibid., 280.

66   Ibid., 281.

67   Ibid.

68   Ibid., 282.

69   Ibid., 283.

70   Ibid.

71   Ibid., 281.

72   "Suit Over Photos," *Globe*, January 14, 1908, 12.

73   "Boys Discover Personal Effects of Ambrose Small in North Toronto Dump," *Toronto Daily Star*, October 11, 1929, 1.

74   "Music and the Drama," *Globe*, April 2, 1892, 10; *Globe*, October 1, 1895, 2.

FOUR: MRS. AMBROSE SMALL

1   Ignatius sometimes went with France, like he told the census taker in 1861. Census of 1861, Canada West, Waterloo, accessed online, Library and Archives Canada.

2   Henry McEvoy, ed., *The Province of Ontario Gazetteer and Directory* (Toronto: Robertson & Cook, 1869), 91.

3   Tristin Hopper, "Everyone Knows John A. Macdonald Was a Bit of a Drunk, but It's Largely Forgotten How Hard He Hit the Bottle," *National Post*, January 9, 2015, https://nationalpost.com/news/canada/everyone-knows-john-a-macdonald-was-a-bit-of-a-drunk-but-its-largely-forgotten-how-hard-he-hit-the-bottle.(Sproat doesn't provide details, but Hopper notes that it was suspected by one historian that MacDonald had "severe acute pancreatitis" that summer. The condition can be caused by gallstones, heavy alcohol consumption, and several other factors.)

4   Alexander Sproat to George-Étienne Cartier, June 1870. No. 3582, Department of Agriculture General Correspondence, RG 17, vol. 38, FINDO17/67166, MIKAN 1972803, LAC.

5   "Metapedia Municipal Council With copy of resolution re misconduct of
     Mr. Kormann's German settlers," August 11, 1874. Department of
     Agriculture General Correspondence, RG 17, vol. 116, FIND017/73019,
     MIKAN 1978664, LAC.

6   1871 census, Bruce South, Carrick, LAC. Accessed at https://www.bac-lac.gc
     .ca/eng/census/1871/Pages/1871.aspx (There is also a Ludwig Kormann
     in this census, but he doesn't appear in other censuses with the family.)

7   According to the 1876 city directory, Ignatius was working in Toronto as a
     butcher, and the growing family soon moved to Yorkville. When the census
     taker came in 1881 to count up the Kormanns, Ignatius was forty-five, the oldest
     son still at home was Frank, who was twenty, and his youngest child was three.
     Theresa was ten years old, right in the middle of the brood. Yorkville offered all
     of the convenience of the city to the south, but had the pure and healthy air of
     the countryside. It was landlocked, and constantly in need of water, but its
     inhabitants resisted annexation by Toronto, because they didn't want to pay
     higher taxes. (They finally gave in by 1883, when Yorkville joined Toronto.)

8   Jordan St. John, "Lost Breweries of Toronto," Toronto: Arcadia Publishing,
     2014, 79.

9   Toronto Illustrated, 1893: Its Growth, Resources, Commerce, Manufacturing
     Interests, Financial Institutions, Educational Advantages and Prospects: Also
     Sketches of the Leading Business Concerns which Contribute to the City's Progress
     and Prosperity: A Brief History of the City from Foundation to the Present Time
     (Toronto: Consolidated Illustrating Co, 1893), 73. Accessed at Archive.org.

10   Jordan St. John (author of Lost Breweries of Toronto), in discussion with the
     author, January 17, 2018.

11   "The Toronto City Directory for 1889," R.L. Polk & Co. (1889), Toronto
     Public Library, online.

12   Mary Eva Kormann, will filed November 15, 1902, RG 22-305, York County
     estate files, 15671, MS584, Reel 1090, AO.

13   "A Timeline of Historic Milestones," Sisters of St. Joseph of Toronto,
     accessed at http://www.csj-to.ca/history. (Theresa is the only Kormann who
     shows up as a student in the archive record of boarding students, but the
     community annals mention her sister as a former pupil in the entry of
     October 27, 1902.)

14   Elizabeth Smyth, "The Lessons of Religion and Science: The Congregation
     of the Sisters of St. Joseph and St. Joseph's Academy, Toronto 1854–1911."
     EdD thesis, University of Toronto, 1990, 210. Here, she is citing Ruth
     Agnew from St. Joseph Lilies 11, no. 2, Centennial Issue, 1851–1951.

15 Smyth, "The Lessons of Religion and Science," 198. (As Smyth notes, if you wanted to graduate in this era, you had to board at the school for at least one term. The archives for the Sisters of St. Joseph only has records for boarders, and not day students, during Theresa's time period.)

16 Ibid., 209.

17 Ibid., 212.

18 Theresa Small, "Her First Lover," *St. Joseph Lilies* 1, no. 2 (September 1912): 83–84. Accessed at Archive.org.

19 Photo is in the collection of the Sisters of St. Joseph of Toronto Archives.

20 Chris Bateman, "That Time Toronto Won the 1887 Baseball Pennant," blogTO, April 12, 2015, https://www.blogto.com/city/2015/04/ that_time _toronto_won_the_1887_baseball_pennant.

21 Some accounts of the Small mystery have noted that Ignatius had an "interest" in the Small family saloon, which is possible. Fred McClement's 1974 book, *The Strange Case of Ambrose Small* (McClelland & Stewart), mentions that Dan Small worked at the Kormann Brewery. I never found any record of that employment in city directories and tax assessments, but they certainly were connected in other ways. The Kormann Brewery was an advertiser in the Toronto Opera House programs of the mid-1890s, after Ignatius's death but before Ambrose and Theresa's marriage.

22 County Marriage Registers, 1869–1928. Series MS932, Reel 73, AO.

23 "The Toronto City Directory 1894," Might Directory Co., 1894, Toronto Public Library, online.

24 The street was initially called Herbert Place when Dan Small first moved in, according to the 1890 city directory.

25 "Music and the Drama," *Globe*, March 3, 1900, 24.

26 *Community Annals of the Sisters of St. Joseph*, vol. 1, October 8, 1901, 290. Sisters of St. Joseph of Toronto Archives.

27 "In the Public Eye," *Toronto Daily Star*, April 24, 1901, 2.

28 Mary Brown, "Ambrose Small a Ghost in Spite of Himself," in *Theatrical Touring and Founding in North America*, ed. L.W. Conolly (Westport, Connecticut and London: Greenwood Press, 1982), 79.

29 Ibid., 83

30 Brockhouse, *The Royal Alexandra Theatre*, 10.

31 "The Music and the Drama: Informal Opening of the New Princess," *Globe*, September 2, 1895, 10.

32   Jamie Bradburn, "The Princess Theatre," Heritage Toronto, January 7, 2013, http://heritagetoronto.org/the-princess-theatre.

33   "In the Public Eye," *Toronto Daily Star*, April 24, 1901, 2.

34   "Over 83,000 Were There," *Globe*, September 3, 1901, 1.

35   "The Music and the Drama," *Globe*, August 29, 1901, 5.

36   Ibid.

37   Mary Eva Kormann, will filed November 15, 1902, RG 22-305, York County estate files, 15671, MS584, Reel 1090, AO.

38   "After a Long Illness," *Globe*, October 21, 1902, 12.

39   "Social Events," *Globe*, November 7, 1902, 9.

40   Careless, *Toronto to 1918*, 138.

41   "Small's Home Life Is Aired in Court," *Globe*, April 11, 1924, 13.

42   "Social Events," *Globe*, March 10, 1903, 9.

43   Careless, *Toronto to 1918*, 124.

44   "Theatre Gone in Smoke," *Globe*, March 26, 1903, 7.

45   "The Music and the Drama," *Globe*, November 3, 1903, 12.

46   Brown, "Ambrose Small a Ghost in Spite of Himself," 82. "They planned to invest in theatre properties; when the Toronto Opera House burned in 1903, they decided to expand and diversify their holdings. The impetus to do so was fortified when Small's partner, C.J. Whitney, died that same year."

47   "Mrs. Small Had Money and Wasn't Husband's," *Toronto Daily Star,* December 7, 1922, 16.

48   Whitney vs. Small, O.J. No. 26, Ontario Supreme Court—Appellate Division, April 6, 1914, Can LII.

49   Ibid. "There does not seem to be any way to ascertain, before referring the accounts, what the surviving partner has actually done since the death of Whitney," the appeal judge said, but he agreed that the death dissolved the partnership.

50   "May Buy the Grand," *Toronto Daily Star*, November 2, 1905, 1.

51   "Miss Jane Porter Killed by Auto," *Toronto Daily Star*, September 4, 1906, 6.

52   "'Follow It as Far as You Like' Says Wife of Millionaire," *Toronto Daily Star*, December 8, 1922, 16.

53   *Community Annals of the Sisters of St. Joseph*, 1, October 26, 1912, 468-469. Sisters of St. Joseph of Toronto Archives.

FIVE: **NAPOLEON AND HIS EMPIRE**

1   McNamara, *The Shuberts of Broadway*, 25.

2   Ibid.

3   Brockhouse, *The Royal Alexandra Theatre*, 66–68.

4   Ibid., 68.

5   Steve Travis, "The Rise and Fall of the Theatrical Syndicate," *Educational Theatre Journal* 10, no. 1 (March 1958): 36.

6   Brockhouse, *The Royal Alexandra Theatre*, 72.

7   McNamara, *The Shuberts of Broadway*, 22.

8   Ibid., 22–23.

9   "Two Leading Managers Dead," *Theatre Magazine Advertiser* IX (May–June 1905). Accessed via Fultonhistory.com. (Article references a "recent interview" with said description.)

10   McNamara, *The Shuberts of Broadway*, 32.

11   "At Least 120 Killed or Injured in Train Wreck," *Toronto Daily Star*, May 11, 1905, 5.

12   Ibid.

13   McNamara, *The Shuberts of Broadway*, 32.

14   "Two Leading Managers Dead."

15   McNamara, *The Shuberts of Broadway*, 41.

16   Ibid., 91.

17   Ibid., 72.

18   Ibid., 60–62.

19   Patrick B. O'Neill, "The British Canadian Theatrical Organization Society and the Trans-Canada Theatre Society," *Journal of Canadian Studies* 15, no. 1 (Spring 1980): 58.

20   *Dictionary of Canadian Biography*, s.v. "Mulock, Cawthra," by Alexander Reford, accessed February 13, 2019, http://www.biographi.ca/en/bio / mulock_cawthra_14E.html. (The money was administered by his father but most was "bequeathed in trust" to Cawthra.)

21   "Toronto's New Theatre: Royal Alexandra a Splendid Model of Construction," *Globe*, August 22, 1907, 12.

22   Brockhouse, *The Royal Alexandra Theatre*, 18. (The suggestion may have come from another man.)

23   1871 Census of Canada. District 47, Toronto East, Subdistrict: St. David's Ward.

24   "The Jews in Toronto," *Globe*, January 21, 1876, 2.

25   Ibid.

26   Brockhouse, *The Royal Alexandra Theatre*, 19.

27   Ibid., 20.

28   Ibid., 69.

29   Hector Charlesworth, "Lawrence Solman," *Saturday Night*, April 4, 1931, 8. (Charlesworth cites this incident in his obituary of Solman, but the exchange is the stuff of legend, as Mora Dianne Guthrie O'Neill points out in her 1976 PhD thesis "A Partial History of the Royal Alexandra Theatre, Toronto, Canada 1907-1939." She notes that the New York Telegraph had a similar take on the exchange, but the Canadian Film Weekly noted that it was Erlanger's business partner Marc Klaw who said the Royal Alex would make a good stable for the "horses of the carriage trade that patronized the Princess." Either way, the Syndicate was sour.)

30   Brockhouse, *The Royal Alexandra Theatre*, 81–85.

31   Anthony Vickery, "Two Patterns of Touring in Canada: 1896 to 1914," *Theatre Research in Canada* 31, no. 1 (2010), https://journals.lib.unb.ca /index.php/TRIC/article/view/18281/19698.

32   Lol Solman to J.J. Shubert, March 20, 1911. Box 180, SA.

33   Ibid.

34   "Toronto had a population of about 300,000 before the war, and—and there were close to 20,000 Jewish people among them. Pogroms and violence had sent Jewish people away from Russia and Europe, and many had settled in Canadian cities like Montreal and Toronto." https://www .jewishvirtuallibrary.org/toronto-canada-virtual-jewish-history-tour.

35   Rev. Jon Coburn, *I Kept My Powder Dry* (Toronto: Ryerson Press, 1950), 122.

36   J.J. Shubert to Lawrence Solman, November 12, 1926. Royal Alexandra Theatre 1923–1926, Box 180, Shubert Archive, New York (hereafter cited as SA). (This letter came later than the era in this chapter, but it reflects the conservative environment of the city.)

37   Lol Solman to Mr. Murry, January 4, 1921. Box 180, SA.

38   Coburn, *I Kept My Powder Dry*, 122.

39   Ibid., 121.

40   A.J. Small to George Nicolai, January 6, 1909. Box 84, SA.

41   Mary Brown, "Ambrose Small: A Ghost in Spite of Himself," 80–81.

42 Ibid., 81. (Additional information about the heat issue from email correspondence with University of Toronto professor Stephen Johnson.)

43 McNamara, *The Shuberts of Broadway*, 73.

44 Patrick B. O'Neill, "The British Canadian Theatrical Organization Society and the Trans-Canada Theatre Society," *Journal of Canadian Studies* 15, no. 1 (Spring 1980): 61.

45 Mary Brown, "Ambrose Small: A Ghost in Spite of Himself," 81. Brown writes that Ambrose was "responsible for the continuity of the Canadian theatrical tradition; without him, the record of the last 75 years would have been quite different."

46 A.J. Small to Lee Shubert, December 22, 1910. Box 2028, SA. (In this letter, Small realizes the Shuberts are not associated with the show that wronged him, as he'd earlier believed.)

47 Michael B. Leavitt, *Fifty Years in Theatrical Management* (New York: Broadway Publishing Co., 1912), 567.

48 Ibid.

49 H. Stuart Raleigh to "My Dear old Sammy," September 14, 1909. Folder 6, Grand Opera House, St. Catharines, SA.

50 "Victim of a Vidocq?" *New York Press*, June 30, 1896, 5. Accessed via Fultonhistory.com.

51 H. Stuart Raleigh to "My Dear old Sammy," SA.

52 Ibid.

53 Ibid.

54 J.J. Shubert to H. Stuart Raleigh, September 17, 1909. Folder 6, Grand Opera House, St. Catharines, SA.

55 Fred McClement, *The Strange Case of Ambrose Small* (Toronto: McClelland & Stewart, 1974), 17.

56 "Man Held in Auto Was Ambrose Small, Witness Declares," *Globe*, March 22, 1923, 1.

57 Charlesworth, *More Candid Chronicles*, 277.

58 Ibid., 276.

59 Ibid., 283.

60 McClement, *The Strange Case of Ambrose Small*, 39–41.

61 Sheila M.F. Johnston, *Let's Go to the Grand! 100 Years of Entertainment at London's Grand Theatre* (Toronto: Natural Heritage Books, 2001), 12.

62 Now called the Grand Theatre, it is one of the only pieces of the A.J. Small empire that still stands. Rebuilt after a fire in 1901, it could seat 1,850. A

renovation in the 1970s modernized most of the building, but the heart of the place is still the same. The proscenium arch and the secret room still exist, but there is no velvet bedspread or tasteful nudes. When I visited the theatre in December 2017, the former love nest of Ambrose Small was a no-nonsense storage room filled with hats. The maintenance man, who has been here since the pre-renovation days, told stories as we twisted through the bowels of the place, pointing out the vent that Ambrose used to peer through to spy on the audience to see if they liked the show. In the newer part of the theatre, staff were preparing for the next show. One member of the wardrobe team motioned to the far side of the room with her head as she nudged a costume through her sewing machine. That's where she saw Ambrose Small a few years ago, she said. Another night, he stole her scissors. It was a short trip for the ghost, because, as I was informed before leaving, Ambrose Small was buried by a willow tree on the nearby Thames River.

63   A.J. Small to Jack Doughty, May 19, no year. Copy. Doughty family collection.

64   Margaret Lovatt-Santon, *Down the Bluffs: A Memoir* (Oro-Medonte, Ontario: Le Temps H&S Times Publishing, 2016), 8.

65   Eliza and Jean were a few years older than Jack, Barbara was younger, but this cohort of Doughtys was close.

66   A.J. Small to Jack Doughty, May 23, 1913. Copy. Doughty family collection.

67   A.J. Small to Mr. Osgood, undated,1908. A.J. Small bookings 1907–1908, Klaw and Erlanger Collection, SA.

68   Charlesworth, *More Candid Chronicles*, 286.

69   Ambrose Small to J.W. Jacobs, June 11, 1908. Box 84, SA.

70   Ambrose Small to J.J. Shubert, December 2, 1911. Box 2028, SA.

71   Lol Solman to Jas. H. Decker, April 13, 1911. Box 180, SA. "Mr. Wiggins, the dramatic editor of the Star, one of our best friends in this City, will be in your city. . . . You will confer a great favor on me if you will take care of him for your different houses. . . . P.S. I would also like you to take care of Mr. Goss of the Toronto World for the same reason."

72   Bilkey, *Persons, Papers and Things*, 30.

73   Ibid., 30.

SIX: **WAR**

1   Christopher Armstrong (professor emeritus of history at York University),

in discussion with the author, March 13, 2018.

2   "Ambrose Small General Correspondence." Shubert Collection, Box 2028, SA.

3   Careless, *Toronto to 1918*, 149.

4   "First Convention Minutes." Chicago, November 26–28, 1915. Series 4, Box 17, Folder 3, International Federation of Catholic Alumnae collection (hereafter cited as IFCA), American Catholic Research Center and University Archives, Washington, D.C. (Many of these concerns were expressed by Rev. J.L. Belford, who spoke at the 1915 IFCA convention in Chicago, held at the Hotel Sherman on November 26 to November 28, 1915.)

5   Archbishop of New York John Farley to Mrs. James J. Sheeran, April 21, 1914. In Elizabeth Rose Kearney, "Pro Deo et Doctrina," *History of the International Federation of Catholic Alumnae*, undated, 12. Series 4, Box 17, Folder 6, IFCA. ("A sketch of the growth of the Federation from its inception to the beginning of the fifth year of its organic life", undated [circa 1919, five years from inception].)

6   "Helping to Canadianize the Young Newcomers," *Globe* (Toronto), February 28, 1914, 10.

7   Kearney, "Pro Deo et Doctrina," 5 and 7.

8   Ibid., 58.

9   Speech, Mr. E.V.P. Schneiderhahn in "IFCA Third Biennial Convention Minutes," May 30 to June 3, 1919, 88-89. Series 4, Box 15, Folder 4: Convention Minutes, IFCA.

10 Ibid., 98. "I would like to move a standing vote of thanks to the speakers," Theresa Small said after the speech as the entire hall gave a standing ovation.

11 Coburn, *I Kept My Powder Dry*, 123.

12 McClement, *The Strange Case of Ambrose Small*, 15.

13 "Second Convention in Maryland." Series 4, Box 18, Folder 8: Second and Fifth Convention Minutes, 1916 and 1922, IFCA.

14 Theresa's speech is in the IFCA report for the year 1916–1917, page 66. Series 6, Box 22, Folder 9: Baltimore Convention 1916, IFCA.

15 Ibid.

16 "A Delightful Alumnae Function," *St. Joseph Lilies*, 1916–1917 5, no. 4 (March 1917): 93. Accessed at Archive.org.

17 "Governor's Conference Minutes 1919," 22. Series 4, Box 17, Folder 5, IFCA.

18 Ibid.

19 "IFCA Third Biennial Convention Minutes." Series 4, Box 15, Folder 4:

May 30 to June 3, 1919, IFCA.

20 Mark G. McGowan, *The Imperial Irish: Canada's Irish Catholics Fight the Great War, 1914–1918* (Montreal/Kingston: McGill-Queen's University Press, 2017), 127.

21 *Community Records of the Sisters of St. Joseph of Toronto, 1914–1932*, vol. 2, December 31, 1914, page 489. Sisters of St. Joseph of Toronto Archives.

22 "Irish Regiment of Canada Correspondence and a Brief History," 1931–1934. Series 2165, File 27, CTA.

23 McGowan, *The Imperial Irish*, 126.

24 "National Annual Meeting of the Imperial Order Daughters of the Empire," May 27 to June 1, 1918, pages 3–21. IODE Canada Archives, Toronto.

25 "I.O.D.E. Educational Work in Toronto," *Echoes* (The Official Organ of the Imperial Order of the Daughters of the Empire) March 1919 issue, 31. IODE Canada Archives, Toronto.

26 "Alumnae Item," *St. Joseph Lilies*, 1918–1919, no. 1 (June 1918): 106, accessed online at archive.org.

27 "Irish Battalion Has Active Woman Manager," undated. Scrapbook 18, Sisters of St. Joseph of Toronto Archives.

28 Ibid.

29 "When the Irish Started," *Irish Canadian*, Toronto, April 1917, 20. Fonds 253, Series 2165, File 11, CTA.

30 McGowan, *The Imperial Irish*, 123.

31 Ibid., 137.

32 Ambrose Small to Chas. Osgood, September 2, 1914, in Klaw and Erlanger collection, Shubert Archive, New York.

33 Anthony Vickery, "Two Patterns of Touring in Canada: 1896 to 1914," *Theatre Research in Canada* 31, no. 1 (2010), https://journals.lib.unb.ca /index.php/TRIC/article/view/18281/19698.

34 McNamara, *The Shuberts of Broadway*, 74.

35 J.J. Shubert to Lol Solman, September 13, 1914. Box 180, SA.

36 J.J. Shubert to Lol Solman, March 2, 1915. Box 180, SA.

37 Clara Smith to Ambrose Small, June 27, 1918, *Toronto Star Weekly*, April 19, 1924, 6.

38 Clara Smith to Ambrose Small, March 18, 1917, *Toronto Star Weekly*, April 19, 1924, 4.

39 Clara Smith to Ambrose Small, March 29, 1917, *Toronto Star Weekly*, April 19,

1924, 4.

40 "Captain Bruce Hunter—Our Chaplain," *The Irish Canadian*, April 1917, 42. Fonds 253, Series 2165, File 11, CTA.

41 Edward Hammond, "O.P.P. memorandum re disappearance of Ambrose Small," page 7, line 46, RG 4-123-0-1, 1936, AO.

42 Ibid.

SEVEN: THE MILLION-DOLLAR MAN

1 "Service Record of Douglas Foster Jennings," Regimental number 36425, RG 150, Accession 1992–93/166, Box 4822-15, Item 479738, LAC.

2 Ibid.

3 Clara Smith to Ambrose Small, August 5, 1918, *Toronto Star Weekly*, April 19, 1924, 4.

4 Clara Smith to Ambrose Small, June 24, 1918, *Toronto Star Weekly*, April 19, 1924, 4.

5 Clara Smith to Ambrose Small, July 26, 1918, *Toronto Star Weekly*, April 19, 1924, 4.

6 Clara Smith to Ambrose Small, August 5, 1918, *Toronto Star Weekly*, April 19, 1924, 4. (She responds to him in the letter.)

7 Clara Smith to Ambrose Small, August 5, 1918. *Toronto Star Weekly*. April 19, 1924, 4.

8 Clara Smith to Ambrose Small, November 4, 1919, *Toronto Star Weekly*, April 19, 1924, 6.

9 Ibid.

10 Ibid.

11 Clara Smith to Ambrose Small, undated letter, c. 1919, *Toronto Star Weekly*, April 19, 1924, 6.

12 Clara Smith to Ambrose Small, undated letter, c. 1919, *Toronto Star Weekly*, April 19, 1924, 6.

13 Ibid.

14 Ibid.

15 Clara Smith to Ambrose Small, November 24, 1919, *Toronto Star Weekly*, April 19, 1924, 6.

16 David Phillips (Environment Canada senior climatologist), in discussion with the author via email, March 14, 2018.

17   Careless, *Toronto to 1918*, 149.

18   Ibid., 152.

19   R.L. Brackin, "Dower Act Needs Radical Amendment," *Globe*, September 18, 1919, 11.

20   Joseph Dyk, "Legal Rights of Wives," *Globe*, March 25, 1931.

21   "Says He Gave Big Check to Small Late Monday," *Toronto Daily Star*, March 22, 1922, 1.

22   Clara Smith to Ambrose Small, November 24, 1919, *Toronto Star Weekly*, April 19, 1924, 6.

23   "Says He Gave Big Check to Small Late Monday," 1.

24   "I joked about it," Mr. Shaughnessy related, "because I recall saying that I ought to give it to Mrs. Small. Mr. Small replied that that would be all right and said he would do that. He handed the cheque to Mrs. Small." "Says He Gave Big Check to Small Late Monday," 1.

25   "Small's Former Cook Insists No 'Mystery Pervaded Household,'" *Toronto Daily Star*, November 6, 1935, 3.

26   Max Braithwaite, "The Rise and Fall of the Dumbells," *Maclean's*, January 1, 1952, 20–40, https://archive.macleans.ca/article/1952/1/1/the-rise-and-fall-of-the-dumbells.

27   Ibid.

28   Johnston, *Let's Go to the Grand!*, 42.

29   "Says He Gave Big Check to Small Late Monday," 1.

30   "Barber's Statement Draws Long Letter from Chief Dickson," *Globe*, March 23, 1922, 13.

31   Edward Hammond, "Brief Circumstances Surrounding the Disappearance of Ambrose J. Small," page 1, RG 4-123-0-1, 1936, AO.

32   "Sure Small Did Not Leave Voluntarily," *Toronto Daily Star*, June 22, 1920, 9.

33   Ibid. (Flock's testimony over the years was consistent on this timeline. He also gave the account to many newspapers.)

34   Weekly theatre listings, *Evening Telegram*, December 1, 1919.

35   Statement of Alfred Elson, given on May 20, 1936. In "Copies of 1919–1921 report and statements regarding the Ambrose Small case; transcriptions of 1936 statements regarding the case," RG 4-123-0-2, AO (1919–1936).

EIGHT: THE DETECTIVE

1   "Ontario Provincial Police Criminal Investigation Records—missing persons

files," RG 23-26-1, AO (1914–1921).

2   "Sure Small did not leave voluntarily," *Star*, June 22, 1920, 9.

3   "Daughter of France Has a Full Program," *Toronto Daily Star*, December 9, 1919, 2.

4   Hammond, "Brief Circumstances Surrounding the Disappearance of Ambrose J. Small," page 10, line 72, RG 4-123-0-1, 1936, AO.

5   Ibid., page 15, line 115.

6   Toronto Police Service, *Proud of Our Past, Confident of Our Future: A History of Policing in Toronto* (Toronto: Toronto Police Service [hereafter cited as TPS], 2000).

7   Ibid.

8   "Annual report of the chief constable of the city of Toronto," 1914, Fonds 2, Series 60, Iten 893, CTA.

9   "Annual report of the chief constable of the city of Toronto," 1918. Fonds 2, Series 60, Item 897, CTA.

10 "Annual report of the chief constable of the city of Toronto," 1914. Fonds 2, Series 60, Item 893, CTA.

11 Greg Marquis, "The Police as a Social Service in Early Twentieth-Century Toronto," Social History. Vol 25, No. 50, November 1992, 263. Marquis notes that Catholic made up about a tenth of the force in 1920, which tracked with the percentage of Catholics in the population.

12 "Annual report of the chief constable of the city of Toronto," 1914. Fonds 2, Series 60, Item 893, CTA.

13 Marquis, 264.

14 "Annual report of the chief constable of the city of Toronto," 1919. Fonds 2, Series 60, Item 898, CTA.

15 Ibid.

16 "First reported disappearance of Ambrose Small." In "Copies of 1919–1921 report and statements regarding the Ambrose Small case; transcriptions of 1936 statements regarding the case," RG 4-123-0-2, AO (1919–1936).

17 "Police School Opens," *Globe*, December 14, 1931, 12.

18 "Detectives Duty Roll," 1915. Fonds 38, Series 148, File 4, CTA (1915).

19 "Drug Crusade Leads to Summoning Doctors: Detectives Claim They Are Unearthing a Serious State of Affairs," *Globe*, November 9, 1915, 6.

20 Dahn D. Higley, *O.P.P.: The History of the Ontario Provincial Police Force* (Ottawa: Queen's Printer, 1984), 29.

21 Ibid., 40.

22   John Wilson Murray, *Memoirs of a Great Canadian Detective: Incidents in the Life of John Wilson Murray* (London: William Heinemann,1904; Toronto: William Collins Sons & Co, 1978), 23.

23   Higley, *O.P.P.: The History of the Ontario Provincial Police Force*, 49.

24   Murray, *Memoirs of a Great Canadian Detective*, 77. (As Murray relates in this case, he listened as the young farmer talked about escaping his burning house, but he noticed a strange burn on the man's neck. It looked like he had branded himself with a poker. "A mere blister would have aroused no suspicion, but he had pressed the iron in so deep that if a flame had inflicted so severe a burn on the back of his neck, it would have scorched the hair off and blistered the back of the head." Murray walked into the husk of the charred house and began his "systematic sifting of the debris," with a crew of locals. He saw the big stove was burned molten on the inside, but not the outside, and found a butcher's knife with a bent tip, two pieces of bone, and a matted bit of bedding. He scooped these items into his evidence bag and took the train back to Toronto, where he asked a professor if he could find traces of blood on the items. The professor ran some tests [Murray doesn't describe these] and determined it was the blood of a female, and the bone fragments came from a spine and an ankle. The farmer was convicted.)

25   Ibid., 21.

26   Careless, *Toronto to 1918*, 100.

27   Metropolitan Toronto Police Force, *Toronto Police Force: A Brief Account of the Force Since Its Re-Organization in 1859 up to the Present Date, Together with a Short Biographical Sketch of the Present Board of Police Commissioners, Prepared to Accompany the Photograph of the Force to Be Sent to the Colonial Exhibition to Be Held in London, England, in May, 1886* (Toronto: E.F. Clark, Printer, 1886), 5. Baldwin Collection, Toronto Reference Library.

28   John C. Weaver, "Crimes, Constables and Courts: Order and Transgression in a Canadian City, 1816-1970," (Montreal: McGill-Queen's University Press, 1995), 171.

29   "Charged with Shoplifting," *Globe*, March 10, 1914, 8.

30   "Grabbed Revolver in Time," *Globe*, July 30, 1912, 9.

31   "Prisoner Did Not Faint: Wife Said He Would," *Globe*, February 28, 1913, 8.

32   "Commits Murder on the Street," *Globe*, March 7, 1910, 1.

33   "Theft of Candy is Charged," *Globe*, April 22, 1910, 4.

34   "Negro was Remanded," *Globe*, July 3, 1909, 5.

35   "Statement of James Cowan and Thomas Flynn re. disappearance of
      A.J. Small," dated December, 17, 1919, but occurred December 16, 1919.
      In "Copies of 1919–1921 report and statements regarding the Ambrose
      Small case; transcriptions of 1936 statements regarding the case," RG
      4-123-0-2, AO (1919–1936).

36   Ibid.

37   McClement, *The Strange Case of Ambrose Small*, 19. (The police notes that
      survive do not give any indication of where they were sitting or drinking
      inside the house.)

38   "First reported disappearance of A.J. Small," summary of interview with
      Theresa Small on December 16, 1919. In "Copies of 1919–1921 report and
      statements regarding the Ambrose Small case; transcriptions of 1936
      statements regarding the case," RG 4-123-0-2, AO (1919–1936).

39   Ibid.

40   Ibid.

41   Ibid.

42   "First reported disappearance of A.J. Small," summary of interview with
      Theresa Small on December 17, 1919. In "Copies of 1919–1921 report
      and statements regarding the Ambrose Small case; transcriptions of 1936
      statements regarding the case," RG 4-123-0-2, AO (1919–1936).

43   Ibid.

44   "First reported disappearance of A.J. Small," summary of interview with
      Theresa Small on December 18, 1919. In "Copies of 1919–1921 report and
      statements regarding the Ambrose Small case; transcriptions of 1936
      statements regarding the case," RG 4-123-0-2, AO (1919–1936).

45   "First reported disappearance of A.J. Small," summary of interview with
      Theresa Small on December 19, 1919. In "Copies of 1919–1921 report and
      statements regarding the Ambrose Small case; transcriptions of 1936
      statements regarding the case," RG 4-123-0-2, AO (1919–1936).

46   S.W. Hicks to E.W.M. Flock, January 5, 1920. In E.W.M. Flock Papers
      1919–1924, Envelope 4, Toronto Reference Library, Ontario, Canada.

47   E.W.M. Flock to H.J. Wright, "RE A.J. Small," January 5, 1920. In E.W.M.
      Flock Papers 1919–1924, Envelope 1, Toronto Reference Library, Ontario,
      Canada.

48   Edward Hammond, "O.P.P. memorandum re disappearance of Ambrose
      Small," 11, point 79, RG 4-123-0-1, AO (1936).

NINE: **THE INVESTIGATION BEGINS**

1   Edward H. Smith, "Baffling Mystery of Missing Canadian Millionaire," *St. Louis Post-Dispatch*, August 1, 1920, 79.

2   Ibid.

3   Ibid.

4   "Thinks Small Has Met with Some Accident," *Buffalo Commercial*, January 6, 1920, 2.

5   "No Light on the Mystery," *Toronto Evening Telegram*, January 9, 1919.

6   "The Worth of a Millionaire," *Toronto Evening Telegram*, January 7, 1920, 18.

7   "Statement of Raphael Savein, re Ambrose J. Small," January 10, 1920. In "Copies of 1919–1921 report and statements regarding the Ambrose Small case; transcriptions of 1936 statements regarding the case," RG 4-123-0-2, AO (1919–1936).

8   Jack Doughty letter to "My Dear Bill," December 7, 1919. Copy. Doughty family collection.

9   "Cannot Locate John Doughty," *Toronto World*, January 10, 1920, 1.

10   "John Doughty Wrote He Was Quitting Show," *Toronto Daily Star*, December 4, 1920, 11.

11   "Statement of James Cowan and Thomas Flynn, re disappearance of A.J. Small," referencing December 31, 1919, interview with Cowan. In "Copies of 1919–1921 report and statements regarding the Ambrose Small case; transcriptions of 1936 statements regarding the case," RG 4-123-0-2, AO (1919–1936).

12   "Statement of James Cowan and Thomas Flynn, re disappeareance of A.J. Small," December 17, 1919 (Dated that way, but includes information from end of December), AO file.

13   Summary of Clara Smith interview, January 10, 1920. In "Copies of 1919–1921 report and statements regarding the Ambrose Small case; transcriptions of 1936 statements regarding the case," RG 4-123-0-2, AO (1919–1936).

14   Ibid.

15   "Statement made to Bud Lennon on or about 9 Months ago by John Dowdey," January 13, 1920. In "Copies of 1919–1921 report and statements regarding the Ambrose Small case; transcriptions of 1936 statements regarding the case," RG 4-123-0-2, AO (1919–1936).

16   Ibid.

17   Ibid.

18   "Re. John Doughty. Statement of Frederick Osborne," taken on January 25, 1920. In "Copies of 1919–1921 report and statements regarding the Ambrose Small case; transcriptions of 1936 statements regarding the case," RG 4-123-0-2, AO (1919–1936).

19   Ibid.

20   "Story of Ernest Reid, 63 Wineva Avenue, re: John Doughty," taken on January 10, 1921. In "Copies of 1919–1921 report and statements regarding the Ambrose Small case; transcriptions of 1936 statements regarding the case," RG 4-123-0-2, AO (1919–1936).

21   Ibid.

22   "Statement of George Kennedy," taken on May 24, 1920. In "Copies of 1919–1921 report and statements regarding the Ambrose Small case; transcriptions of 1936 statements regarding the case," RG 4-123-0-2, AO (1919–1936).

23   "Statement of William Wampole," undated. In "Copies of 1919–1921 report and statements regarding the Ambrose Small case; transcriptions of 1936 statements regarding the case," RG 4-123-0-2, AO (1919–1936).

24   Ibid.

25   Margaret Lovatt-Santon, *Down the Bluffs*, 9. Jack also lived at 26 Langley Avenue for a time, during his second marriage.

26   "Lean to Abduction Theory," *Toronto Telegram*, January 13, 1920.

27   "Statement of Mrs. Eliza Lovatt, 8 Kingswood Road, Toronto Re – John Doughty," taken on January 24, 1920. In "Copies of 1919–1921 report and statements regarding the Ambrose Small case; transcriptions of 1936 statements regarding the case," RG 4-123-0-2, AO (1919–1936).

28   Summary of William Doughty statement, taken on February 26, 1920. In "Copies of 1919–1921 report and statements regarding the Ambrose Small case; transcriptions of 1936 statements regarding the case," RG 4-123-0-2, AO (1919–1936).

29   "RE: John Doughty," summary of interview with Eliza Lovatt on May 4, 1920. In "Copies of 1919–1921 report and statements regarding the Ambrose Small case; transcriptions of 1936 statements regarding the case," RG 4-123-0-2, AO (1919–1936). (Jack Doughty married Connie Spears in 1917, but it was a tumultuous union. A baby girl had been born in 1918, but she died a few days after her birth, and the couple eventually split. Connie told Detective Mitchell that Jack had "affections" for another woman, and there were many "unkindnesses" toward her.

30   Jean Doughty (in police court, December 30, 1920). In Rex vs. John
      Doughty, RG 22-5871, General Sessions of the Peace, County of York,
      File 224-20, AO.

31   "Doughty Family Meant to Hand Bonds to Raney," *Toronto Daily Star*,
      March 23, 1921, 2.

32   Ibid.

TEN: **ABSENTEE**

1   "Here's $50,000 Reward for You If You Find This Missing Millionaire,"
      Saskatoon Daily Star, August 7, 1920, 9.

2   "Would Protect Estates of Disappearing Men," April 23, 1920. *Newspaper
      Hansard* at AO.

3   Ibid.

4   "Accounts Passed Regarding Estate Ambrose Small," *Toronto Daily Star*,
      November 23, 1921, sec. 2, 1.

5   Ibid.

6   Edward H. Smith, "Baffling Mystery of Missing Canadian Millionaire,"
      St. Louis Post-Dispatch, August 1, 1920, 81.

7   "States Small was discussed by men in park," *Globe*, June 10, 1920, 9.

8   Correspondence, medium to E.W.M. Flock, April 14, 1922. In E.W.M. Flock
      Papers 1919–1924, Envelope 1, Toronto Reference Library, Ontario, Canada.

9   "Theatre Man Is Approached on Kidnapping," *Globe*, June 24, 1920, 9.

10   "Hopeless Cripple Is Believed to Be Lost Millionaire," *Press and Sun-Bulletin*
      (Binghamton, New York), August 15, 1921, 1.

11   "That Wisconsin Clue Turns Out Worthless," *Globe*, October 22, 1920, 8.

12   C.E.M. Churchill to Deputy Attorney General Edward Bayly, October 24,
      1920, "A.G.O.: Letters from Cranks," RG 4-32, AO (1920).

13   "That Wisconsin Clue Turns Out Worthless," 8.

14   "A.G.O.: Letters from Cranks," RG 4-32, AO (1920).

15   "Alumnae Notes," *St. Joseph Lilies*, 1920–1921 9, no. 4 (March 1921), 112.
      Accessed at Archive.org.

16   Ibid., 114–115.

17   Toronto City Police note on anonymous letters about Theresa Small, recorded
      June 14, 1920. In "Copies of 1919–1921 report and statements regarding the
      Ambrose Small case; transcriptions of 1936 statements regarding the case,"
      RG 4-123-0-2, AO (1919–1936).

18   "Re Mr. Small's safety deposit box, Dominion Bank, King and Yonge," dated
      May 7, 1920. In "Copies of 1919–1921 report and statements regarding the
      Ambrose Small case; transcriptions of 1936 statements regarding the case,"
      RG 4-123-0-2, AO (1919–1936).

19   Ibid.

20   "Says Doughty Had Attorney Power," *Toronto World*, March 3, 1921, 12.

21   Ibid. (It would later be revealed that Theresa was "given" the other $200,000
      by Ambrose in celebration of the deal—which corresponds with the
      December 1 visits. The amount that Doughty was alleged to have taken at
      some points in police notes appears as $150,000, but at the later trial, the
      figure was $105,000.)

22   "Returns True Bill Against Doughty," *Globe*, January 7, 1921, 6.

23   "Re – The story of Charles Roach about A.J. Small," May 22, 1920. In
      "Copies of 1919–1921 report and statements regarding the Ambrose Small
      case; transcriptions of 1936 statements regarding the case," RG 4-123-0-2,
      AO (1919–1936).

24   Ibid.

25   Ibid.

26   Ibid.

27   "RE: John Doughty," summary of interview with Eliza Lovatt on May 4, 1920.
      In "Copies of 1919–1921 report and statements regarding the Ambrose Small
      case; transcriptions of 1936 statements regarding the case," RG 4-123-0-2, AO
      (1919–1936).

28   "Two Warrants Issued for Small's Secretary," *Toronto Daily Star*, June 18, 1920, 1.

29   Smith, "Baffling Mystery of Missing Canadian Millionaire," 81.

30   "Police Seek John Doughty," *Star*, June 19, 1920, 28.

ELEVEN: **THE BALLAD OF CHARLES BENJAMIN COOPER**

1   "The Creation of Willamette Falls," Museum of the Oregon Territory,
      Oregon City. Visited September 27, 2017.

2   "Native Land Rights and the Reservation System," Museum of the Oregon
      Territory, Oregon City. Visited September 27, 2017.

3   "Oregon, Country, Territory, State, City," Museum of the Oregon Territory,
      Oregon City. Visited September 27, 2017.

4   "Oregon City Municipal Elevator," Museum of the Oregon Territory, Oregon
      City. Visited September 27, 2017.

5   "Doughty Tells His Own Story to the *Star*," *Toronto Daily Star*, November 27, 1920, 1.

6   "Doughty Was Well Liked by People He Lived With," *Oregon Daily Journal* (Portland), November 24, 1920, 2. (One Oregon newspaper account notes the Strain family lived at Centre Street, but the 1920 U.S. Census shows the Strain family at Bluff Street, with several boarders living with them. The census was taken in January 1920, and Jack Doughty/Charles Benjamin Cooper was not listed—he arrived in Oregon City later that winter, according to his account. The *Toronto Daily Star*, in its coverage, gave the address as 306 Bluff Street.)

7   He mentions his pay bump in his post-arrest train interviews.

8   "Stray Shorthand Note Gave Doughty a Boost," *Toronto Star*, November 25, 1920, 1.

9   "Doughty Taken into Custody," *Statesman Journal* (Salem, Oregon), November 24, 1920, 1.

10   "Arrested When He Bared His Head," *Boston Post*, December 5, 1920, 56. (The story of how Doughty was spotted had several iterations. In another one, he came into the mill on a Sunday to do the time cards, and wasn't wearing his hat.)

11   Ibid.

12   "Unfair Treatment of Men in Custody," *Toronto Daily Star*, December 2, 1920, 2. (At a public commission, Toronto Police Inspector Guthrie explained the provision to pay for investigation costs outside of the province is an archaic holdout in the Criminal Code. The costs were reimbursed by the Crown attorney if a guilty conviction was secured, but the government would pay none of the out of province costs until that time.)

13   "Doughty Cheerful; Says that Arrest Is Load off Mind," *Toronto World*, November 24, 1920, 1.

14   Ibid., 2.

15   "Doughty Tells His Own Story to the *Star*," 2.

16   Austin Mitchell, examined by Mr. Greer at Police Court, December 30, 1920, page 2. In Rex vs. John Doughty, RG 22-5871, General Sessions of the Peace, County of York, File 224-20, AO.

17   "Doughty on Way East to Answer Charge of Theft," *Oregon Daily Journal* (Portland), November 24, 1920, 2.

18   Ibid.

19   "Doughty Tells Story of Life in the West," *Toronto Daily Star*, November 24, 1920, 1.

20   W.H. Kesterton, *A History of Journalism in Canada* (Toronto: McClelland & Stewart, 1967), 86.

21   "Doughty on Way East to Answer Charge of Theft," 2.

22   Ibid.

23   "Doughty Doubts Small Is Alive," *Oregon Daily Journal* (Portland), November 25, 1920, 1.

24   "Mrs. A.J. Small Not Surprised at Doughty's Arrest," *Toronto World*, November 24, 1920, 1.

25   "Doughty Tells Why He Changed His Name," *Toronto Daily Star*, November 27, 1920, 1.

26   "Goes Back to Tell Mystery of Millionaire," *Bismarck Daily Tribune*, November 26, 1920, 8.

27   "The Northwest: A Baltimorean's Interesting Description of a Trip Across the Continent," *The Sun* (Baltimore), August 27, 1898, 6.

28   "Doughty Tells His Own Story to the *Star*," 1.

29   Ibid.

30   E.W. Flack, "Veil of Mystery Draws Tighter over Small Case," *Oregon Sunday Journal* (Portland), December 5, 1920, 12.

31   "Statement of John Doughty," November 28, 1920. In Rex vs. John Doughty, RG 22-5871, General Sessions of the Peace, County of York, File 224-20, AO.

32   Ibid.

33   Ibid.

34   Ibid.

35   "Doughty Is Confident Can Prove Innocence," *Toronto Daily Star*, November 29, 1920, 11.

TWELVE: **HOMECOMING**

1   "Recovery of Sister Gladdens J. Doughty," *Toronto Daily Star*, November 29, 1920, 12.

2   "John Doughty Is Received on Arrival as an Old Friend," *Toronto Daily Star*, November 29, 1920, 1.

3   Ibid.

4   Ibid., 2.

5   "105,000 in Bonds Found at Mrs. Lovatt's Home," *Toronto Daily Star*, November 29, 1920, 1. (The details about the chisel and hammer came later—police were still being coy at this point.)

6   Lindsay Scotton, "A Quiet Revolutionary," *Toronto Star*, September 14, 1989, L1 and L4. Scotton quotes a *Montreal Daily Witness* article of 1897.

7   Ibid.

8   *Dictionary of Canadian Biography*, s.v. "Denison, George Taylor (1839–1925)," by Norman Knowles, accessed October 26, 2018, http://www.biographi.ca/en/bio/denison_george_taylor_1839_1925_15E.html.

9   Ibid.

10   Ibid.

11   Ibid.

12   "Doughty Is Remanded But Bail Is Refused," *Toronto Daily Star*, November 29, 1920, 2.

13   "105,000 in Bonds Found at Mrs. Lovatt's Home," *Toronto Daily Star*, November 29, 1920, 1. (The details about the chisel and hammer came later—police were still being coy at this point.)

14   "No Clue to A.J. Small," *Toronto Daily Star*, December 9, 1920, 2.

15   "Doughty Receives No Visitors at the Jail," *Toronto Daily Star*, November 30, 1920, 2.

16   "Remember Doughty," *Toronto Daily Star*, December 13, 1920, 18.

17   "Second Charge Stands against Jack Doughty," *Globe*, January 4, 1921, 6.

THIRTEEN: JACK DOUGHTY ON TRIAL

1   McClement, *The Strange Case of Ambrose Small*, 87.

2   "Keenly Interested in Fate of Jack Doughty," *Toronto World*, March 23, 1921, 12.

3   "Doughty Faces Judge and Jury on Theft Charge," *Toronto Daily Star*, March 22, 1921, 1.

4   Ibid.

5   "Isidore F. Hellmuth," Tennis Hall of Fame, Tennis Canada website, accessed October 15, 2018, http://www.tenniscanada.com/hall-of-fame/isidore-f-hellmuth.

6   Constance Backhouse and Nancy Backhouse, *The Heiress vs. the Establishment: Mrs. Campbell's Campaign for Legal Justice* (Vancouver: UBC Press for Osgoode Society for Canadian Legal History, 2004), 82. (For more on Hellmuth's reputation, see page 265, note 2. The book is a reprint of Elizabeth Campbell's legal odyssey for her mother's estate, with detailed commentary in the footnotes from legal scholars Constance and Nancy Backhouse.)

7   Lawyers for the Crown were hired on a part-time basis and sometimes for one signal case, legal scholar Constance Backhouse wrote in an email to the author. Ontario didn't move to a system of full-time Crowns until later in the twentieth century.

8   J. Patrick Boyer, *A Passion for Justice: How 'Vinegar Jim' McRuer Became Canada's Greatest Law Reformer* (Toronto: Blue Butterfly, 2008), 67.

9   "Reserve decision on Appeal Leave for John Doughty," *Toronto Daily Star*, May 2, 1921, 1.

10   "Says Doughty Had Proposed to Kill Small," *Globe*, March 23, 1921, 1.

11   Ibid.

12   "A.J. Small's Last Known Movements Told by Wife," *Toronto Daily Star*, March 23, 1921, 3.

13   "Says Doughty Had Proposed to Kill Small," *Globe*, March 23, 1921, 1.

14   "A.J. Small's Last Known Movements Told by Wife," *Toronto Daily Star*, March 23, 1921, 3.

15   "Says Doughty Had Proposed to Kill Small," 1. (In his charge to the jury, Judge Denton told jurors to ignore the evidence of Fred Daville, concerned by the way the printer's story had grown more detailed since police court. "I would not punish a mouse on the evidence of that man," Denton said.)

16   "A.J. Small's Last Known Movements Told by Wife," 3.

17   "Says Doughty Had Proposed to Kill Small," 1.

18   Ibid.

19   "A.J. Small's Last Known Movements Told by Wife," 3.

20   Ibid.

21   Ibid.

22   "Says Doughty Had Proposed to Kill Small," 1.

23   "A.J. Small's Last Known Movements Told by Wife," 3.

24   Ibid.

25   "Says Doughty Had Attorney Power," *Toronto World*, March 23, 1921, 12.

26   "Doughty Family Meant to Hand Bonds to Raney," *Toronto Daily Star*, March 23, 1921, 1.

27   Ibid., 2.

28   Ibid., 2.

29   "Says Doughty Thought Bonds Safe in Vault," *Globe*, March 24, 1921, 1.

30   "Judge Decides Case Must Go to the Jury," *Toronto Daily Star*, March 24, 1921, 3.

31   Ibid.

32   "Jury Finds Doughty Guilty of Bond Theft," *Toronto Daily Star*, March 24, 1921, 1.

33   Ibid.

34   "Doughty Guilty of Stealing Bonds," *Toronto World*, March 25, 1921, 12.

35   "Doughty within Attorney Power Says Hellmuth," *Toronto Daily Star*, March 24, 1921, 2.

36   "Doughty Guilty of Stealing Bonds," *Toronto World*, March 25, 1921, 12.

37   "Doughty within Attorney Power Says Hellmuth," *Toronto Daily Star*, March 24, 1921, 2.

38/   "Jury Finds Doughty Guilty of Bond Theft," *Toronto Daily Star*, March 24, 1921, 1.

39   "The Twelve Men Who Found Jack Doughty Guilty," *Toronto World*, March 25, 1921, 1.

40   "On Way to Kingston, Doughty Tells of Jail," *Toronto Daily Star*, May 14, 1921, 1.

41   "Doughty Alimony Judgment Stands," *Globe*, April 16, 1921, 15.

42   "Doughty Taken to Kingston without Family's Knowledge," *Toronto Daily Star*, May 14, 1921, 21.

43   "Five Justices Agree, Deny Doughty Appeal," *Toronto Daily Star*, May 6, 1921, 1.

44   "Doughty to Serve Six Years in Pen: Appeal for Leniency by Counsel Because Bonds Are Recovered," *Globe*, May 10, 1921, 6.

45   "Drop Kidnap Charge against J. Doughty?" *Toronto Daily Star*, May 7, 1921, 4. (The *Star* noted that because there was no retrial on the theft conviction, it was rumoured the Crown would accept a not guilty plea without a trial.)

46   "On Way to Kingston, Doughty Tells of Jail," 1.

47   "On Way to Kingston, Doughty Tells of Jail," *Toronto Daily Star*, May 14, 1921, 1.

48   Ibid.

49   Ibid.

50   "John Doughty." In Historical Inmate Ledgers, Kingston Penitentiary, rg 73, Volume 562, File 17-8, Item 750, LAC.

51   "John Doughty." In the *Convict Register & Description Book*, Kingston Penitentiary, Catalog CR-92-001, Correctional Services of Canada Museum.

52 Cameron Willis, "Summary of Information." (Description of Kingston prison and practices at the time provided by Willis, research assistant at the Correctional Services of Canada Museum, in email of September 1, 2017.)

53 "Doughty Taken to Kingston without Family's Knowledge," 21.

54 Anonymous letter to Clara Brett Martin, April 1921. Doughty family collection. Transcribed by Carol Doughty.

FOURTEEN: THE FORGOTTEN SISTERS AND THE NOTORIOUS AGITATOR

1   Registers of incoming correspondence to the Department of the Attorney General, RG 4-31, vol. 45, AO (1920).

2   Registers of incoming correspondence to the Department of the Attorney General, RG 4-31, vol. 45, Entry D985, AO (1920).

3   "Sisters of Ambrose J. Small Approach Attorney-General," *Toronto World*, April 17, 1920.

4   McClement, *The Strange Case of Ambrose Small*, 31.

5   "Re- Disappearance of Ambrose Small," undated, Ambrose Small Missing persons file, Toronto Police Museum. (No paperwork survives from these hearings in the OPP files at the Ontario Archives.)

6   Chief Constable Sudbury to commissioner APP, April 22, 1921. In "No. 132 Sullivan P" VII.23 GRI975.0125/351, PAA.

7   Samuel Dickson to Alfred Cuddy, April 15, 1922. In "No. 132 Sullivan P" VII.23 GRI975.0125/351, Provincial Archives of Alberta, Edmonton (hereafter cited as PAA).

8   Alfred Cuddy to Samuel Dickson, April 21, 1922. In "No. 132 Sullivan P" VII.23 GRI975.0125/351, PAA.

9   "Information from the Service File of Patrick Crowley Sullivan." In "No. 132 Sullivan P" VII.23 GRI975.0125/351, PAA.

10 Patrick Sullivan to chief commissioner APP, January 20, 1919. In "No. 132 Sullivan P" VII.23 GRI975.0125/351, PAA.

11 "Information from the Service File of Patrick Crowley Sullivan." In "No. 132 Sullivan P" VII.23 GRI975.0125/351, PAA.

12 H.N. Trickey to commanding officer APP, Peace River, Alberta, July 26, 1919. In "No. 132 Sullivan P" VII.23 GRI975.0125/351, PAA.

13   "Woman Accused of Murder of Husband at Grande Prairie," *Peace River Record*, October 24, 1919, 1.

14   Lottie Trollee, "Alberta's She Devil," *Thunder*, Thunder Publishing Co. (Toronto), June 6, 1931, 13. At Thomas Fisher Rare Book Library, Rare Book M-10 00244. (This was a Patrick Sullivan–associated magazine, and probably written by Sullivan himself under a pen name.)

15   Ibid.

16   Ibid.

17   Lottie Trollee, "Alberta's She Devil," *Thunder*, Thunder Publishing Co. (Toronto) June 13, 1931,13. At Thomas Fisher Rare Book Library, Rare Book M-10 00244.

18   "Hythe Murder Case Held at Grande Prairie," *Grande Prairie Herald*, January 20, 1920, 1.

19   "Woman Accused of Murder of Husband at Grande Prairie," *Peace River Record*, October 24, 1919, 1.

20   Superintendent APP to Chief Belanger, Montreal Police, October 27, 1920. In "No. 132 Sullivan P" VII.23 GR1975.0125/351, PAA.

21   "Re Patrick Sullivan Constable Reg. No. Using Seditious Language," Beaver Lodge Department, November 17, 1919. In "No. 132 Sullivan P" VII.23 GR1975.0125/351, PAA.

22   "Re. Complaint by Mrs. M.E. Johnson, Hythe, Alta, against Const. P Sullivan," November 17, 1919. In "No. 132 Sullivan P" VII.23 GR1975.0125/351, PAA.

23   Inspector E Division to superintendent APP, December 5, 1919. In "No. 132 Sullivan P" VII.23 GR1975.0125/351, PAA.

24   Superintendent APP to Inspt. McDonnell, Peace River, December 8, 1919. In "No. 132 Sullivan P" VII.23 GR1975.0125/351, PAA.

25   "Hythe Murder Case Held at Grand Prairie," January 10, 1920, Grande Prairie Herald, 1. (Henrietta Dougherty's lawyer said it was self-defence. Jack had been a "raging" mad man with "homicidal tendencies" who tortured and attacked his wife. Henrietta shot him to save herself.)

26   "Murdered in May! Another Northern Crime," *Peace River Standard and Farmer's Gazette*, October 23, 1919, 1.

27   Patrick Sullivan to Col. Bryan, February 18, 1920. In "No. 132 Sullivan P" VII.23 GR1975.0125/351, PAA.

28   Ibid.

29   Superintendent APP to Patrick Sullivan, February 27, 1920. In "No. 132

Sullivan P" VII.23 GR1975.0125/351, PAA.

30   Ibid.

31   Superintendent APP to A.J. Cawdron, RCMP, December 14, 1920. In "Royal
     Canadian Mounted Police—Request of Pat Sullivan to be appointed to
     investigate disappearance of A.J. Small," Department of Justice fonds, MIKAN
     1364262, LAC.

32   James Irvine to Superintendent APP, April 29, 1920. In "No. 132 Sullivan P"
     VII.23 GR1975.0125/351, PAA.

33   Patrick Sullivan to James Irvine, November 25, 1920. In "No. 132 Sullivan P"
     VII.23 GR1975.0125/351, PAA.

34   Superintendent APP to Editor, Jack Canuck, November 3, 1920. In "No. 132
     Sullivan P" VII.23 GR1975.0125/351, PAA. (According to another letter
     in Sullivan's thick file, *Jack Canuck* decided against publishing the rest of the
     series after taking a look at his record.)

35   Patrick Sullivan to James Irvine, November 25, 1920. In "No. 132 Sullivan P"
     VII.23 GR1975.0125/351, PAA.

36   Superintendent APP to Chief Belanger, Montreal Police, October 27, 1920.
     In "No. 132 Sullivan P" VII.23 GR1975.0125/351, PAA.

37   Superintendent APP to chief constable Sudbury Police, April 26, 1921.
     In "No. 132 Sullivan P" VII.23 GR1975.0125/351, PAA.

38   McClement, *The Strange Case of Ambrose Small*, 122.

39   Ibid.

40   Sullivan, "The Ambrose J. Small Mystery—Startling Revelations by Patrick
     Sullivan," *On Guard*, undated, circa 1923, 6. In "Royal Canadian Mounted
     Police—Request of Pat Sullivan to be appointed to investigate disappearance
     of A.J. Small," Department of Justice fonds, MIKAN 1364262, LAC.

41   Ibid.

42   "Are Seeking Order Demanding Answers," *Globe*, November 25, 1922, 22.

43   Ibid.

44   J.M. Ferron, "The Masters," *Law Society of Upper Canada Gazette* 22, no. 4
     (December 1988): 342–45, Law Society of Ontario Archive.

45   Sullivan, "The Ambrose J. Small Mystery," 6.

46   Ibid., 7.

47   Patrick Sullivan, "A Common-Sense Kind of Discourse," *On Guard*, undated
     newspaper clippings (circa 1923); Sullivan, "The Ambrose J. Small Mystery,"
     8. In "Royal Canadian Mounted Police—Request of Pat Sullivan to be
     appointed to investigate disappearance of A.J. Small," Department of Justice
     fonds, MIKAN 1364262, LAC.

48   "Proving Small's Death May Not Take 7 Years," *Toronto Daily Star*,
     December 1, 1922, 3.

49   Ibid.

50   Ibid.

51   "Millionaire's Will Now Approaching Final Settlement," *Globe*, February 5,
     1923, 11.

52   "Jurist Dean of Toronto Passes Away," *Globe*, May 12, 1943, 4.

53   "All Ranks and Classes Mourn Tilley's Passing," *Toronto Daily Star*, June 11,
     1942, 10.

54   Constance Backhouse and Nancy L. Backhouse, *The Heiress vs. the
     Establishment*. (This book is an annotated account of Elizabeth Campbell's
     legal odyssey for an accounting of her mother's estate, and involved many
     lawyers involved in the Small case. The authors provide annotations and
     biographical material in the footnotes. This additional information about
     Slaght's wild side comes from page 263, note 32.)

55   Backhouse and Backhouse, *The Heiress vs. the establishment: Mrs. Campbell's
     campaign for legal justice*, 242–43, note 30.

56   "Detective Asserts He Knows Place of Small's Burial," *Globe*, March 21,
     1923, 13.

57   "Extract of evidence given by Austin Richardson Mitchell," undated (circa
     March 1923), pages 1–13, in Ambrose Small missing person file, Toronto
     Police Museum.

58   Ibid.

59   Ibid.

60   "Argues Small's Death Is Practically Proved," *Toronto Daily Star*, March 22,
     1923, 1.

61   "Refuses to Rule A.J. Small Dead," *Globe*, March 28, 1923, 15.

62   H. Addington Bruce, "Forgotten Flights," *Toronto Daily Star*, April 29, 1924, 25.

63   "Fugues," *Lancet*, August 7, 1915, 292–93.

64   H. Addington Bruce, "Forgotten Flights," *Toronto Daily Star*, April 29, 1924, 25.

65   Ibid.

66   "Small Litigation Is Finally Ended," *Globe*, June 6, 1923, 17.

FIFTEEN: SMALL VS. SMALL

1   "Justice W.A. Logie Is Taken by Death," *Globe*, June 7, 1933, 1.

2   "Claim 1903 Small Will Is the Only Genuine One," *Toronto Daily Star*,

April 10, 1924, 1.

3   Ibid.

4   Photo: "Figures in Legal Battle for A.J. Small Fortune," *Toronto Daily Star*, April 12, 1924, 8.

5   "Small's Home Life Is Aired in Court," *Globe*, April 11, 1924, 13.

6   Ibid.

7   "Vanished Theatre Magnate's Widow Describes the Conspiracy to Link Her Name with a Mystery Man," *Toronto Daily Star*, April 12, 1924, 9.

8   "Banked a Million, Then Vanished," *Olean Evening Times Herald*, October 5, 1932, sec. 2, 1. (The local press did not print the letters in their daily coverage, only the most basic snippets. The *Star*'s weekly magazine published all of them—which can be found in earlier chapters of this book. This story in 1932 from an American paper also contained one of the letters published by the *Star*.)

9   "Vanished Theatre Magnate's Widow Describes the Conspiracy to Link Her Name with a Mystery Man," *Toronto Daily Star*, April 12, 1924, 8.

10   "Vanished Theatre Magnate's Widow Describes the Conspiracy to Link Her Name with a Mystery Man," *Toronto Daily Star*, April 12, 1924, 9.

11   "Court Probes Business Relations of Mr. and Mrs. Small Checks Details of Disappearance," *Toronto Daily Star*, April 29, 1924, 10.

12   "Vanished Theatre Magnate's Widow Describes the Conspiracy to Link Her Name with a Mystery Man," *Toronto Daily Star*, April 12, 1924, 8.

13   Ibid.

14   Ibid., 9.

15   Ibid.

16   Ibid.

17   Ibid.

18   "Mr. T. Herbert Lennox Not 'Mysterious Mr. X,'" *Toronto Daily Star*, April 15, 1924, 1.

19   "Attempt to Settle Small Will Dispute Is Not Successful," *Globe*, April 29, 1924, 13.

20   "Court Probes Business Relations of Mr. and Mrs. Small Checks Details of Disappearance," *Toronto Daily Star*, April 29, 1924, 10.

21   Ibid., 11.

22   Ibid.

23   "Small Sisters Each Get the Income on $100,000 Percy, Madeleine Same," *Toronto Daily Star*, April 29, 1924, six o'clock edition, 1.

24   Ibid.

25   Gideon Grant to Hon. Ernest Lapointe, August 29, 1925. In "Royal
     Canadian Mounted Police—Request of Pat Sullivan to be appointed to
     investigate disappearance of A.J. Small," Department of Justice fonds,
     MIKAN 1364262, LAC.

26   Ibid.

27   Ibid.

28   Pat Sullivan to Ernest Lapointe, October 1, 1925. In "Royal Canadian Mounted
     Police—Request of Pat Sullivan to be appointed to investigate disappearance
     of A.J. Small," Department of Justice fonds, MIKAN 1364262, LAC.

29   Supt. H.M. Newson (commanding officer, western Ontario district RCMP) to
     Col. Cortlandt Starnes, RCMP commissioner, November 7, 1925. In "Royal
     Canadian Mounted Police—Request of Pat Sullivan to be appointed to
     investigate disappearance of A.J. Small," Department of Justice fonds, MIKAN
     1364262, LAC.

30   Alfred Cuddy to Lieut. Col. W.C. Bryan, Commissioner APP, April 25, 1924.
     In "No. 132 Sullivan P" VII.23 GR1975.0125/351, PAA.

31   Alfred Cuddy to Lieut. Col. W.C. Bryan, Commissioner APP, May 16, 1924.
     In "No. 132 Sullivan P" VII.23 GR1975.0125/351, PAA.

SIXTEEN: DOUGHTY'S FREEDOM

1   Cameron Willis, "Summary of Information." (Description of Kingston prison
    and practices at the time provided by Willis, research assistant at the
    Correctional Services of Canada Museum, in email of September 1, 2017.)

2   "Doughty to Be Freed Early in New Year," Globe, November 18, 1925, 17.
    (In 1923, the clemency branch of the federal justice department turned down
    Doughty's request for early release, but this article notes that he had earned
    a few months off for good behaviour.)

3   W. Hilyard Smith (Protestant chaplain of Kingston Penitentiary) to Judge
    Denton, July 22, 1925. In Rex vs. John Doughty, RG 22-5871, General
    Sessions of the Peace, County of York, File 225-20, AO.

4   Denton memo, undated. In Rex vs. John Doughty, RG 22-5871, General
    Sessions of the Peace, County of York, File 224-20, AO.

5   "Doughty Breathes Air of Freedom Once More Today," Toronto Daily Star,
    February 3, 1926, five o'clock edition, 1.

6   "Sisters Welcome Home Small's Old Secretary," *Toronto Daily Star*, February 4, 1926, 3.

7   Ibid.

8   Ibid.

9   Ibid.

10 Ibid.

11 "Small, Ambrose: case." In Premier Howard Ferguson correspondence, RG 3-6-0-1294, AO (1926).

12 Small vs. Holmes, RG 22-5800, Case 863-1936, Supreme Court of Ontario, May 1936. (Pat Sullivan mentions his sister living in Boston in his preliminary interview.)

SEVENTEEN: THERESA SMALL MAKES SOME FRIENDS

1   "Shutting out Harsh World Mrs. Small's Only Shield against Barbs of Gossip," *Toronto Telegram*, November 12, 1935. Box 1, Clipping File 7: "Mrs. Ambrose Small newspaper and magazine clippings." Archives of the Sisters of Service, Toronto (hereafter cited as SOS).

2   Ibid.

3   John Herd Thompson and Allen Seager, *Canada 1922–1939: Decades of Discord* (Toronto: McClelland & Stewart, 1985), 171.

4   Robert B. Scott, "Professional Performers and Companies," *Later Stages— Essays in Ontario Theatre from the First World War to the 1970s*, eds. Ann Saddlemyer and Richard Plant (University of Toronto Press, 1997), 31.

5   Lee Shubert to H.W. Beauclerk, December 19, 1921. Trans Canada 1407, Shubert Collection, Box 377, SA.

6   "Mrs. Ambrose Small Offers More Money: But Trans-Canada Theatres, . . ." *Globe*, July 17, 1923, 3.

7   Ibid.

8   "Earnings Maintained by Famous Players," *Globe*, October 20, 1925, 6.

9   "Secures Season Lease of Grand Opera House," *Globe*, September 1, 1923, 2.

10 Ibid.

11 "An Old Theatre Passes," *Globe*, November 30, 1927, 4.

12 Ibid.

13 Jeanne Beck, *To Do and to Endure: The Life of Catherine Donnelly, Sister of Service* (Toronto: Dundurn Press, 1997), 107.

14 Ibid., 47.

15 *The Canadian Encyclopedia*, s.v. "History of Settlement in the Canadian Prairies," by Gerald Friesen, February 7, 2006, https://www.thecanadianencyclopedia.ca/en/article/prairie-west.

16 Carol Goar, "Canada Starved Aboriginal People into Submission: Goar," *Toronto Star*, June 10, 2014, https://www.thestar.com/opinion/ commentary /2014/06/10/canada_starved_aboriginal_people_into_ submission_goar.html.

17 James Daschuk, *Clearing the Plains: Disease, Politics of Starvation, and the Loss of Aboriginal Life* (Regina: University of Regina Press, 2013), 125.

18 Beck, *To Do and to Endure*, 60.

19 Beck, *To Do and to Endure*, 80.

20 Felix Devine to Archbishop Neil McNeil, August 30, 1920. MNAH09.94, Archives of the Roman Catholic Archdiocese of Toronto (ARCAT). (Devine wrote a note at the top of the letter in red ink: "Don't approach Theresa Small about this. If you need to, talk to her lawyer, but don't mention my name.")

21 Beck, *To Do and to Endure*, 133.

22 "Yearly Report, year ending April 30, 1927" (Edson mission), series 6-10, Box 1, File 2, SOS.

23 "At the New Novitiate," *The Field at Home* 4, no. 3 (April 1928), SOS.

24 George Daly to Theresa Small, August 7, 1927. Series 5-01, Box 1, File 3, SOS.

25 May 1930 and June 1931 entries, Sisters of Service Annals. Series 5-01, Oversized Box 1, File 1, SOS.

26 June 21, 1934 entry in Sisters of Service Annals. Series 5-01, Oversized Box 1, File 1, SOS.

EIGHTEEN: ONE MORE CHARLATAN

1 "Small Slain; Crime Nearly Solved, Says Criminologist," *Winnipeg Tribune*, September 10, 1928, 1.

2 H. Blair Neatby, "King, William Lyon Mackenzie," in *Dictionary of Canadian Biography*, vol. 17, University of Toronto/Université Laval, 2003–, accessed March 24, 2019.

3 "Can Find Ambrose Small with His Sister's Help," *Toronto Daily Star*, March 14, 1922, 4.

4 Gurston S. Allen, "Hypnotism and Its Legal Import," *Canadian Bar Review* 12 (1934): 91.

5 Ibid.

6   Ibid., 92.

7   "Langsner a Mystery: Uses Latent Powers," *Toronto Daily Star*, October 3,
     1928, 36.

8   "Deny Langsner Known in Vienna or in New York," *Toronto Daily Star*,
     September 13, 1928, 1.

9   "Provincial Authorities Very Little Impressed by Langsner's Finds," *Globe*,
     October 25, 1928, 1.

10   "Austrian Criminologist Would Attempt Solve Ambrose Small Mystery,"
     Toronto Daily Star, July 27, 1928, 2.

11   "Provincial Authorities Very Little Impressed by Langsner's Finds," 1.

12   Ibid.

13   Ibid.

14   Ibid.

15   "Langsner Quits His Enquiry into Ambrose Small Mystery," *Winnipeg
     Tribune*, November 13, 1928, 1.

16   200 Society to Archbishop Neil McNeil, November 28, 1928. MNAH17.105
     ARCAT.

17   F.D. Jacob, "Hypnotism Is Boomerang Says Expert of Langsner," *Toronto Daily
     Star*, November 28, 1928, 14.

18   Ibid.

19   "Latent Light Expert Branded as Faker by Police Records," *Globe*, December 29,
     1928, 15.

20   Ibid., 16.

21   Ibid.

22   Ibid.

23   Gordon Sinclair, "'Doctor' Langsner Back in Limelight in Native Poland,"
     Toronto Daily Star, September 26, 1930, 1.

24   Ibid., 2.

25   Ibid.

NINETEEN: **SKYSCRAPER CITY**

1   Pierre Berton, *The Great Depression: 1929–1939* (Toronto: McClelland &
     Stewart, 1990), 26.

2   Ibid., 25.

3   "Plan 26-storey Skyscraper for Gayety Theatre Site," *Toronto Daily Star*,

July 5, 1929, 20.

4 "Downtown Toronto Is Now Experiencing a Wonderful Boom," *Globe*, December 3, 1927, 15.

5 "Completed Hotel Plans to Show New Structure 29 Stories in Height," *Toronto Daily Star*, December 2, 1927, 8.

6 "Grand Opera House Lane Revives Grand Memories," *Toronto Daily Star*, June 23, 1928, 8.

7 "Historic Stuff at Old Grand," *Evening Telegram*, November 30, 1927.

8 Ibid.

9 "Eight Years Fail to Solve 'Amby' Small's Disappearance," *Evening Telegram*, December 2, 1927, 1.

10 Ibid.

11 "Wreckers of Grand Opera House Report Odd Happenings in Night," *Globe*, June 28, 1928, 13.

12 Tax Assessment for Ward 3, Division 4, City of Toronto, 1929 for 1930, page 260, CTA.

TWENTY: **BEHOLD THE MAN OF GOD**

1 Agreement of sale for *The Thunderer* between A.M. Orpen and Patrick Sullivan, September 7, 1926. SC 272, Ralph Browne Collection, CTA.

2 "Whew! — The Stink!" *Thunderer*, January 11, 1930, 3. In "E.N. Armour, Crown Attorney, Toronto: Re prosecution of the Editor of the 'The Thunderer,'" RG 4-32, AO.

3 Susan E. Houston, "A Little Steam, a Little Sizzle and a Little Sleaze: English Language Tabloids in the Interwar Period," *Papers of the Bibliographic Society of Canada* 40, no. 1 (2002): 37.

4 Ibid., 59.

5 Sullivan, "Come Out You Hounds," 7.

6 "We Demand Arrest of Corti," *Thunderer*, undated. In "E.N. Armour, Crown Attorney, Toronto: Re prosecution of the Editor of the 'The Thunderer,'" RG 4-32, AO (1929).

7 "Whew! What a Smell!" *Thunderer*, February 1, 1930, 3. In "E.N. Armour, Crown Attorney, Toronto: Re prosecution of the Editor of the 'The Thunderer,'" RG 4-32, AO.

8   Attorney General W.H. Price to George Vale, May 7, 1929. In "E.N. Armour, Crown Attorney, Toronto: Re prosecution of the Editor of the 'The Thunderer,'" RG 4-32, AO. (A citizen wrote to the attorney general to advise him of the "obscene" matter in *The Thunderer*, and Price replied that if they prosecuted, the publication would be better known, better to pay it "little attention. . . . It is comparatively unknown and I think will die a natural death.")

9   "AJ Small Mystery Resurrected Again by Woman's Story," *Globe*, October 18, 1929, 13.

10   "Didn't Visit Sullivan," *Toronto Daily Star*, January 21, 1930, 1.

11   Rex vs. Patrick Sullivan, Supreme Court of Canada criminal indictment files, York Winter assizes 1930, RG 22-517, AO.

12   "Behold the man of God!" *Thunderer*, January 11, 1930, 2. In "E.N. Armour, Crown Attorney, Toronto: Re prosecution of the Editor of the 'The Thunderer,'" RG 4-32, AO. (The attack evidently came in an earlier edition, which had been suppressed—and not included in the archival file. The Attorney General's office seems to have been alerted to this issue in late December.)

13   "John Bruce Hunter," Canada, Military Honours and Awards Citation Cards 1900–1961. Ancestry.com, 2012.

14   Letter to the editor, *Banner and Time*, undated. From Eva Birss, sent to Bruce Hunter, January 17, 1930. In "Correspondence received re: Thunderer article 1930," 2017.019C4-4, United Church of Canada Archives, Toronto.

15   I.A. Humphries to Attorney General Price, December 21, 1929. In "E.N. Armour, Crown Attorney, Toronto: Re prosecution of the Editor of the 'The Thunderer,'" RG 4-32, AO (1929).

16   "Patrick Sullivan Arrested on Obscene Charge," *Toronto Daily Star*, January 9, 1930, 1.

17   "Arrest Editor Thunderer," *Evening Telegram*, January 9, 1930, 1.

18   "Oh! the Scandal!" *Thunderer*, January 11, 1930, 1. In "E.N. Armour, Crown Attorney, Toronto: Re prosecution of the Editor of the 'The Thunderer,'" RG 4-32, AO (1929).

19   "Behold! The Man of God!" *Thunderer*, January 11, 1930, 2. In "E.N. Armour, Crown Attorney, Toronto: Re prosecution of the Editor of the ' The Thunderer,'" RG 4-32, AO (1929).

20   Ibid.

21   Eric Armour to A.W. Rogers, January 23, 1930. In "E.N. Armour, Crown Attorney, Toronto: Re prosecution of the Editor of the 'The Thunderer,'" RG 4-32, AO (1929).

22   Letter to Rev. J. Bruce Hunter, January 15, 1930, in "Correspondence Received re: Thunderer article 1930," 2017.019C4-4. United Church of Canada Archives, Toronto.

23   Ibid.

24   "Confidence Voiced in London Minister," *Globe*, January 14, 1930, 2.

25   Ibid.

26   In "Correspondence received re: *Thunderer* article 1930," 2017.019C4-4, United Church of Canada Archives, Toronto.

27   Ibid.

28   Ibid.

29   "Confidence Voiced in London Minister," 2.

30   Sullivan, "Come Out You Hounds," 7.

31   W.N. Manning TO AG W.H. Price, January 25, 1930. In "E.N. Armour, Crown Attorney, Toronto: Re prosecution of the Editor of the 'The Thunderer,'" RG 4-32, AO (1929).

32   Judge Dan O'Connell, "Reasons for sentencing Patrick Sullivan," May 29, 1930. In Rex vs. Patrick Sullivan, RG 22-5870, Case 19-30, AO.

33   Sheila Gail Browne, *On this Corner 1896–1996: A History of Metropolitan United Church, London, Ontario* (London: Metropolitan United Church, 1996), 39.

TWENTY-ONE: **THE OLD ORDER IS GONE**

1   *Dictionary of Canadian Biography*, s.v. "Bennett, Richard Bedford," by P.B. Waite, accessed March 4, 2019, http://www.biographi.ca/en/bio/bennett_richard_bedford_17E.html.

2   Thompson and Seager, Canada 1922–1939, 262.

3   "William Marchington, "Tories Are Rocked by Bennett Speech, Cabinet May Split," *Globe*, January 4, 1935, 1. (It wasn't that out of character. Back in the late 1920s, when his government was in opposition, Bennett had supported contributory old age pensions and unemployment insurance.)

4   *Dictionary of Canadian Biography*, s.v. "Bennett, Richard Bedford," by P.B. Waite, accessed March 4, 2019, http://www.biographi.ca/en/bio/bennett_richard_bedford_17E.html.

5   Thompson and Seager, *Canada 1922–1939*, 261.

6   Ibid., 262.

7   "Likens Bennett's New Policy to Conjurer's Rabbit Trick," *Toronto Daily Star,*
     January 4, 1935, 1.

8   "Doubt, Opposition Greet Bennett Plan," *Toronto Daily Star,* January 7,
     1935, 3.

9   Ibid.

10   February 8, 1935, Diaries of Prime Minister William Lyon Mackenzie King,
     MG26-513. Accessed online at Library and Archives Canada, April 16, 2019.

11   Coralie van Paassen, "Knife at Jew's Throat 24 Hours after Ballot Is Threat
     in Saarland," *Toronto Daily Star,* January 12, 1935, 1.

12   *Encyclopedia Brittanica,* s.v. "Saarland," by Alison Eldridge, accessed
     February 20, 2018, https://www.britannica.com/place/Saarland.

13   M.H. Halton, "Thousands in Saar Marked for Punishment by Nazis,"
     Toronto Daily Star, January 12, 1935, 2.

14   Van Paassen, "Knife at Jew's Throat," 3.

15   Summaries of Kormann family economic outlook circa 1935. Series 2-09.2,
     Box 1, File 10, SOS.

16   "Shutting Out Harsh World Mrs. Small's Only Shield against Barbs of
     Gossip," *Toronto Telegram,* November 12, 1935. Box 1, Clipping File 7:
     "Mrs. Ambrose Small newspaper and magazine clippings," SOS.

17   Ibid.

18   "Alumnae Notes," *St. Joseph Lilies* 20, no. 4 (March 1932): 85 and 96.
     Accessed online at Archive.org. Theresa attends a party for a new priest,
     and throws a dinner dance for her sister at the King Edward. These are the
     last mentions of Theresa Small in the journal until her death. On October 3,
     1933, the *Toronto Daily Star* ran a small item that Theresa was "critically ill"
     and confined to her home.

19   "Mrs Small Ill," *Thunder,* June 9, 1934, 13. Special Collections, Thomas
     Fisher Rare Book Library. , Rare Book M-10 00244. (The *Thunder* was under
     new management, but Sullivan was still writing for it. In a May 13, 1933
     issue there was a note announcing new management of the tabloid, assuring
     readers that "Pat Sullivan, the former editor has agreed to continue to write
     those vigorous articles by which *Thunder* has become so well known.")

20   Peter T. McGuigan, "Cardinal James McGuigan: Tormented Prince of the
     Church" (Master's thesis, St. Mary's University, 1995, page v), http://library
     2.smu.ca/ handle/01/22170#.W5VxfJNKgWo.

21   Ibid., 125.

22   September 23, 1935 entry in Sisters of Service Annals. Series 5-01,
      Oversized Box 1, File 1, SOS.

23   Thompson and Seager, *Canada 1922–1939*, 264.

24   Ibid., 266.

25   Ibid., 274.

26   Ibid.

27   October 14–16, 1935, entries in Sisters of Service Annals. Series 5-01,
      Oversized Box 1, SOS.

28   "Shutting Out Harsh World Mrs. Small's Only Shield against Barbs of
      Gossip," *Toronto Telegram*, November 12, 1935, SOS.

29   "Crowd Church at Burial of Mrs. Small," *Telegram*, October 17, 1935.
      "Mrs. Ambrose Small newspaper and magazine clippings," File 7, Box 1, SOS.

30   J.A.C. Cameron Discipline Committee Report (redacted), November 15,
      1934. Law Society of Ontario Archive.

31   Fr. Edward Jackman, ed., "The Growth of Catholic Cemeteries in the
      Archdiocese of Toronto," in *A Quiet Gentle Surprise: A History of Saint
      Michael's Cemetery* (Toronto: Toronto Catholic Cemeteries Association,
      1980), 12.

32   Sisters of Service Annals, October 21, 1935, Series 5-01, Oversized Box 1,
      File 1, SOS.

33   Ibid.

34   Sisters of Service Annals, October 26, 1935, Series 5-01, Oversized Box 1,
      File 1, SOS.

35   Ibid.

36   Mark McGowan, *Imperial Irish: Canada's Irish Catholics Fight the Great War,
      1914–1918* (Kingston: McGill-Queen's University Press, 2017), 259.

37   McGowan, 258.

38   McGowan, 261.

39   Correspondence from Martin J. Quinn, President, Catholic Taxpayers
      Association of Ontario to Archbishop Neil McNeil, May 5, 1933, ARCAT,
      Archbishop Neil McNeil Fonds, MNAE21.09.

40   Bilkey, 12.

41   "Would Block Small Will Until Domestic Located," *Telegram*, November 4,
      1935. "Mrs. Ambrose Small newspaper and magazine clippings," File 7,
      Box 1, SOS.

42   "Maid Tells Strange Act of Mrs. Small," *Telegram*, November 5, 1935.
      "Mrs. Ambrose Small newspaper and magazine clippings," File 7, Box 1, SOS.

43   Ibid.

44   *Dictionary of Canadian Biography*, s.v. "Monk, Maria," by Philippe Sylvain,
      accessed June 26, 2018, http://www.biographi.ca/en/bio/monk_maria_7E.html.

45   McClement, *The Strange Case of Ambrose Small*, 21.

46   "Small's Former Cook Insists No 'Mystery Pervaded Household,'" *Toronto
      Daily Star*, November 6, 1935. "Mrs. Ambrose Small newspaper and magazine
      clippings," File 7, Box 1, SOS.

47   "Ambrose Small's Remains Not in Cellar, Maid Says," *Toronto Daily Star*,
      November 7, 1935. "Mrs. Ambrose Small newspaper and magazine
      clippings," File 7, Box 1, SOS.

48   "No Signs of Dying Message States Mrs. Small's Nurse," *Toronto Daily Star*,
      November 8, 1935, 1.

TWENTY-TWO: **THE WILL**

1   Theresa Small, will filed April 17, 1936, RG 22, York County Estate Files,
      73336, Reel 313, MS584, AO, and "Estate of Theresa Small Approximate
      Inventory as of October 14, 1935" in Series 2-09.2, File 1, Box 1, SOS.

2   It was unclear when Theresa made her real estate investments. For the
      properties on Adelaide Street next to the old Grand Opera House, the tax
      rolls don't show a change of ownership linked to Theresa until 1936, a year
      after her death. City archives staff said the rolls are reliable because that's
      how the city taxed people, after all. According to a column dedicated to real
      estate transactions in the Toronto Star, Theresa bought a vacant lot on the
      north side of Adelaide Street west of Yonge in November 1930 from John F.
      Snarr for $90,000, but then sold that to "Stainton and Evis" for $1.00.
      Research at the Land Registry Office has not yielded answers as to the exact
      dates of her purchases.

3   F.L. Morton to Arthur J. Holmes, March 19, 1936. Series 2-09.2, Box 1, File
      3, SOS.

4   Fr. George Daly to Archbishop McGuigan, March 22, 1936. Series 2-09.2,
      Box 1, File 3, SOS.

5   Memo in Master's file (apparently furnished by A.J. Holmes), circa 1949.
      Series 2-09.2, Box 1, File 6, SOS.

6   Will of Theresa Small, filed April, 17, 1936, RG 22-305 York County Estate
     Files, 73336. MS 584, Reel 313, AO.

7   S.G. Crowell to Mr. O'Brien, January 7, 1936. Series 2-09-2, Box 1, File 2,
     SOS.

8   Ibid.

9   A. Kelly to Arthur Holmes, September 14, 1936. Series 2-09-2, Box 1,
     File 2, SOS.

TWENTY-THREE: **CONFESSION**

1   Pre-trial examination of Patrick Sullivan, May 30, 1936, in Small vs.
     Holmes, RG 22-5800, Case 863-1936, Supreme Court of Ontario, May
     1936, 43, AO.

2   Ibid., 31.

3   Ibid., 59.

4   Purported confession of Theresa Small, undated. Series 2-09.2, Box 1, File 3, SOS.

5   Pre-trial examination of Florence Small, May 30, 1936, Small vs. Holmes, RG
     22-5800, Case 863-1936, Supreme Court of Ontario, May 1936, 127–128, AO.

6   S.G. Crowell to W.J. O'Brien Esquire, June 5, 1936. Series 2-09.2, Box 1,
     File 3, SOS.

7   Fr. George Daly to Reverend Sisters of Service, October 19, 1936.
     Series 2-09.2, Box 1, File 3, SOS.

8   Fr. George Daly to Reverend Sister Barton, November 15, 1936.
     Series 2-09.2, Box 1, File 3, SOS.

9   "Counsel Denies Suggesting Pay for Refreshing Memory," *Toronto Daily Star*,
     November 25, 1936, 1 and 2.

10   "Mrs. Small Voiced Threats Involving Mate, Court Told," *Evening Telegram*,
     November 20, 1936, SOS.

11   Justice Nicol Jeffrey, "Reasons for Judgment in the Supreme Court of Ontario
     Small v. Holmes (1936)," Series 2-09.2 Box 1, File 10, SOS, 10.

12   Det. Sgt. J.J McIlrath notes on Small V. Holmes, November 20, 1936, 7. In
     Ambrose Small missing persons file, Toronto Police Museum.

13   "Mitchell Got Lots of Money AJ Small's Sister Charges," *Toronto Telegram*,
     November 23, 1936, newspaper collection, SOS.

14   Det. Sgt. J.J McIlrath to John Chisholm, Inspector of Detectives, "Re: The
     Small sisters vs. executors of Theresa Small estate," November 28, 1936, 2.

In Ambrose Small missing persons file, Toronto Police Museum. (The police were also watching what Sullivan said about Mitchell. On the stand, Sullivan was more careful than he'd ever been in his tabloids. According to an article in the *Evening Telegram* on November 24, 1936, Sullivan said that the money that Mitchell received ("$200 here, $300 there") was "money for expenses and running down clues." "Then you make no reflection on the character of Inspector Mitchell, or doubt his honesty of purpose?" the lawyer asked. "I do not," Sullivan replied.

15 "Reasons for Judgment," Small vs. Holmes, RG 22-5800, Case 863-1936, Supreme Court of Ontario, November 1936, 19. Series 2-09.2, Box 1, File 10, SOS.

16 "Witnesses tell of murder plot in Small action," *Globe*, November 17, 1936, 14. (Shields used "coal-hole" during his preliminary interview in May to refer to the basement of the theatre.)

17 "Mrs. Small Voiced Threats Involving Mate, Court Told," *Evening Telegram*, November 20, 1936, SOS.

18 "Reasons for Judgment," 10.

19 Ibid., 11.

20 Ibid., 18.

21 Ibid., 21.

22 Fr. George Daly to Reverend and Dear Sisters, November 27, 1936. Series 2-09.2 Box 1, File 3, SOS.

23 Sisters of Service Annals, November 27, 1936, Series 5-01.1. Oversized Box 1, File 1.

TWENTY-FOUR: **THE LAST SMALL**

1 Memo from S.E. Parker to executors, October 8, 1936. Series 2-09, Box 1, File 10, SOS.

2 Memo in Master's file, Series 2-09, Box 1, File 6, SOS.

3 Fr. George Daly to George Keogh, October 20, 1944. Series 2-09, Box 1, File 10, SOS.

4 Fr. George Daly to Mrs. J.H. Logan, October 31, 1938. Series 2-01, Box 3, File 15, SOS.

5 Fr. George Daly to John Collins, April 8, 1937. Series 2-01, Box 3, File 15, SOS.

6   Eric Brown to George Daly, January 19, 1939. Series 2-01, Box 3, File 15, SOS.

7   *Time* magazine to Fr. George Daly, June 10, 1942. Series 2-01, Box 3, File 16, SOS.

8   Fr. George Daly to Charles Kelz, May 13, 1954. Series 2-09.2, Box 1, File 4, SOS.

9   Charles J. Kelz to lawyers for the Theresa Small estate, May 11, 1955, Series 2-09.2, File 4, Box 1, SOS.

10   Charles J. Kelz to Fr. George Daly, May 20, 1954, Series 2-09.2, File 4, Box 1, SOS.

11   Fr. George Daly to Charles Kelz, May 21, 1954. Series 2-09.2, Box 1, File 4, SOS.

12   "In the matter of the estate of Theresa Small late of the City of Toronto, in the County of York, Widow, Deceased: Report," May 11, 1954, 5. Series 2-09.2, Box 1, File 4, SOS.

13   "Judgement in the matter of the estate of Theresa Small," May 11, 1954, Supreme Court of Ontario, by F.G. Cushing, master. Series 2-09.2 File 4, Box 1, SOS. The judgement says Madeleine was entitled to 29.9 per cent of payout and Percy 20.2 per cent.

14   Charles Hutchings, in discussion with the author, March 20, 2019.

15   Charles Hutchings and Nancy Hutchings, in discussion with the author, August 11, 2017. Her descendants are not certain about the exact settlement Madeleine received from Theresa's estate, but between that and support from her ex-husband, she was comfortable, her grandson says.

16   Madeleine might have stayed anonymous forever, but she applied for an Ontario birth certificate in the 1970s. That document confirmed that she was the daughter of Daniel and Josephine Small.

17   Charles Hutchings, in discussion with the author, August 11, 2017.

18   Charles Hutchings, in discussion with the author, March 20, 2019.

TWENTY-FIVE: **DINNER WITH THE DOUGHTYS**

1   "Memorandum of agreement between John Doughty and George D. Lovatt of the first part and Eliza Lovatt of the second part, May 27, 1927." Doughty family collection.

2   Margaret Santon, in discussion with the author, November 21, 2017.

3   Ibid.

4   Bruce Doughty, in discussion with the author, December 20, 2018.

5   "Figured in Ambrose Small Case, John Doughty, 71, Dies," *Toronto Daily Star*, August 13, 1949, 2.

6   Margaret Santon, in discussion with the author, November 21, 2017.

7   Michael Ondaatje, *In the Skin of a Lion* (Toronto: McClelland & Stewart, 1987), 57.

8   Ibid., 95.

9   Ibid., 214.

10   "Says He Saw Small Down in Juarez City," *Globe*, April 26, 1923, 13.

11   W.H. Kesterton, *A History of Journalism in Canada* (Toronto: McClelland & Stewart, 1967), 194.

TWENTY-SEVEN: **THE HAMMOND REPORT**

1   "Police Renew Probe New Records Filed," *Toronto Daily Star*, May 6, 1936, 2.

2   Fred McClement, *Strange Case of Ambrose Small*, 47.

3   Dahn D. Higley, *O.P.P.: The History of the Ontario Provincial Police Force* (Toronto: The Queen's Printer): 1984, 118, 126-127. (Hammond comes across as a stubborn, righteous character in Higley's history. Higley mentions an episode in 1921 where Hammond was suspicious that several Ontario Temperance Act officers were corrupt and disloyal, along with their superior, Chief Provincial Inspector Ayearst, "but he was unable at the time to offer more than tentative substantiation of his allegations," Higley writes. Also that year, Hammond and an "Inspector Collison" had such a feud going that both men were summoned into the office of the commissioner, an investigation was ordered, and Collison was asked to resign, and Hammond was demoted for a time to the O.T.A. enforcement branch. In 1922, he was back in the force's good graces, it seems, given the job of chasing down an OPP constable who had stolen money from other senior officers and "fled the city." In 1923, he was part of a "posse" of 30 OPP officers who hunted down Leo Rogers, a young man who had shot and killed a North Bay police constable. One OPP officer died in the manhunt, but Rogers was ultimately killed as well, and Hammond was one of many who were "commended in Police orders," Higley writes on page 150.)

4   Edward L. Hammond, O.P.P. memorandum re disappearance of Ambrose Small, RG 4-123-0-1, 2. AO (1936). (The first three pages of this document are a letter explaining the report, hereafter called Hammond Letter. The rest is the Hammond Report, hereafter called "Hammond Report.")

5   Ibid.

6   Hammond Report, 17, line 128.

7   Hammond Letter, 2.

8   Hammond Report, 5, 35-37, and 6, 35.

9   Ibid., 5, 38.

10   Ibid., 6, 41.

11   Ibid., 7, 47-48.

12   Ibid., 6, 42.

13   Ibid., 6, 44.

14   Ibid., 6, 40.

15   Ibid., 4, 27, and "Witnesses Tell of Murder Plot in Small Action," *Globe*, November 17, 1936, 14.

16   Hammond Report, 13, 89.

17   Ibid., 13, 89-91.

18   Ibid., 13, 91.

19   Ibid., 13, 92.

20   Ibid., 14, 100.

21   Ibid., 14, 97.

22   Ibid., 7, 52.

23   Ibid., 10, 69.

24   Ibid., 14, 111.

25   Ibid. (Telegrams from Doughty to Trans-Canada in the Toronto Police files associated with the Hammond Report say on November 25 that it is "impossible to leave before Sunday." A telegram sent by Doughty to his Montreal boss on December 1, 1919 at 6:57 p.m. says he has been "unable to clean up matter," but will leave tomorrow.)

26   Doughty as quoted by Harry Dahn, in statement to Toronto Police, April 20, 1920, in "Copies of 1919-1921 report and statements regarding the Ambrose Small case; transcriptions of 1936 statements regarding the case," RG 4-123-0-2. AO (1919-1936).

27   Hammond Report, 15, 117.

28   Ibid., 17, 124.

29   Ibid., 15, 114.

30   "Comments of Inspector Austin Mitchell, Toronto Police Department, on Small Disappearance and on source documents," RG 4-123-0-3, 14a. AO (1936). (Hereafter called Mitchell response.)

31   Ibid., 13.

32   Ibid., 14a.

33   Ibid., 15.

34   Ibid., 9.

35   Ibid., 7.

36   Ibid., 7.

37   Ibid., 14a.

38   Ibid., 16.

39   Ibid., 13.

40   Ibid., 10.

41   Ibid., 16.

42   Ibid., 13.

43   Hammond Report, 11, 78.

44   Ibid., 2, 10.

45   Ibid., 11, 76.

46   Ibid., 7, 49.

47   Ibid.

48   Ibid., 8, 53.

49   Mitchell response, 5.

50   Ibid., 4.

51   Ibid., 4.

52   Ibid., 10.

53   Ibid., 5.

54   Ibid., 10.

55   "Unsolved Murder of Ambrose J. Small Disgrace to the British Empire,"
     Thunderer, June 29, circa 1929, 3. In "E.N. Armour, Crown Attorney,
     Toronto: Re prosecution of the Editor of the 'The Thunderer,'" RG 4-32,
     AO (1929).

56   Hammond Report, 4, 29.

57   Ibid., 8, 58.

58   Ibid., 5, 35.

59   Ibid., 5, 31.

60   Ibid., 5, 32.

61   Ibid., 10, 73.

62   Ibid., 5, 32.

63   Ibid., 6, 87-88.

64   Untitled story in *On Guard*, page 7 in "Royal Canadian Mounted Police—
     Request of Pat Sullivan to be appointed to investigate disappearance of
     A.J. Small," Department of Justice fonds, MIKAN 1364262, LAC.

65   Hammond Report, 11, 74.

66   Hammond Report, 20-155.

67   Hammond Report, 17-123.

68   Mitchell response, 11.

69   Ibid., 8.

70   Ibid. (This 9:30 home time was not in his initial case notes.)

71   Ibid.

72   Ibid., 14.

73   Ibid., 21.

74   "Trial Date Is Fixed for Flynn-Small Case," *Toronto Daily Star*, January 20,
     1921, 2.

75   "Dismisses Action of Thomas Flynn," *Globe*, December 29, 1921, 8.

76   "Man Held in Auto Was Ambrose Small Witness Declares," *Globe*, 1.

77   Hammond Report, 10, 70.

78   Mitchell response, 13.

79   Hammond, 2.

80   Statement of Alfred Elson, given on May 20, 1936. In "Copies of 1919–1921
     report and statements regarding the Ambrose Small case; transcriptions of
     1936 statements regarding the case," RG 4-123-0-2, AO (1919–1936).

81   Mitchell response, 21.

82   Ibid.

83   Hammond Report, 17, 140.

84   Ibid., 19, 151.

85   Ibid., 20, 156.

86   "Statement of Burton Keyser," September 1, 1936, in Hammond Report.

87   Hammond Report, 18, 140.

88   Ibid.

89   Hammond Report, 18, 143.

90   Ibid., 19, 148.

91   Mitchell response, 18.

92   Ibid., 21.

93   Ibid., 19.

94   Ibid., 20.

95   Ibid., 19.

96   Ibid., 20.

97   Ibid., 2.

TWENTY-EIGHT: **ANNIHILATION OF THE I**

1   Robert Thomas Allen, "What Really Happened to Ambrose Small," *Maclean's*, January 15, 1951, 13.

2   "Sullivan Objects to Catholic Judge in Obscenity Case," *Toronto Daily Star*, March 25, 1930, 1.

3   Pre-trial examination of Patrick Sullivan, May 30, 1936, in Small vs. Holmes. RG 22-5800, Case 863-1936, Supreme Court of Ontario, 6.

4   Justice Nicol Jeffrey, "Reasons for Judgment," Small vs. Holmes, November 1936. Series 2-09.2, Box 1, File 10, 20, SOS.

5   Kenneth Cragg, "Two drown in Wasaga Car Plunge," *Globe and Mail*, October 28, 1939, 1.

6   Jessie MacTaggart, "She Wanted a Fling at Life I Feared a Dreadful Fate," *Toronto Daily Star*, October 30, 1939, 19.

7   Ibid.

8   Ibid.

9   Kenneth Cragg, "Two Drown in Wasaga Car Plunge," *Globe and Mail*, October 28, 1939, 1.

10   "Gertrude Small Died of Shock Not Drowned, River Yields Husband," *Toronto Daily Star*, October 30, 1939, 17, 32.

11   "Bridal Pair's Death Is Puzzle to Police," undated newspaper story in clipping file, SOS.

12   "Gertrude Small Doped, Sister Says at Inquest; Drowned, Reply Experts," *Globe and Mail*, January 5, 1940, 4.

13   Cragg, "Two Drown in Wasaga Car Plunge," 1.

14   "Gertrude Small Burial Is with Anglican Rites," *Globe and Mail*, November 1, 1936, 4, SOS.

15   There is conflicting information about Mitchell's birth. One census puts it at 1874, another 1876.

16   Alfred Tennyson, "Crossing the Bar," in Austin Mitchell funeral booklet. Originally published 1889. Toronto Police Museum.

17 "Sherlock at Work," *Thunder*, Thunder Publishing Co. (Toronto), July 11, 1931, at Thomas Fisher Rare Book Library, Rare Book M-10 00244, 2.

18 Browne family records. Fonds 2, Series 89, File 115, CTA.

19 "Disappearance of Her Brother Remains Mystery," *Globe and Mail*, March 20, 1953, 7.

20 "Says She Gave Gift to Small," *Globe*, May 24, 1922, 13.

21 1920 U.S. Federal census.

22 "Woman's Letters to Small Full of Endearing Terms," *Toronto Star Weekly*, April 19, 1924, 4–6.

23 "Clara Jennings against D Foster Jennings," State of Minnesota, County of Hennepin, District Court, fourth judicial district, May 10, 1922, Case No. 197143.

24 Browne Family records. Fonds 2, Series 89, File 115, CTA.

25 Ibid.

26 Justice Nicol Jeffrey, "Reasons for Judgment," 11.

27 "Cremation," *Thunder*, October 31, 1931, 14. Thomas Fisher Rare Book Library, Rare Book M10 00244.

28 "Finally Admit Can't Find Ambrose Small," *Toronto Daily Star*, December 14, 1960, 2.

29 Assorted correspondence. Ambrose Small missing person file, TPS Museum.

30 Individual to Toronto Police, August 18, 1976. Ambrose Small missing persons file, Toronto Police Museum. (Individual does not say his father's name, but voters lists show that he lived with his parents in Timmins. Voter records are sporadic, but his father is listed as late as 1958; he is no longer on the voter's list in 1962. His death occurred sometime in that window.)

31 Victor Telford response, September 1, 1976. Ambrose Small missing persons file, Toronto Police Museum.

TWENTY-NINE: **ENIGMA**

1 Robert Thomas Allen, "What Really Happened to Ambrose Small," *Maclean's*, January 15, 1951, 33.

2 McClement, 158.

3 "Copy: Treasury department Succession Duty office—Estate of Ambrose Small." Series 2-09.2, Box 1, File 3, SOS.

4   Interview with Margaret Santon, January 28, 2019.

5   Justice Nicol Jeffrey, "Reasons for Judgment in the Supreme Court of Ontario, Small v. Holmes (1936), in Series 2-09.2, Box 1, File 10, SOS, 7.

6   Interview with Joe Small, September 12, 2017. Joe didn't agree with his relatives. He doesn't think that Theresa was involved in the disappearance.

7   Interview with Joe Small, September 12, 2017.

8   Michael Swan, "Visitors Trying to Get Behind St. Michael's Cemetery Gates," *Catholic Register*, October 26, 2011, https://www.catholicregister.org/home/canada/item/13215-visitors-trying-to-get-behind-st-michael%E2%80%99s-cemetery-gates.

9   Interview, Catholic Cemeteries, March 19, 2019.

10   Josephine Small died in 1950. In 1933, when Dan Small died, she buried her husband with his first wife, Ellen. Josephine kept the home on Moss Park Place as a rental property, and she continued to live in the couple's Kendal Avenue home with her aging bachelor son, Percy. When she died in 1950, she gave $15,000 to a nurse and $100 to a Catholic church, and divided the rest of her $28,000 estate between her children, Percy and Madeleine. Instead of being buried with her husband, she was buried with her sister, Theresa Small, in the unmarked grave at the opposite end of the cemetery.

ACKNOWLEDGEMENTS

———————————◇———————————

had no idea how sprawling this story would become. Thanks to everyone who helped me make sense of it.

Thank you to the descendants for sharing your family stories: Chuck and Nancy Hutchings, Joe Small, Margaret and Rick Santon, Bruce, Carol, Colin and Nancy Doughty and Aaron Sheedy.

Thanks to the historians and experts who were generous with time and knowledge including Mark McGowan, Elizabeth Smyth, Janis Barlow, Victor Russell, Scott James, Antje Dietze, Stephen Johnson, Jeanne Beck, Susan Houston, Greg Marquis, Jordan St. John, Paul Moore, Christopher Armstrong, Anthony Vickery, Jim Phillips, and Constance Backhouse.

I was lucky enough to be a Massey College journalism fellow in 2016–2017, where I learned many research skills that helped me with this book. Thank you for that opportunity.

So many archivists and librarians helped find the paper trail. MC Havey at the Sisters of Service, Linda Wicks at the Sisters of St. Joseph of Toronto, Sylvia Wang and the staff at the Shubert Archive, the good people at the Toronto Archives, Ontario Archives, and Thomas Fisher Rare Book Library, Alan Walker and the Special Collections staff at the Toronto Reference Library, Paul Leatherdale at the Law Society of Ontario Archives, Erin Bienert at the Archives of the Roman Catholic Archdiocese of Toronto, Elizabeth Mathew at the United Church of Canada Archives, Shane MacDonald with the Catholic University Archives, Norina D'Agostini at the Toronto Police Museum and Discovery Centre, Kathryn Watts in records management at the Toronto Police Service, Carson Murphy at the Peace River Museum, Archives and Mackenzie Centre, Cameron Willis at Canada's Penitentiary Museum, and Johna Heintz at the Museum of the Oregon Territory. Thanks to the people who welcomed me into their homes and businesses associated with this story, like the Grand Theatre in London.

Thanks to the authors who wrote the books that helped me understand Toronto, the theatre world, policing, and the justice system—you'll find their names in the notes.

Thanks to those who make history accessible online. I relied on city directories (digitized by the Toronto Public Library), fire insurance maps (digitized by Nathan Ng at http://goadstoronto. blogspot.com), and biographies of fascinating people at the *Dictionary of Canadian Biography*. (Their entry on Ambrose Small, written by Kathleen Fraser, gave me a great list of sources to start my research.) Fultonhistory.com was a great resource for New York newspapers.

Thanks to Douglas Glover and the non-fiction crew at Banff in October 2017. Thank you to my first-draft readers for their helpful feedback: Tim Shufelt, Heather McCalden, Matt Carter, Amy Dempsey, and Martha Webb.

To my wonderful friends, thank you for asking me how the book was going and sending emails and texts that brightened my days. Wendy Gillis, thanks for letting me borrow your jacket for my author photo. Thanks to Richard Lautens for taking that photo.

To the Shufelts, thanks for your encouragement. To my parents, thank you for riding out the highs and lows of this book with me, as you always do, no matter what. Dad, I know that every time you asked, "Is the book done yet?" the answer always pained you more than me. Thanks for asking, it lightened the load.

Thanks to the *Toronto Star* for the photos, for encouraging my love of archival research, and for allowing me time away for this project. Every day reporters write the first draft of history, and I relied on the *Star*'s work, along with dozens of newspapers across North America. Please support your local newspaper.

To the team at McClelland & Stewart: Jared Bland, thank you for your instant enthusiasm for this story. Jenny Bradshaw, thank you for wrestling this book into submission with me. Thanks to Andrew Roberts for the beautiful cover and page design, and to Terri Nimmo for your work on the cover. Thanks to Tara Tovell for the copyedit, Erin Kern for proofreading, and Lloyd Davis for the index. Thanks to Joe Lee and Kimberlee Hesas for your help with the manuscript. Thanks to my agent, Martha Webb, for putting this all in motion, and to Shona Cook at Penguin Random House Canada for the publicity help.

This book was written in so many places. At Dineen before work, the Massey College library on the weekends, and libraries across Ontario, including my home branch in Forest, Ontario. Thank you for the quiet.

Lastly, to Tim. Thank you for bringing me back to the present tense.

INDEX

———————◇———————

Note: Page numbers in *italics* refer to photographs and illustrations. Page numbers followed by n refer to footnotes.